SUCCESS IN MATHS

SiM

pupil's book

Rob Kearsley Bullen
Andrew Edmondson
Tony Ward

G1

LONGMAN

CONTENTS

HOW TO USE THIS BOOK

This book is divided into Chapters and Topics.
A Chapter is a bit like a week's work.
A Topic is a bit like one lesson.

Topics are made out of these sections

What's it called?	What's it for?	Notes
Learn About It	Learning new things and getting new facts and information.	You might get this from your teacher or read it in the book.
Try It Out	'Having a go' at what you just learned.	These questions are usually quite easy.
Practice	Using what you have learned to answer questions and solve problems.	These questions get a bit harder. You might have to think a bit before you answer them.
Further Practice	'Having another go' if you found this topic difficult.	Usually, these are more like **Try It Out**.
Finished Early?	Using what was in the topic to investigate something or solve a harder problem.	You do this when you've finished your Practice. It's at the back of the book.

Sometimes there's a section called **Learn More About It**.
This happens when there's a lot to learn, so it's split into two parts.
You get another chance to **Try It Out** here too.

In the book there are icons (little pictures) that help you

 You need some equipment or special paper.

 There is a special sheet to go with the exercise.

 There is something to watch out for. It could be a trick question. It could be a mistake you might make.

 The page number tells you where to find **Finished Early?** for the topic you're doing.

 You will be working with somebody else.

 You can use a calculator.

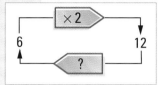

You will often see **number machines**.
Sometimes you just have to do what they tell you.
Sometimes you have to find out what they do.

Word Check
quadrilateral a shape with 4 straight sides

regular a shape with all sides the same and all angles the same

square a regular quadrilateral

This box tells you what words mean.

Key Fact
The angle sum of a triangle is always 180°.

This box tells you how to do something or gives you important information. You should always try to remember things from these boxes.

Example   What is 4^4?

Working $4^4 = 4 \times 4 \times 4 \times 4$
$= 16 \times 16$
$= 256$

Answer $4^4 = 256$

These boxes show you how to do the questions in an exercise.

1 Numbers and Number Names

In this chapter you will learn …
1. how to change figures to words and words to figures
2. the correct words for putting things in order
3. how letters are used in Roman numerals

1 Numbers and Words

Learn About It

These are the correct names for the numbers up to 20.

1	one	2	two	3	three	4	four
5	five	6	six	7	seven	8	eight
9	nine	10	ten	11	eleven	12	twelve
13	thirteen	14	fourteen	15	fifteen	16	sixteen
17	seventeen	18	eighteen	19	nineteen	20	twenty

Here are some more numbers, up to 100.

30	thirty	40	forty	50	fifty	60	sixty
70	seventy	80	eighty	90	ninety	100	one hundred

26 is written **twenty-six**. There is a **hyphen** (-) between **twenty** and **six**.

135 is written **one hundred and thirty-five**. Note the **and** between **hundred** and **thirty**.

Add these to your list. You also need to know how to spell **thousand** and **million**.

We have special words for some numbers. For example, **pair** stands for 2 and **dozen** for 12.

Word Check
figures numbers written using 1, 2, 3, 4, 5, 6, 7, 8, 9 and 0

Try It Out

A Andy had to write some numbers in words for his homework.

1 a free   b for   c sevun   d eihgt
2 a twelfe   b sixteeen   c ninteen   d twentey
3 a twenty-too   b thirty three   c faurty-six
4 a one hunred and two
   b five hundred forty four
   c two thousnd

Copy any that are correct (right) and rewrite any that are wrong.

Write each one in figures as well.

Example	elevan
Answer	eleven (11)

Practice

B

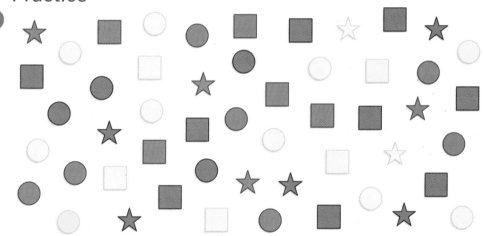

Answer the questions in sentences. Put the answer in figures after each sentence.

Example	How many stars are there?
Answer	There are eleven stars. (11)

How many of these can you see?

1 red circles   2 yellow stars
3 blue squares   4 yellow circles
5 circles   6 squares
7 red shapes   8 blue shapes
9 yellow shapes   10 shapes

C This is a map Shakti made of her street.

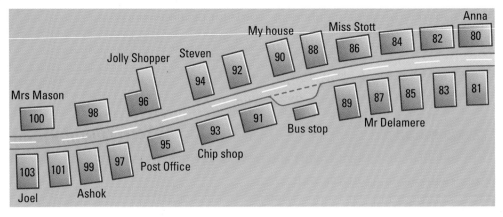

Write each answer as a sentence, using figures.

Example	Who lives at number ninety-four?
Answer	Steven lives at number 94.

1 What number does Shakti live at?

2 Who lives at number one hundred and three?

3 Who lives at number eighty-seven?

4 What is at number ninety-six?

5 What is at number ninety-five?

6 Who lives at number one hundred?

7 Who lives next door to number one hundred and one?

8 What is in between number eighty-nine and number ninety-one?

9 What is at number ninety-three?

10 Shakti doesn't know who lives in the houses without names. Write **in words** three house numbers like this.

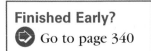

Finished Early?
Go to page 340

Further Practice

D

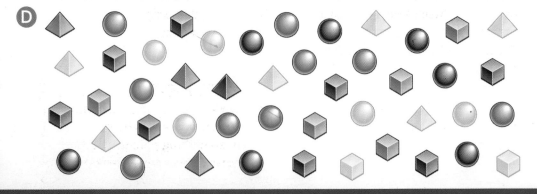

Answer the questions in sentences. Put the answer in figures after each sentence.

> **Example** How many balls are there?
> **Answer** There are twenty-one balls. (21)

How many of these can you see?

1 yellow pyramids   **2** purple cubes   **3** blue balls
4 purple pyramids   **5** cubes   **6** pyramids
7 yellow shapes   **8** blue shapes   **9** purple shapes
10 shapes

> **Finished Early?**
> 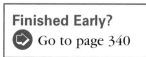 Go to page 340

② Numbers for Ordering

Learn About It

Here are some numbers used for putting things in order.

1	first	1st		8	eighth	8th
2	second	2nd		9	ninth	9th
3	third	3rd		10	tenth	10th
4	fourth	4th		11	eleventh	11th
5	fifth	5th		12	twelfth	12th
6	sixth	6th		13	thirteenth	13th
7	seventh	7th				

Notice that the number gets the same ending as the word, so
    second → **2nd**, **fourth** → **4th**.

Here are some more.

20	twentieth	20th		80	eightieth	80th
21	twenty-first	21st		100	hundredth	100th
22	twenty-second	22nd		101	hundred-and-first	101st
23	twenty-third	23rd		1000	thousandth	
24	twenty-fourth	24th		1 000 000	millionth	
30	thirtieth	30th				

Word Check

ordering number a number that tells you where something comes in a list

Try It Out

E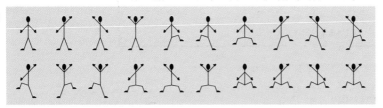

Example	What position in the row is ⚇
Answer	⚇ is twentieth.

What position is:

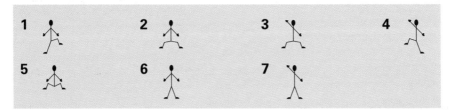

What is in these places?

8 fourth   **9** sixteenth   **10** thirteenth

11 sixth   **12** twelfth   **13** eleventh

14 eighteenth

Practice

F Here is the alphabet.

A B C D E F G H I J K L M N O P Q R S T U V W X Y Z

Copy out the alphabet and use it to answer the questions.

Which letters are in these places?

Example	second
Answer	The second letter is B.

1 fifth   **2** eighth   **3** fifteenth

4 twentieth   **5** twenty-fourth   **6** eleventh

7 third

Which place are these letters in?

Example	A
Answer	A is the first letter.

8 F   **9** J   **10** Y   **11** P   **12** U   **13** K   **14** C

G This is how the even numbers begin.

2   4   6   8   10   12 ...

What is the ...

1 third even number   **2** fifth even number

3 seventh even number   **4** tenth even number

5 twentieth even number?

What position in the even numbers is ...

6 8   **7** 12   **8** 16   **9** 24   **10** 50?

> **Finished Early?**
> ➡ Go to page 340

Further Practice

H

Draw the symbols that are in these places.

1 second   **2** ninth   **3** thirteenth

4 twentieth   **5** sixth   **6** seventeenth

Which position is each symbol in?

7 —   **8** ✳   **9** ⌣

10 ○   **11** ═   **12** ⌄

I Here is the start of a list of numbers.

5   6   7   8   9   10 ...

What is the ...

1 fourth number   **2** sixth number   **3** seventh number

4 ninth number   **5** twentieth number?

What position in the list is ...

6 7   **7** 9   **8** 12   **9** 17   **10** 30?

> **Finished Early?**
> ➡ Go to page 340

P 3 Roman Numerals

Learn About It

1 About two thousand years ago, the Romans used the letters of their alphabet to write their numbers. They used simple letters that could easily be carved in stone.

They used the letter **I** to stand for 1. **II** stands for 2

and **III** stands for 3.

2 The Romans had a rule. You can't use more than **three** of the **same** letter together, so you can't write **IIII** for 4.

The letter **V** stands for 5. To write 4, you use '1 before 5', **IV**.

3 Draw a table in your book to record the different numbers.

Put in the numbers you have seen so far.

From now on, add new numbers to the table as you read.

4 6 is written '1 after 5', **VI**.

7 and 8 follow the same pattern. Make them.

You can't use **VIIII** to make 9 because of the rule in step 2.

Try to find an answer to the problem. Hint: 10 is written **X**.

5 Now make the numbers from 11 to 20. Hint: 20 is **XX**.

6 50 is written **L** and 100 is **C**.

Write the numbers 30, 40, … up to 100.

7 To go further, you need to know that **D** stands for 500.

Write the numbers 200, 300 and so on.

To finish the hundreds, you need to know that **M** stands for 1000.

You can also use small letters. 45 is written **xlv**.

Word Check

Roman numeral a number written using an old system of letters, still used today

Try It Out

J Write these in modern numbers.

Example	XXI
Working	XX = 20, I = 1
Answer	21

1 XII   **2** XXIX   **3** xli

4 LXXVII   **5** XCV   **6** civ

7 cccxl   **8** CDXVI   **9** dcclxviii

10 MDCLXXXIV

K Write these in Roman numerals. Use capital letters.

1 25   **2** 52   **3** 68   **4** 99   **5** 146

6 555   **7** 941   **8** 1033   **9** 1939   **10** 2001

Practice

L Roman numerals are often used for years in dates. These were the years when some of England's kings and queens were born and died.

Copy the table, and write the dates in Roman numerals.

Copy this table, and write the dates in modern numbers.

	King/queen	Born	Died
1	William I	1027	1087
2	Richard III	1452	1485
3	Henry VIII	1491	1547
4	Elizabeth I	1533	1603
5	Charles II	1630	1685

	King/queen	Born	Died
6	Anne	MDCLXVI	MDCCXIV
7	George III	MDCCXXXVIII	MDCCCXX
8	Victoria	MDCCCXIX	MCMI
9	Edward VII	MDCCCXLI	MCMX
10	Elizabeth II	MCMXXVII	–

Further Practice

M Here is a shopping list written in Roman numerals.
Write it out using modern numbers.

1 pack of XII toilet rolls

2 VI apples

3 breakfast flakes (D grams)

4 orange squash (LXXV centilitres)

5 CCCXX grams cheese

6 roll of XXIV refuse bags

7 VIII slices of bacon

8 pack of V CLXXX-minute videotapes

9 MD gram tub of ice cream

10 CCXL tea bags

Finished Early?
➡ Go to page 341

2 Place Value and Rounding

> In this chapter you will learn ...
> **1** what the columns and positions in the decimal system mean
> **2** what a digit means within a number
> **3** how to round off numbers to the nearest ten or hundred

P 1 Positions and Columns

 A strip of centimetre squared paper about 7 cm wide

Learn About It

Our number system is called the **decimal** system. It is based on **tens**. This is probably because we have ten fingers and thumbs.

A **digit** is a 1, 2, 3, 4, 5, 6, 7, 8, 9 or 0 used as part of a number.

In the decimal system, it is important that the digits in a number are in the correct **places**.

18 is not the same as 81!

18 has one ten and eight units.

81 has eight tens and one unit.

The place of a digit is often called a **column**. This is because numbers are written underneath each other when you do sums.

The object on the right is called a **decimalizer**.

It is a table showing the names of the first seven columns.

Each column is 1 cm wide.

millions	hundred thousands	ten thousands	thousands	hundreds	tens	units

NUMBER SKILLS Know the names of the digits and the concept of place value in numbers with 1 or 2 s.f.

1 Copy the decimalizer carefully onto your strip of squared paper.

2 The units column of your decimalizer strip must always go over the last digit of the number. Try putting it on this number.

4	0	0	0	0

The 4 is in the ten-thousands column. All the other digits are zeroes. So this number is **forty thousand**.

3 Now try this one.

2	3	0	0	0	0

The 2 is in the hundred-thousands column and the 3 is in the ten-thousands column. All the other digits are zeroes. So this number is **two hundred and thirty thousand**.

A number written in words can be changed into figures. Your strip can help.

4 Suppose you want to write down **six thousand**. Lay the decimalizer on a piece of paper. The 6 has to go in the thousands column, so write it under this heading. All the other digits will be zeroes, so put a zero under every other column. Copy the answer into your book.

5 Use your strip to help you write the number **seventy-five thousand**.

Try It Out

Centimetre squared paper

A For each question, copy the number and use your decimalizer strip to write it in words.

1	2	0	0	0			
2	5	0	0				
3	8	0	0	0			
4	3	0	0	0	0		
5	9	0					
6	1	3	0	0	0	0	
7	7	2	0	0	0		
8	2	5	0	0	0	0	0
9	6	3					
10	3	7	0	0	0		

B For each question, copy the number, then use your decimalizer
strip to help you write it in figures.

Example   fifteen thousand
Working

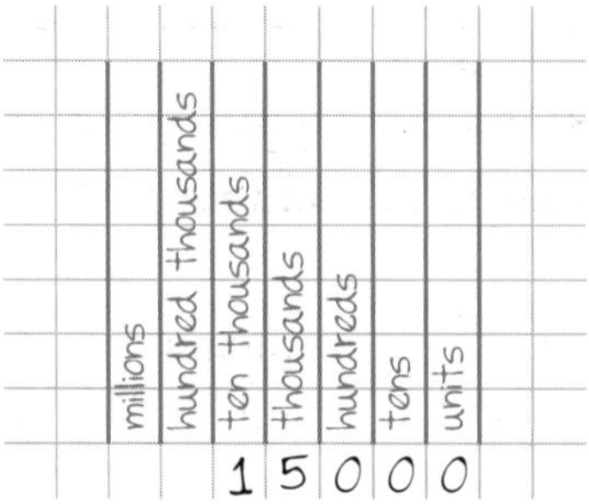

millions	hundred thousands	ten thousands	thousands	hundreds	tens	units
		1	5	0	0	0

Answer   fifteen thousand = 15 000

1 five thousand
2 eighty thousand
3 twenty
4 three hundred thousand
5 four million
6 fifty-three thousand
7 nine hundred and ninety thousand
8 four hundred and ten
9 eleven thousand
10 one million, eight hundred thousand

Practice

C These are readings from some cars showing their mileage.
Use your decimalizer to write down the mileage in words.

Example   0 0 7 2 0 0
Working   Ignore the zeroes at the beginning. The number is 7200.
Answer   007200 = seven thousand, two hundred miles

1 0 0 0 0 5 2 0   2 0 2 6 0 0 0

3 1 2 0 0 0 0   4 0 0 4 7 0 0

5 0 0 0 0 2 4

D Use your decimalizer to write out these numbers.

Example	a 2 in the hundreds column and a 7 in the thousands column
Answer	7200

1 a 6 in the thousands column and a 3 in the ten-thousands column

2 an 8 in the hundred-thousands column and a 7 in the ten-thousands column

3 a 5 in the millions column

4 a 3 in the tens column and a 7 in the hundreds column

5 a 1 in the hundred-thousands column and an 8 in the millions column

E Make up a number using the parts given.

Example	500 and 6000
Working	You need 6 in the thousands, 5 in the hundreds, and zeroes in the tens and units.
Answer	6500

1 300 and 4000

3 500 and 60

5 4000 and 80 000

7 60 000 and 600

9 5000, 600 and 30

2 60 000 and 500 000

4 500 and 6000

6 200 000 and 7000

8 500 and 90 000

10 5000, 60 000 and 300 000

Finished Early?
➡ Go to page 341

Further Practice

F For each question, copy the number and use your decimalizer strip to write it in figures.

1 three hundred

2 eight thousand

3 twenty thousand

4 five hundred thousand

5 five million

6 thirty-five thousand

7 one hundred and ninety thousand

8 seven hundred and forty

9 fifteen thousand

10 three million, one hundred thousand

G The table on page 18 shows the population of some countries. Write a sentence to describe each line.

Example	Question 1.
Answer	The population of Antigua is eighty-five thousand.

Question	Country	Population
1	Antigua	85 000
2	Belize	190 000
3	Dominica	81 000
4	Faeroes	45 000
5	Gambia	880 000
6	Malta	350 000
7	Sierra Leone	4 100 000
8	Sweden	8 500 000
9	Switzerland	6 700 000
10	Zimbabwe	9 400 000

Finished Early?
➡ Go to page 341

T 2 Digits

Learn About It

These are the correct names for different sizes of numbers.

1	one
10	ten
100	one hundred
1000	one thousand
10 000	ten thousand
100 000	one hundred thousand
1 000 000	one million
1 000 000 000	one billion (thousand million)
1 000 000 000 000	one trillion (million million)

Digits mean different things depending on where they are in a number.

Look at the number 676.

The first 6 stands for 600 (six hundred). It is in the hundreds column.

The second 6 stands for 6 (six). It is in the units column.

Zeroes are important too. Without them, you couldn't tell the difference between 63, 630, 603, 6300, 6030, 6003 or even 603 000!

Word Check

digit a 1, 2, 3, 4, 5, 6, 7, 8, 9 or 0 used as part of a number

place/column the position of a digit in a number

value the number that a digit is 'worth' when it is in a column

Try It Out

H Write down the value of the coloured digits, in words and in figures.

Each number has two coloured digits.

Example	23 705
Answer	Red: three thousand (3000)
	Blue: seven hundred (700)

1 6570

2 10 822

3 32 046

4 180 343

5 566 002

6 1 042 240

7 8 765 432

8 1 760 000

9 625 501

10 21 536 300

Practice

I Put the numbers in each cloud into order, smallest to largest.

Write them in figures *and* in words, in two columns.

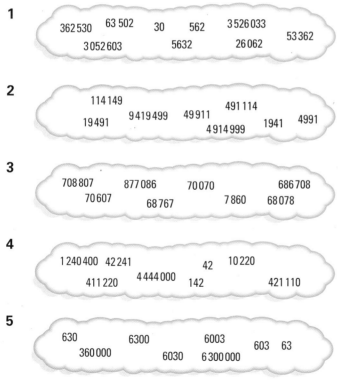

1

362 530   63 502   30   562   3 526 033   53 362

3 052 603   5632   26 062

2

114 149   491 114

19 491   9 419 499   49 911   1941   4991

4 914 999

3

708 807   877 086   70 070   686 708

70 607   68 767   7860   68 078

4

1 240 400   42 241   42   10 220

411 220   4 444 000   142   421 110

5

630   6300   6003   603   63

360 000   6030   6 300 000

Finished Early?

➡ Go to page 341

Further Practice

J This table shows the sizes of some computer disks.

Type of disk	Size in kilobytes
Floppy disk	1440
Small hard disk	40 9**60**
Zip cartridge	102 **4**00
CD-ROM	**76**0 000
Normal hard disk	2 400 000
Large hard disk	9 **1**00 000

1 Write down the value of each **red** digit, in figures *and* in words.

2 Find the digit in the table that is worth the number given.

Copy out the number and underline the digit.

> **Example**   two thousand
> **Answer**   102 400

(a) forty
(b) nine hundred
(c) forty thousand
(d) one hundred thousand
(e) nine million
(f) four hundred thousand

K These are the distances to some faraway galaxies, in kiloparsecs (a kiloparsec is about 32 000 000 000 000 000 km!).

Galaxy	Distance
Andromeda	704
Sombrero Hat	4 427
Hydra Cluster	555 600
The Whirlpool	11 420
Black Eye	13 580
M33	725
NGC 4552	11 070

Copy the table. Put the galaxies in order, nearest to farthest.

> **Finished Early?**
> ➡ Go to page 341

3 Rounding

Learn About It

Rounding to the nearest ten

Look at this number line.

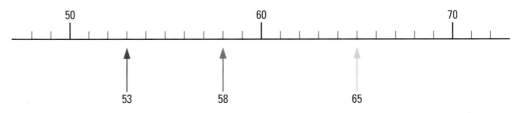

53 is in between 50 and 60. It is closer to 50 than 60, so you round **down**. You say that 53, rounded to the nearest ten, is 50.

58 is in between 50 and 60. It is closer to 60 than 50, so you round **up**. You say that 58, rounded to the nearest ten, is 60.

65 is **exactly** halfway between 60 and 70. If this happens, you round **up**. So you say that 65, rounded to the nearest ten, is 70.

A number rounded to the nearest ten is not as **accurate** as the original number.

Rounding to the nearest hundred

Look at this number line.

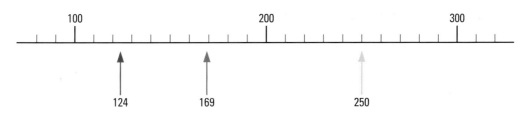

124 is in between 100 and 200. It is closer to 100 than 200, so you round **down**. You say that 124, rounded to the nearest hundred, is 100.

169 is in between 100 and 200. It is closer to 200 than 100, so you round **up**. You say that 169, rounded to the nearest hundred, is 200.

250 is **exactly** halfway between 200 and 300. If this happens, you round **up**. So you say that 250, rounded to the nearest hundred, is 300.

A number rounded to the nearest hundred is less accurate than one rounded to the nearest ten.

Word Check

accurate how close a number is to being exact

to round to make a number less accurate by writing the nearest 10 or 100 instead

Try It Out

L Round these numbers to the nearest 10.
You can use the number line to help.

Example	26
Working	26 is between 20 and 30, but nearer to 30.
Answer	26 rounded to the nearest ten is 30.

1 52	**2** 36	**3** 88
4 24	**5** 31	**6** 45
7 85	**8** 93	**9** 97
10 4	**11** 122	**12** 178
13 264	**14** 598	**15** 835

M Round these numbers to the nearest 100.
You can use the number line to help.

Example	264
Working	264 is between 200 and 300, but nearer to 300.
Answer	264 rounded to the nearest hundred is 300.

1 130	**2** 180	**3** 640
4 370	**5** 880	**6** 148
7 151	**8** 698	**9** 350
10 47	**11** 1530	**12** 2007
13 3185	**14** 7050	**15** 2964

Practice

N These are rounding machines. They tell you that you have to round

a number to the nearest ten R(10) , or

the nearest hundred R(100) . Use them on

the numbers in the questions.

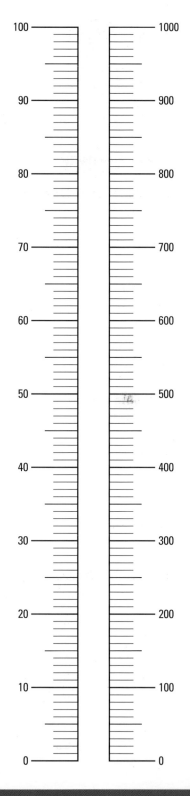

NUMBER SKILLS **Know when a number is closer to a particular multiple of 10 or 100**

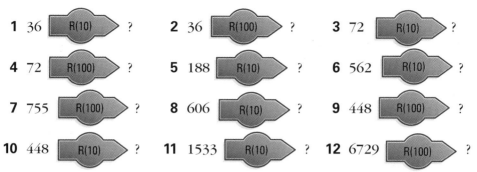

1 36 R(10) ? **2** 36 R(100) ? **3** 72 R(10) ?

4 72 R(100) ? **5** 188 R(10) ? **6** 562 R(10) ?

7 755 R(100) ? **8** 606 R(10) ? **9** 448 R(100) ?

10 448 R(10) ? **11** 1533 R(10) ? **12** 6729 R(100) ?

The table shows the number of words in some newspaper stories.
Copy and complete it.

Story	Number of words	Rounded to nearest 10	Rounded to nearest 100
BAND SPLIT UP	234		
TRAIN CRASH	417		
NEW HOSPITAL WARD	662		
FOOTBALL REPORT	310		
TREE STOLEN!	81		
TV HIGHLIGHTS	139		
POLITICAL COMMENT	225		
LOCAL CLUB NEWS	150		
CHARITY FUN RUN	405		
IN BRIEF	42		

Finished Early?
Go to page 342

Further Practice

The table shows the number of fossils found in some rock samples.
Copy and complete it.

Sample	Number of fossils	Rounded to nearest 10	Rounded to nearest 100
A	342		
B	174		
C	626		
D	105		
E	18		
F	350		
G	252		
H	501		

Finished Early?
Go to page 342

Unit 1 *All About Numbers*
Summary of Chapters 1 and 2

- Here is a list of numbers, ordering numbers and Roman numerals.

1	one	1st	first	I
2	two	2nd	second	II
3	three	3rd	third	III
4	four	4th	fourth	IV
5	five	5th	fifth	V
6	six	6th	sixth	VI
7	seven	7th	seventh	VII
8	eight	8th	eighth	VIII
9	nine	9th	ninth	IX
10	ten	10th	tenth	X
11	eleven	11th	eleventh	XI
12	twelve	12th	twelfth	XII
13	thirteen	13th	thirteenth	XIII
20	twenty	20th	twentieth	XX
22	twenty-two	22nd	twenty-second	XXII
30	thirty	30th	thirtieth	XXX
90	ninety	90th	ninetieth	XC
100	one hundred	100th	one hundredth	C
104	one hundred and four	104th	one hundred and fourth	CIV

- The position of a digit in a number is important. It decides what the digit is worth.

- When rounding to the nearest ten, round **up** if the units are 5 or more. Otherwise round down.

- When rounding to the nearest hundred, round **up** if the tens are 5 or more. Otherwise round down.

Addition and Subtraction

In this chapter you will learn ...
- **1** how to add and subtract three-digit and four-digit numbers
- **2** how to add and subtract larger numbers

1 Up to Four Digits

Learn About It

There are lots of different ways to add numbers.

Look at this question: **add 245 + 381**. Three different people will show you how they do it.

1 Janice does it like this. She adds each digit of 381 by splitting it into 1, 80 and 300.

245 + 1 = 246
246 + 80 = 326
326 + 300 = 626.

Try doing **473 + 255** like this.

Word Check

digit a figure used as part of a number

sum the result of adding numbers together

plus the + sign

carry add 1 or more to the next column when digits in the amount get bigger than 9

2 Huw adds **245 + 381** like this. He adds the hundreds, tens and units separately, then adds these together to get the answer.

200 + 300 = 500
40 + 80 = 120   } 500 + 120 + 6 = 626
5 + 1 = 6

Try doing **264 + 641** Huw's way.

3 Mary adds **245 + 381** like this. She sets it out in columns and adds the columns up from right to left. She carries any extra tens or hundreds into the next column.

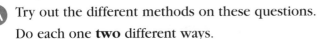

```
  2 4 5          2 4 5          2 4 5
+ 3 8 1        + 3 8 1        + 3 8 1
───────        ───────        ───────
      6            2 6          6 2 6
                 1              1
```

units: tens: hundreds:
5 + 1 = 6   4 + 8 = 12   2 + 3 = 5
                write 2 here, carry   you would write 5 here but you
                1 to hundreds   need to add the 1 carried from
                                     before, so write 6 here

Try doing **657 + 216** Mary's way.

Word Check

place/column a position in a number where a digit can be put

Try It Out

A Try out the different methods on these questions.

Do each one **two** different ways.

1 27 + 51   **2** 46 + 37   **3** 72 + 41

4 153 + 89   **5** 256 + 144   **6** 648 + 337

Learn More About It

Look at this question: **subtract 435 − 267**. The same people have their own ways of doing this, too.

1 Janice does it like this. She subtracts each digit of 267 by splitting it into 7, 60 and 200.

435 − 7 = 428

428 − 60 = 368

368 − 200 = **168**.

Try doing **473 − 255** like this.

2 Huw subtracts **435 − 267** like this. He works from the smaller number to the bigger one in steps. This is called **counting on**.

(to next 10) (to next 100) (to final 100) (final 10s) (final units)

267 | +3 ⟩ 270 | +30 ⟩ 300 | +100 ⟩ 400 | +30 ⟩ 430 | +5 ⟩ 435

To find the answer, Huw adds together all the numbers he had to add on to 267 to reach 435.

$3 + 30 + 100 + 30 + 5 = 100 + 60 + 8 = 168$.

Try doing **641 − 264** Huw's way.

3 Mary subtracts **435 − 267** like this. She sets it out in columns and subtracts the columns from right to left. She borrows tens or hundreds from the next column if the top number isn't big enough.

Try doing **657 − 276** Mary's way.

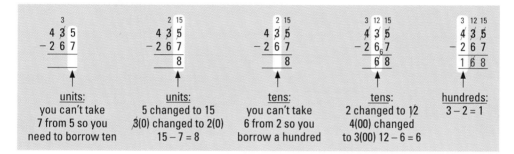

| units:
you can't take
7 from 5 so you
need to borrow ten | units:
5 changed to 15
3(0) changed to 2(0)
15 − 7 = 8 | tens:
you can't take
6 from 2 so you
borrow a hundred | tens:
2 changed to 12
4(00) changed
to 3(00) 12 − 6 = 6 | hundreds:
3 − 2 = 1 |

Word Check

difference the result of subtracting numbers

minus the − sign

borrow use a ten or hundred from the next column when the digit you are subtracting is too big

Try It Out

B Try out the different methods on these questions.
Do each one **two** different ways.

  1 58 − 35   **2** 64 − 28   **3** 126 − 83   **4** 150 − 95

Practice

C Shelley is in charge of the money for a charity. At the end of each day, she writes down the amount of money people have given. She also works out how much money she has collected so far. Copy the table on page 28 and fill in the gaps in her sheet.

Day	Amount	Total so far
Mon	£265	£621
Tue	£124	£
Wed	£318	£
Thu	£576	£
Fri	£	£1832
Sat	£	£2166
Sun	£	£2505

D In each question, one answer is different from the other two.
Find the 'odd one out'.

> **Example**   **(a)** 45 + 28   **(b)** 16 + 58   **(c)** 95 – 22
> **Working**   **(a)** 45 + 28 = 73
>   **(b)** 16 + 58 = 74
>   **(c)** 95 – 22 = 73
> **Answer**   **(b)** is the odd one out.

1 **(a)** 32 + 71   **(b)** 65 + 38   **(c)** 165 – 61

2 **(a)** 162 + 188   **(b)** 425 – 175   **(c)** 627 – 277

3 **(a)** 1056 + 3111   **(b)** 6143 – 2056   **(c)** 4141 – 54

4 **(a)** 428 + 2197 + 169   **(b)** 1444 + 1444 – 144   **(c)** 3443 – 149 – 500

> **Finished Early?**
> ➡ Go to page 343

Further Practice

E Use the method you prefer to answer these.

1 62   [+ 51]▷ ?   **2** 144   [+ 83]▷ ?

3 571   [+ 62]▷ ?   **4** 627   [+ 264]▷ ?

5 316   [+838]▷ ?   **6** 62   [– 28]▷ ?

7 144   [+ 82]▷ ?   **8** 571   [– 144]▷ ?

9 627   [+ 289]▷ ?   **10** 1248   [– 529]▷ ?

> **Finished Early?**
> ➡ Go to page 343

② Large Numbers

Learn About It

This section is about adding and subtracting larger numbers. These have more than four digits. You can use any of the methods you know.

Here are the sum and difference of two numbers worked out in columns.

Example Find the sum of 265 848 and 1 571 400.

Working Add the numbers.

```
      2 6 5 8 4 8
  +  1 5 7 1 4 0 0
     1 8 3 7 2 4 8
        1     1
```

Answer 1 837 248

Example Find the difference between 265 848 and 1 571 400.

Working Subtract the smaller number from the bigger one.

```
              10  13  9
          6   0   3 10 10
     1 5  7   1   4  0  0
   -   2  6   5   8  4  8
     1 3 0 5  5  5  2
```

Answer 1 305 552

Try It Out

Continent	Area (sq km)
Africa	30 264 000
Antarctica	13 209 000
Asia	44 250 000
Europe	9 907 000
North America	24 398 000
Oceania	8 534 000
South America	17 793 000

1 Find the area of …
   (a) Europe and Antarctica together;   (b)   Africa and Asia together.

2 Find the difference in area between …
   (a) Europe and Oceania;   (b)   North and South America.

3 Add up all the continents to find the total land area of the Earth.

4 In question 1(b) you found the area of Africa and Asia together.

   Do the other continents add up to more than that, or less?

Practice

G This table shows how many people live in some British cities – their **population**.

City	Population
Belfast	280 972
Birmingham	2 500 400
Cardiff	272 600
Edinburgh	423 213
Glasgow	654 542
Leeds	1 984 700
Liverpool	1 376 800
London	6 378 000
Manchester	2 445 200
Newcastle upon Tyne	1 087 000

1 (a) Find the total population of the Scottish cities, Edinburgh and Glasgow.
   (b) One other city's population is very close to this total. Which is it, and what is the difference?

2 Birmingham is the next biggest city after London. What is the difference in population?

3 (a) What is the total population of Leeds, Liverpool and Manchester?
   (b) Is this more or less than London? What is the difference?

4 What is the total population of *all* these cities?

5 The total population of the UK is 56 467 000. How many people do *not* live in the cities in the table?

H This picture shows part of the Solar System. Each planet's **distance** from the Sun is marked.

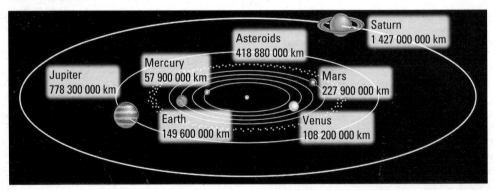

1 Work out the width of each planet's orbit. Add each **distance** to itself.

Example	Mercury	
Working	57 900 000 + 57 900 000	
Answer	115 800 000 km	

2 Work out how wide the gaps between the orbits are. Take one distance away from the other.

Example	Mercury to Venus
Working	108 200 000 – 57 900 000
Answer	50 300 000 km

Finished Early?
Go to page 343

Further Practice

The table shows how many people are employed by some big car makers.

Country	Company	People employed
USA	General	765 700
	Mord	358 939
Germany	Denz	326 288
	Volker	260 548
France	Reneot	188 936
	Peugeault	160 600

1 Work out the total number of people working for …
   (a) the American car makers;
   (b) the German car makers;
   (c) the French car makers.

2 Work out how many more people work …
   (a) in the American companies than the German ones;
   (b) in the American companies than the French ones;
   (c) in the German companies than the French ones.

Finished Early?
Go to page 343

Multiplication

In this chapter you will learn ...
1. that knowing your multiplication tables is important
2. how to multiply by 10 or 100
3. how to multiply any number by a single digit
4. how to multiply any two numbers together

T 1 Multiplication Tables

Learn About It

Suppose you want to buy 4 chews at 6 pence each. How much will it cost?

You often need to work out things like this. To help, you learn a few simple facts. These are your **multiplication tables**.

The result of multiplying numbers is called the **product**.

Make sure that you know your multiplication tables before you start these questions.

Word Check

multiplication table a list showing 1 × a number, 2 × it, 3 × it, and so on.

product the result of multiplying numbers

Try It Out

A Andrew did some tables questions. He wrote the answers down but forgot to write out the questions. Write his work out properly.

Example	8
Answer	4 × 2 = 8

1	10	2	15	3	28	4	40	5	64
6	48	7	56	8	18	9	24	10	30
11	54	12	32	13	72	14	36	15	49
16	12	17	27	18	35	19	63	20	81

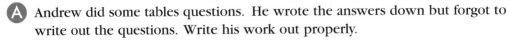

Practice

B Use multiplication tables to answer these questions. Show the working before you write down the answer.

Example	Annalee has 4 shelves in her room. Each shelf holds 8 folders. How many folders can she put on her shelves?
Working	$4 \times 8 = 32$
Answer	She can put 32 folders on her shelves.

1 There are 7 pairs of socks in my drawer. How many socks are there?

2 Ms Eastwood took 7 pupils to a museum. The tickets were £5 each. How much did it cost altogether?

3 Errol is decorating his bathroom. He bought 3 packs of tiles. Each pack has 4 tiles in it. How many tiles did he buy?

4 In a car park each row of spaces can hold 8 cars. There are 8 rows. How many cars can park there?

5 'Pentos' come in packs of 5. Susie bought 6 packs. How many Pentos did she buy?

6 A mandolin is an instrument with 8 strings. A music shop has 6 mandolins in the window. How many strings is that altogether?

7 Triangles have 3 corners. How many corners will 9 separate triangles have?

8 A chess board has 8 rows, each with 8 squares. How many squares are there on a chess board?

C Evans Toiletries send items all over the country. They put items into boxes, then pack the boxes into cases. Copy and complete the table.

Item	Items in a box	Boxes in a case	Items in a case
Soap	8	6	
Hairspray	4	9	
Flannel	6	5	
Towel	3	8	
Sponge	9	5	

Finished Early?
➡ Go to page 344

Further Practice

D Each number machine has **5** numbers that are fed into it. Copy the table and fill in the last column. The first one has been done for you.

Question	Input numbers	Machine	Output numbers
1	6, 4, 7, 9, 5	× 2	12, 8, 14, 18, 10
2	4, 3, 9 , 6, 8	× 4	
3	8, 3, 6, 5, 7	× 5	
4	9, 2, 7, 3, 4	× 9	
5	3, 8, 7, 4, 9	× 6	
6	4, 7, 9, 2, 8	× 7	

E Some friends work out how much money they have saved. Copy and complete the table.

Name	Amount each week	Number of weeks	Amount saved
Jody	£3	8	
Glyn	£5	6	
Linh	£6	7	
Gareth	£4	9	
Faith	£7	5	

Who saved the most?

Finished Early?
➡ Go to page 344

P 2 Multiply by 10 or 100

Learn About It

Multiply by 10

1 Our number system is based on tens. This makes it easy to multiply by 10.

Multiplying by 10 turns **units** into **tens**. This shows what happens when you do 6 × 10.

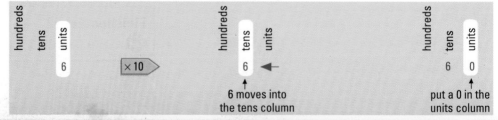

hundreds tens units
6 × 10 hundreds tens units 6 ◄
6 moves into the tens column

hundreds tens units 6 0
put a 0 in the units column

NUMBER SKILLS Understand the concept of multiplication, know multiplication facts to 9 × 9

2 Multiplying by 10 turns **tens** into **hundreds**. This shows what happens when you work out 25×10.

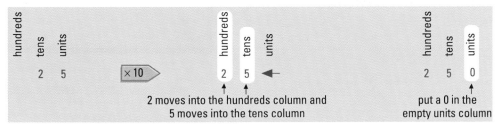

2 moves into the hundreds column and
5 moves into the tens column

put a 0 in the
empty units column

There is a simple rule to help you do this.

This works with any whole number.

So $108 \times 10 = 1080$.

Key Fact

To multiply a whole number
by 10, put **0** onto the end.

3 Multiply these numbers by 10.

(a) 5   (b) 9   (c) 14   (d) 46   (e) 221

Multiply by 100

4 Multiplying by 100 is just the same as multiplying by 10 and then multiplying by 10 again.

Multiplying by 100 turns **units** into **hundreds**. This shows what happens when you work out 3×100.

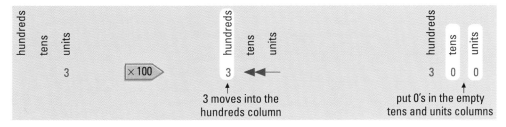

3 moves into the
hundreds column

put 0's in the empty
tens and units columns

5 Multiplying by 100 turns **tens** into **thousands**. This shows what happens when you work out 71×100.

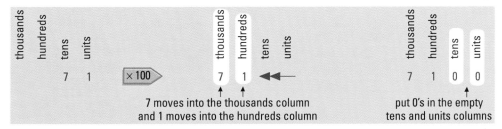

7 moves into the thousands column
and 1 moves into the hundreds column

put 0's in the empty
tens and units columns

There is a simple rule to help you do this.

This works with any whole number. So $449 \times 100 = 44\,900$.

Key Fact

To multiply a whole number by 100, put **00** onto the end.

6 Multiply these numbers by 100.

(a) 3   (b) 8   (c) 16

(d) 32   (e) 166

Word Check

zero, nought 0

Try It Out

F **1** Multiply each of these numbers by 10.

Example	34
Working and answer	$34 \times 10 = 340$ *(Put 0 onto the end of 34.)*

(a) 7   (b) 4   (c) 12   (d) 25   (e) 36

(f) 78   (g) 102   (h) 166   (i) 470   (j) 1609

2 Multiply each of these numbers by 100.

Example	91
Working and answer	$91 \times 100 = 9100$
	(Put 00 onto the end of 91.)

(a) 8   (b) 3   (c) 13   (d) 24   (e) 37

(f) 77   (g) 103   (h) 165   (i) 480   (j) 1608

Learn More About It

If you can multiply by 10 and 100, there are lots of other things you can do.

1 You can work out 3×20, because 20 is just 2×10.

$$3 \times 20$$

is the same as $3 \times 2 \quad \times 10$

is the same as $6 \qquad \times 10 \ = 60$.

2 You can work out 700×4. Find 7×4 first, then put the 00 from 700 onto the end:

$$700 \times 4$$

is the same as $7 \times 4 \quad \times 100$

is the same as $28 \qquad \times 100 \ = 2800$.

3 You can work out 80×60. Find 8×6 first, then put 0 onto the end **twice** because **both** numbers have 0 at the end.

$$80 \times 60$$

is the same as $8 \times 6 \qquad \times 10 \times 10$

is the same as $48 \qquad \times 10 \times 10 \quad = \textbf{4800}$.

 4 Be careful! You might think that 40×50 is 200, but it isn't:

$4 \times 5 = 20$.

Put 00 onto the end: 2000.

So $40 \times 50 = \textbf{2000}$.

Try It Out

Ⓖ Work these out using step 1, 2, 3 or 4 above.

1 (a) 5×30 **(b)** 6×40 **(c)** 3×70

   (d) 60×6 **(e)** 30×9 **(f)** 80×5

2 (a) 7×200 **(b)** 3×800 **(c)** 4×500

   (d) 900×7 **(e)** 800×8 **(f)** 200×9

3 (a) 50×70 **(b)** 30×80 **(c)** 60×20

   (d) 40×40 **(e)** 70×70 **(f)** 50×60

Practice

Ⓗ In each question, two answers are the same and the other is different. Find the 'odd one out'.

 There is one trick question!

Example	**(a)** 2×300 **(b)** 60×10 **(c)** 40×20
Working	**(a)** $2 \times 3 = 6$ (*Put 00 onto the end.*) 600
	(b) $60 \times 10 = \mathbf{600}$ (*Put 0 onto the end of 60.*)
	(c) $4 \times 2 = 8$ (*Put 0 and 0 onto the end.*) 800
Answer	**(c)** is the odd one out.

1 (a) 40×20 **(b)** 10×80 **(c)** 400×4

2 (a) 300×6 **(b)** 9×200 **(c)** 110×10

3 (a) 60×10 **(b)** 200×5 **(c)** 30×20

4 (a) 70×40 **(b)** 200×7 **(c)** 700×2

5 (a) 4×100 **(b)** 80×5 **(c)** 20×20

6 (a) 500×7 **(b)** 60×60 **(c)** 70×50

7 (a) 120×100 **(b)** 30×40 **(c)** 6×200

8 (a) 49×100 **(b)** 70×70 **(c)** 20×490

I Work out how much you would pay for these things.
Copy and complete the tables. Put your working underneath.

Item	Cost each week	Number of weeks	Total cost
Garden shed	£9	50	
Patio	£30	60	
Garage extension	£60	40	
Small car	£30	200	
Family car	£40	300	

Finished Early?
➡ Go to page 344

Further Practice

J Each number machine has five input numbers. Copy the table, then
work out the output numbers. Put your working underneath the table.

Question	Input numbers	Machine	Output numbers
Example	10, 20, 30, 40, 50	× 2	20, 40, 60, 80, 100
1	6, 4, 7, 9, 5	× 10	
2	4, 3, 9, 6, 8	× 100	
3	80, 30, 60, 50, 70	× 3	
4	90, 20, 70, 30, 40	× 7	
5	300, 800, 700, 400, 900	× 8	
6	40, 70, 90, 20, 80	× 20	
7	30, 70, 60, 20, 50	× 60	
8	8, 9, 3, 5, 4	× 500	

K Each question has two multiplications. Work them out, then write *same* if they
give the same answer or *different* if they don't.

1 (a) 6×10 (b) 30×2 **2** (a) 10×8 (b) 4×20
3 (a) 4×100 (b) 10×40 **4** (a) 100×7 (b) 80×10
5 (a) 5×40 (b) 4×50 **6** (a) 2×60 (b) 40×3
7 (a) 80×3 (b) 4×60 **8** (a) 90×7 (b) 56×10
9 (a) 6×600 (b) 900×4 **10** (a) 2×800 (b) 100×12

Finished Early?
➡ Go to page 344

③ Multiply by a Digit

Learn About It

If you know your tables and can multiply by 10 or 100, you can multiply any number by a single digit.

Two different people will show you how they do it.

1 Look at this question: **52 × 3**.

Huw does it like this.

×	50	2
3	**150**	**6**

> ### Key Fact
> When you multiply numbers, you can do it in any order.

He uses the box method.

He splits 52 up into 50 + 2 and puts these above his boxes.

The answers go in the boxes.

Now he adds them up. 150 + 6 = 156.

So **52 × 3 = 156**.

Here is another one. **4 × 173**.

Huw thinks it is easier to multiply a big number by a small number. 4 × 173 gives the same answer as 173 × 4, so he does 173 × 4 instead.

×	100	70	3
4	**400**	**280**	**12**

400 + 280 + 12 = 692.

So **173 × 4 = 692**.

2 Now try 64 × 5 and 6 × 218 this way.

3 Janice does **52 × 3** like this. She works in columns.

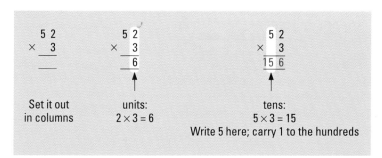

5 2 × 3	5 2 × 3 ——— 6	5 2 × 3 ——— 15 6
Set it out in columns	units: 2 × 3 = 6	tens: 5 × 3 = 15 Write 5 here; carry 1 to the hundreds

This is how Janice does 4×173.

Her method works better with 173×4 too, so she does it this way round.

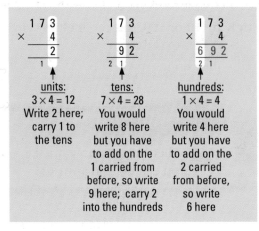

```
  1 7 3          1 7 3          1 7 3
×     4        ×     4        ×     4
─────────      ─────────      ─────────
      2            9 2          6 9 2
  1              2  1          2  1
```

units:	tens:	hundreds:
$3 \times 4 = 12$	$7 \times 4 = 28$	$1 \times 4 = 4$
Write 2 here; carry 1 to the tens	You would write 8 here but you have to add on the 1 carried from before, so write 9 here; carry 2 into the hundreds	You would write 4 here but you have to add on the 2 carried from before, so write 6 here

4 Now try 6×35 and 338×4 this way.

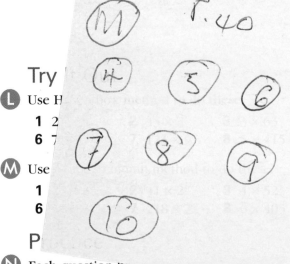

p.40

M

4   5   6

7   8   9

10

Try

L Use H

1 2

6 7

$\quad \times 81$ **5** 27×4

688×3 **10** 1217×8

M Use

1

6

73×3 **5** 3×35

177×9 **10** 8×1366

P

N Each question has two ... use either method to find the answers. Work them out, then write *same* they give the same answer or *different* if they don't.

1 (a) 24×7 (b) 21×8 **2** (a) 45×8 (b) 6×75
3 (a) 62×3 (b) 6×36 **4** (a) 81×6 (b) 54×9
5 (a) 99×8 (b) 88×9 **6** (a) 2×111 (b) 37×6
7 (a) 7×225 (b) 185×9 **8** (a) 833×4 (b) 476×7
9 (a) 8×265 (b) 5×424 **10** (a) 1554×9 (b) 2431×6

⊙ Use the method you prefer to answer these questions.

Some sixth-form students were talking about what they earned in the summer holidays. Copy and complete the table. Put your working underneath the table.

Student	Wages per week	Number of weeks	Total earned
Scott	£126	5	
Elaine	£86	6	
Grace	£165	6	
Claire	£99	7	
Jacob	£215	3	
Hani	£120	5	

Who earned the most?

> **Finished Early?**
> ⇨ Go to page 344

Further Practice

Ⓟ Use the method you prefer to answer these.
Remember to 'turn the question round' if you have to.

1 21×4	**2** 32×3	**3** 42×2	**4** 6×51	**5** 62×4
6 2×84	**7** 3×63	**8** 33×5	**9** 46×7	**10** 29×3
11 4×57	**12** 9×28	**13** 94×8	**14** 3×176	**15** 135×4
16 2×277	**17** 633×7	**18** 9×528	**19** 6×1048	**20** 5533×5

Ⓠ Work out how much it costs to buy all the issues of these magazines.

Magazine	Cost per issue	Number of issues	Total cost
Good Food Guide	£3	36	
Which Car?	£5	24	
Computer Gamer	£6	42	
Medical Matters	£28	9	
CD Heaven	£4	104	
Model Mart	£5	75	

> **Finished Early?**
> ⇨ Go to page 344

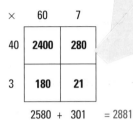

T 4 Multiply b...

Learn Abou...

These diagrams sh...
67×43 and $329 \times$...

×	60	7
40	2400	280
3	180	21

2580 + 301   = 2881

×	20	9
20	6000	400	180
6	1800	120	54

7800 + 520 + 234   = 8554

These diagrams show how
Janice would do them
using long multiplication.

```
    6 7
  × 4 3
  2 0₂1
  2 6₂8 0
  2 8 8 1
```

```
    3 2 9
  ×   2 6
  1 9₁7₅4
  6 5₁8 0
  8 5 5 4
    1  1
```

Try It Out

R Use Huw's box method to do these.

Remember that you can change the order of the numbers if you like.

1 21×14 **2** 43×28 **3** 63×63 **4** 16×815 **5** 287×49 **6** 1707×55

S Use Janice's column method to do these.

Remember that you can change the order of the numbers if you like.

1 43×13 **2** 41×32 **3** 74×52 **4** 735×35 **5** 82×306 **6** 28×2516

Practice

T In each question, two answers are the same and the other is different.
Find the 'odd one out'. Use the method you prefer to work them out.

There is one trick question!

Example	(a) 26×16	(b) 28×15	(c) 35×12

Working	2 6
	× 1 6
	1 5₃6
	2 6 0
	4 1 6
	  1
		2 8
		× 1 5
		1 4₄0
		2 8 0
		4 2 0
		  1
			3 5
			× 1 2
			7₁0
			3 5 0
			4 2 0
			  1

Answer	(a) is the odd one out		

1 **(a)** 21×35 **(b)** 29×25 **(c)** 49×15

2 **(a)** 56×44 **(b)** 39×66 **(c)** 77×32

3 **(a)** 78×14 **(b)** 84×13 **(c)** 36×32

4 **(a)** 132×11 **(b)** 44×33 **(c)** 121×12

5 **(a)** 561×85 **(b)** 935×51 **(c)** 65×733

Ⓤ **1** Here are the weekly wages of some workers. There are 52 weeks in a year. Calculate how much each earns in a year.

(a) £85 **(b)** £108 **(c)** £165 **(d)** £251

2 These are four people's monthly salaries. There are 12 months in a year. Calculate how much each person earns in a year.

(a) £466 **(b)** £609 **(c)** £945 **(d)** £1264

3 A floor tile has an area of 225 square cm. Find the area in square cm covered by these.

(a) 16 tiles **(b)** 25 tiles **(c)** 36 tiles **(d)** 64 tiles

Ⓥ Work these out one step at a time.

Example	$43 \times 24 \times 32$
Working	$$\begin{array}{r} 43 \\ \times 24 \\ \hline 1\,7{\scriptstyle1}2 \\ 860 \\ \hline 1032 \\ {\scriptstyle 1} \end{array} \qquad \begin{array}{r} 1032 \\ \times \quad 32 \\ \hline 2064 \\ 30960 \\ \hline 33024 \\ {\scriptstyle 1\ 1} \end{array}$$
Answer	$43 \times 24 \times 32 = 33\,024$

1 $15 \times 16 \times 17$ **2** $24 \times 18 \times 12$ **3** $35 \times 27 \times 14$

4 $46 \times 75 \times 36$ **5** $123 \times 45 \times 67$ **6** $21 \times 22 \times 23 \times 24$

Further Practice

Ⓦ Each number machine has three input numbers. Copy the table, then work out the output numbers. Put your working underneath the table.

	Input numbers	Machine	Output numbers
1	26, 33, 52	× 13	
2	75, 102, 146	× 15	
3	68, 307, 555	× 23	
4	116, 230, 783	× 35	
5	69, 217, 981	× 69	

Finished Early?
➪ Go to page 345

5 Division

In this chapter you will learn ...
- **1** how to divide any number by a single digit
- **2** how to divide a number by 10 or 100
- **3** how to divide any number by a two-digit number

T 1 Divide by a Digit

Learn About It

Dividing any number by a single digit is easy if you know your tables.

You work from left to right. You try to divide each digit in turn.

This is how to work out $72 \div 3$.

$7 \div 3 = 2\,r\,1$ $12 \div 3 = 4$

$$
\begin{array}{r}
2 \\
3\overline{)7\,^12}
\end{array}
\qquad
\begin{array}{r}
2\ 4 \\
3\overline{)7\,^12}
\end{array}
$$

makes 2
into 12

The answer is $72 \div 3 = 24$.

Here is $364 \div 5$.

$3 \div 5 = 0\,r\,3$ $36 \div 5 = 7\,r\,1$ $14 \div 5 = 2\,r\,4$

$$
\begin{array}{r}
0 \\
5\overline{)3\,^36\ 4}
\end{array}
\qquad
\begin{array}{r}
0\ 7 \\
5\overline{)3\,^36\,^14}
\end{array}
\qquad
\begin{array}{r}
0\ 7\ 2\,r\,4 \\
5\overline{)3\,^36\,^14}
\end{array}
$$

makes 6   makes 4   you have reached
into 36   into 14   the last digit, so this
                                  is the remainder

The answer is 364 ÷ 5 = 72 remainder 4.

Notice how the remainders are carried along to the next digit each time.

Word Check

divide share out or split up into equal parts

division dividing

remainder what is left over if you can't divide exactly

carry move a number from one column to another

per 'in a' or 'every': 4 times per year means 4 times every year

Try It Out

A Work out the answers to these. Check your answer by multiplying.

1 2)4 6   **2** 2)9 2   **3** 3)8 4   **4** 3)4 8 6   **5** 5)6 4 3

6 7)2 4 5   **7** 4)7 4   **8** 9)5 7 6   **9** 8)4 1 5   **10** 6)2 4 6 8

B Set these out properly, then find the answers.

1 243 ÷ 3   **2** 432 ÷ 4   **3** 2166 ÷ 2   **4** 2166 ÷ 5   **5** 724 ÷ 4
6 791 ÷ 7   **7** 2553 ÷ 9   **8** 152 ÷ 8   **9** 714 ÷ 6   **10** 6040 ÷ 5

Practice

C Here is a cloud full of divisions. Some of them have the same answers.

686 ÷ 3   14 ÷ 4   9)2061   1142 ÷ 5

446 ÷ 5   7)84   9)108   2)179   1832 ÷ 8

24 ÷ 2   627 ÷ 7

538 ÷ 6   4)357   6)20   268 ÷ 3

8)716   2)458   6)1370

29 ÷ 9   1603 ÷ 7

Work out the answers, then put the divisions with the same answers into groups. There are **six** groups.

Example 14 ÷ 4 and 29 ÷ 9 would be in the same group because they have the same answer: 3 r 2.

Copy and complete the table when you have the answers.

Answer 3 r 2				
14 ÷ 4 29 ÷ 9				

D For each question, write a division, then work out the answer.

Example	In a hockey league, 128 matches are played in 8 weeks. How many matches are played each week?
Working	128 ÷ 8
	$\begin{array}{r} 0\ 1\ 6 \\ 8\overline{)1\ ^12\ ^48} \end{array}$
Answer	16 matches have to be played each week.

1 Jeannette wants to put 84 model cars into 6 boxes equally. How many cars go in each box?

2 Mrs Almond is putting out biscuits for a party. She has 95 biscuits. 7 biscuits go on each plate.
  (a) How many plates does she need?
  (b) How many biscuits will be left over?

3 Harold is decorating cakes. Each cake needs 8 strawberries. Harold has 100 strawberries.
  (a) How many cakes can he decorate?
  (b) How many strawberries will be left over?

4 Marlon has 384 stickers. There are 4 stickers on a sheet. How many sheets has he bought?

5 A garden centre uses 1155 litres of water per week on its plants. How much is this per day?

6 A bike factory has 4596 wheels in stock. How many bikes can be fitted with wheels?

7 Each file on Jamie's disk takes up 5 kilobytes. He has used 1325 kilobytes. How many files are there on his disk?

8 Fatima worked out that if she watched all of her videos it would take 387 hours. All the videos are 3 hours long. How many videos does she own?

Finished Early?
Go to page 345

Further Practice

E Each number machine has five input numbers. Copy the table, then work out the output numbers. Put your working underneath. Some answers have remainders.

Question	Input numbers	Machine	Output numbers
1	48, 59, 71, 84, 98	÷ 2	
2	78, 72, 66, 59, 54	÷ 4	
3	120, 135, 242, 247, 325	÷ 5	
4	99, 113, 227, 326, 418	÷ 3	
5	648, 536, 440, 312, 257	÷ 6	
6	218, 263, 314, 337, 381	÷ 9	
7	764, 624, 531, 440, 355	÷ 8	
8	1021, 2149, 3650, 4235, 8368	÷ 7	

Finished Early?
➡ Go to page 345

❷ Divide by 10 or 100

Learn About It

Divide by 10

1 Our number system is based on tens. This makes it very easy to divide by 10. Dividing by 10 turns **tens** into **units**. This shows what happens when you do 70 ÷ 10.

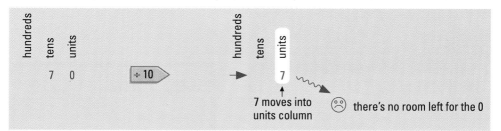

hundreds	tens	units		hundreds	tens	units
	7	0	÷ 10 →			7

7 moves into units column

😞 there's no room left for the 0

2 Dividing by 10 turns **hundreds** into **tens**. This shows what happens when you do 360 ÷ 10.

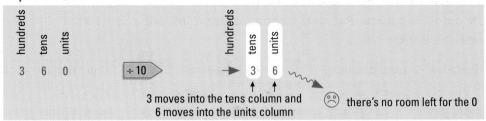

3 moves into the tens column and 6 moves into the units column

there's no room left for the 0

There is a simple rule to help you do this (see Key Fact).

This works with any whole number. So 2040 ÷ 10 = 204.

> ## Key Fact
>
> To divide a whole number by 10, take **0** off the end.

Divide by 100

3 Dividing by 100 is the same as dividing by 10 and then dividing by 10 again.

Dividing by 100 turns **hundreds** into **units**. This shows what happens when you do 400 ÷ 100.

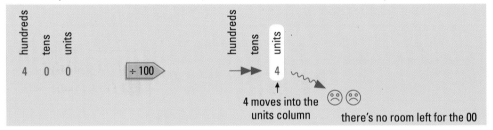

4 moves into the units column

there's no room left for the 00

4 Dividing by 100 turns **thousands** into **tens**. This shows what happens when you do 6200 ÷ 100.

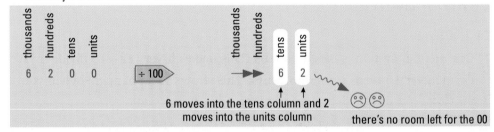

6 moves into the tens column and 2 moves into the units column

there's no room left for the 00

There is a simple rule to help you do this (see Key Fact).

This works with any whole number. So 55 800 ÷ 100 = 558.

> ### Word Check
> zero, nought 0

> ## Key Fact
>
> To divide a whole number by 100, take **00** off the end.

Try It Out

F **1** Divide each of these numbers by 10.

> **Example**   380
> **Working and answer**   380 ÷ 10 = **38** *(Take 0 off the end of 380.)*

(a) 80   (b) 60   (c) 130   (d) 290   (e) 320
(f) 740   (g) 1050   (h) 1630   (i) 3500   (j) 15 090

2 Divide each of these numbers by 100.

> **Example**   8200
> **Working and answer**   8200 ÷ 100 = **82** *(Take 00 off the end of 8200.)*

(a) 600   (b) 300   (c) 1800   (d) 2400   (e) 3900
(f) 7700   (g) 10 200   (h) 16 600   (i) 52 000   (j) 270 500

Learn More About It

If you can divide by 10 and 100, there are lots of other things you can do.

1 Dividing by 20 is the same as dividing by 10, then dividing by 2.

So it's easy to do 840 ÷ 20.
$$840 ÷ 20$$
is the same as   840 ÷ 10   ÷ 2
is the same as   84   ÷ 2   = **42**

2 To do 3600 ÷ 400, do this:
$$3600 ÷ 400$$
is the same as   3600 ÷ 100   ÷ 4
is the same as   36   ÷ 4   = **9**

Try It Out

G Work these out using what you have learned in this section.

1 (a) 180 ÷ 30   (b) 240 ÷ 40   (c) 1050 ÷ 70
(d) 3540 ÷ 60   (e) 1080 ÷ 90   (f) 3550 ÷ 50

2 (a) 600 ÷ 200   (b) 3200 ÷ 800   (c) 4000 ÷ 500
(d) 9100 ÷ 700   (e) 44 800 ÷ 800   (f) 297 000 ÷ 900

Practice

(H) In each question, two answers are the same and the other is different. Find the 'odd one out'.

There is one trick question!

Example	**(a)** $200 \div 10$
	(b) $60 \div 30$
	(c) $40 \div 20$
Working	**(a)** $200 \div 10 = 20$ (Take 0 off the end.)
	(b) $60 \div 30 = 6 \div 3 = 2$ (*Take 0 off the end, then divide.*)
	(c) $40 \div 20 = 4 \div 2 = 2$ (*Take 0 off the end, then divide.*)
Answer	**(a)** is the odd one out.

1 **(a)** $400 \div 20$ **(b)** $80 \div 10$ **(c)** $160 \div 20$
2 **(a)** $1200 \div 100$ **(b)** $3600 \div 300$ **(c)** $2400 \div 20$
3 **(a)** $280 \div 40$ **(b)** $35\,000 \div 500$ **(c)** $420 \div 60$
4 **(a)** $7000 \div 70$ **(b)** $10\,000 \div 100$ **(c)** $8000 \div 800$
5 **(a)** $80 \div 10$ **(b)** $720 \div 90$ **(c)** $12\,000 \div 100$
6 **(a)** $4200 \div 100$ **(b)** $4800 \div 200$ **(c)** $1260 \div 30$
7 **(a)** $8400 \div 400$ **(b)** $840 \div 10$ **(c)** $1050 \div 50$
8 **(a)** $1080 \div 60$ **(b)** $1330 \div 70$ **(c)** $190 \div 10$
9 **(a)** $24\,000 \div 800$ **(b)** $300 \div 10$ **(c)** $2700 \div 90$
10 **(a)** $28\,800 \div 200$ **(b)** $7200 \div 30$ **(c)** $14\,400 \div 100$

Further Practice

(I) Each number machine has five input numbers. Copy the table, then work out the output numbers. Put your working underneath.

> **Finished Early?**
> ➡ Go to page 346

Question	Input numbers	Machine	Output numbers
1	60, 40, 70, 910, 5200	÷ 10	
2	400, 300, 2900, 6000, 85 500	÷ 100	
3	240, 360, 600, 4500, 27 000	÷ 30	
4	140, 490, 700, 3500, 42 000	÷ 70	
5	320, 800, 7200, 4000, 9600	÷ 80	
6	400, 1000, 2400, 6200, 10 800	÷ 200	

Question	Input numbers	Machine	Output numbers
7	1200, 7200, 6000, 24 000, 55 200	÷ 600	
8	8000, 9000, 10 500, 35 000, 46 500	÷ 500	
9	3600, 54 000, 90 000, 81 000, 135 000	÷ 90	
10	16 000, 20 000, 40 000, 60 000, 300 000	÷ 400	

Finished Early?
➡ Go to page 346

❸ Divide by Two Digits

Learn About It

To divide by a two-digit number, you need to know …

(a) how to divide by a single digit
(b) how to multiply larger numbers
(c) how to subtract numbers.

There are two ways of dividing. The first is a bit like 'dividing by a digit' on page 44. This is how you would divide 3133 by 13. It helps to have the 13× table handy.

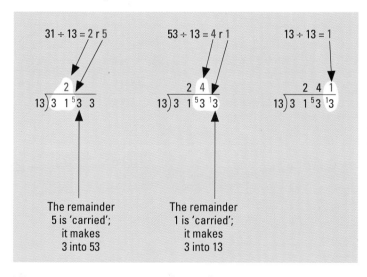

The remainder 5 is 'carried'; it makes 3 into 53

The remainder 1 is 'carried'; it makes 3 into 13

The 13 × table

$1 \times 13 = 13$
$2 \qquad 26$
$3 \qquad 39$
$4 \qquad 52$
$5 \qquad 65$
$6 \qquad 78$
$7 \qquad 91$
$8 \qquad 104$
$9 \qquad 117$

The second way is called **long division**. It takes up a lot of space, but it's easier to work out the remainders. The second way to do $3133 \div 13$ is shown on the next page.

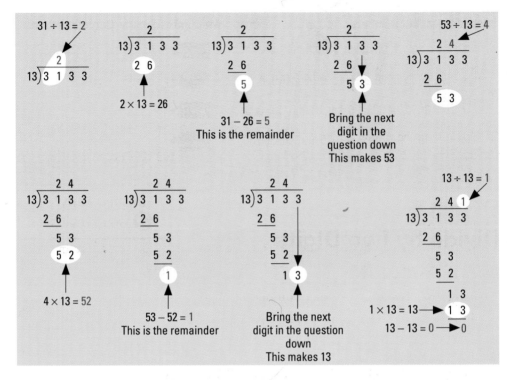

Here's 9802 ÷ 58 done both ways. First the short way:

$$58\overline{)9\ 8\ {}^{40}0\ 2}\quad\overset{1}{}$$

$$58\overline{)9\ 8\ {}^{40}0\ {}^{52}2}\quad\overset{1\ 6}{}$$

$$58\overline{)9\ 8\ {}^{40}0\ {}^{52}2}\quad\overset{1\ 6\ 9}{}$$

Then the long way. Only the finished one is shown.

The 58 × table		
1 ×	58 =	58
2		116
3		174
4		232
5		290
6		348
7		406
8		464
9		522

Try It Out

J Work these out using the methods you like.

1 These divide exactly.

(a) $275 \div 11$ (b) $585 \div 15$ (c) $4727 \div 29$

(d) $13\ 516 \div 62$ (e) $961 \div 31$

2 These have remainders.

(a) $366 \div 12$ (b) $4107 \div 17$ (c) $833 \div 25$

(d) $2777 \div 77$ (e) $25\ 049 \div 51$

Practice

K **1** To turn months into years, divide by 12. How many years are there in …
(a) 384 months (b) 1128 months (c) 3228 months?

2 To turn hours into days, divide by 24. How many days are there in …
(a) 888 hours (b) 1392 hours (c) 8760 hours?

3 To turn weeks into years, divide by 52. How many years are there in …
(a) 936 weeks (b) 1820 weeks (c) 8528 weeks?

4 The planet Saturn takes 29 years to orbit the Sun once. How many times will it orbit the Sun in …
(a) 400 years (b) 600 years (c) 1000 years (d) 2500 years?

What do the remainders mean?

To divide by 230, you can divide by 10 first, then by 23. Use this idea to help you fill in the table.

Example	$7360 \div 230$
Working	$7360 \div 10 = 736$ (*Take 0 off the end.*)
	$736 \div 23 = 32$ (*Use the method you like.*)
Answer	$7360 \div 230 = 32$

L Each number machine has two input numbers. Copy the table, then work out the output numbers. Put your working underneath.

Question	Input numbers	Machine	Output numbers
1	10 350, 23 690	÷ 230	
2	14 040, 46 980	÷ 540	
3	25 410, 12 100	÷ 110	
4	43 200, 321 600	÷ 1200	

> **Finished Early?**
> ➡ Go to page 346

Further Practice

M Each question has two divisions. Work them out, then write *same* if they give the same answer or *different* if they don't.

1 (a) 168 ÷ 12   (b) 154 ÷ 11
2 (a) 169 ÷ 13   (b) 195 ÷ 15
3 (a) 343 ÷ 17   (b) 383 ÷ 19
4 (a) 444 ÷ 21   (b) 499 ÷ 23
5 (a) 875 ÷ 25   (b) 816 ÷ 24
6 (a) 1368 ÷ 38   (b) 1242 ÷ 31
7 (a) 2750 ÷ 55   (b) 3050 ÷ 61
8 (a) 2880 ÷ 72   (b) 1745 ÷ 43

> **Finished Early?**
> Go to page 346

Unit 2 *The Four Operations*
Summary of Chapters 3, 4 and 5

- Additions and subtractions come in families of four,
  e.g. $4 + 3 = 7$, $3 + 4 = 7$, $7 - 4 = 3$, $7 - 3 = 4$.
- You can add numbers by …
  - adding a digit at a time of the second number to the first
  - adding the hundreds, tens and units separately, then adding the answers together
  - adding in columns.
- You can subtract numbers by …
  - subtracting a digit at a time of the second number from the first
  - counting on
  - subtracting in columns.
- Knowing your multiplication tables can help you solve many simple problems.
- To multiply by 10, add 0 to the end of the number.
- To multiply by 100, add 00 to the end of the number.
- To multiply any number by any other number, you can …
  - use the box method
  - set it out in columns.
- Multiplications and divisions come in families of four,
  e.g. $4 \times 3 = 12$, $3 \times 4 = 12$, $12 \div 4 = 3$, $12 \div 3 = 4$.
- In division, you work from **left** to **right**.
- To divide by 10, take 0 from the end of the number.
- To divide by 100, take 00 from the end of the number.
- To divide any number by any other number, you can use short division or long division.

6 Types of Shape

In this chapter you will learn about …
1. different types of shape
2. two-dimensional shapes
3. three-dimensional shapes

1 Flat or Solid?

Learn About It

There are many different types of shape.

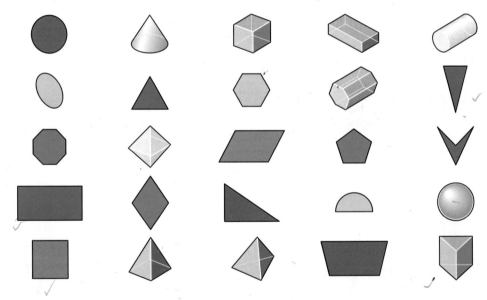

1. Write down the names of any of these that you know. Write them in one column. You will be writing other things next to the names later.

2. Ask about any names you don't know.

3. Some shapes are **flat** (two-dimensional or **2D**). Some are **solid** (three-dimensional or **3D**). Go through your list. After each name, write **2D** or **3D**. Ask if you don't know what to write.

   Example Square 2D

4 Some shapes are made of **straight** parts only. Some have **curved** parts.
Go through your list. After each '2D' or '3D', write **S** for straight or **C** for
curved. Ask if you don't know what to write.

Example *Square 2D S*

5 After each 'S' or 'C', write the name of something with this shape.

Example *Square 2D S Handkerchief*

> **Word Check**
> ....
> **flat/2D shape** covers a
>   surface but doesn't fill
>   up space
> **solid/3D shape** fills up space

Try It Out

A **1** Draw four **different** flat shapes that have 3 **vertices** (corners).
Mark the vertices first, with small dots, then join them up.

2 Draw six **different** flat shapes that have 4 vertices.

3 You can copy the shapes from Learn About It on page 56.
   (a) Draw a sketch of a cuboid. How many
      vertices does it have?
   (b) Draw a triangular prism. How many
      vertices does it have?

> **Word Check**
> ....
> **vertex** a corner of a flat
>   or solid shape
> **vertices** corners

Practice

B Here is a set of flat shapes.

a   b   c   d   e   f   g

Here is a set of solid shapes.

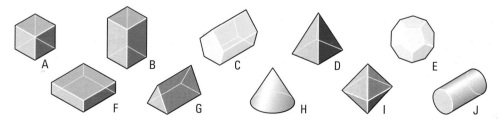

A   B   C   D   E   F   G   H   I   J

1 Each flat shape has been used to make some of the solid ones. For each flat shape, write down which solid shapes it has been used in.
   Example a A, D (*Not finished – there may be more*)

2 Each solid shape is made using the flat shapes. For each solid shape, write down which flat shapes it uses.
   Example D a, d (*Finished – that's all*)

> **Finished Early?**
> ➡ Go to page 346

Further Practice

C Divide a page into four rectangles. Write these headings in the rectangles as shown.

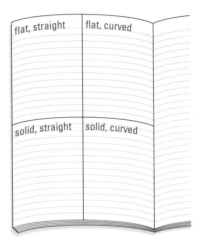

Work through this list of shapes. Write each one in the correct part of your page. Look at the pictures of shapes on page 56 to help you.

circle	ellipse	octagon
rectangle	square	cone
equilateral triangle	octahedron	rhombus
square-based pyramid	cube	hexagon
parallelogram	right-angled triangle	oval
tetrahedron	cuboid	hexagonal prism
pentagon	semicircle	trapezium
cylinder	isosceles triangle	quadrilateral
sphere	triangular prism	kite

> **Finished Early?**
> ➡ Go to page 346

② Two Dimensions

Learn About It

Any flat shape with straight sides or edges is called a **polygon**.
These are **all** polygons.

Sides	3	4	5	6	7	8
Name	Triangle	Quadrilateral	Pentagon	Hexagon	Heptagon	Octagon
Regular						
Convex (irregular)						
Concave (irregular)						

Some other names are: 9 sides – **nonagon**, 10 sides – **decagon**,
11 sides – **undecagon**, 12 sides – **dodecagon**.

Polygons with all their sides and angles the same are called **regular**.

A **convex** polygon has corners that all point outwards. A **concave** polygon
has one or more pointing inwards.

Convex pentagon   Concave pentagon

Here are two more flat shapes.

circle

semi circle

Quadrilaterals have 4 straight sides.

There are different names for different kinds of quadrilateral.

Square   Rectangle   Parallelogram   Rhombus   Kite   Trapezium

Word Check

polygon a flat shape with straight sides

convex all corners pointing outwards

concave some corners pointing inwards

Try It Out

Polygon Game

A die, dotted paper

How to start

Use a quarter of a sheet of dotted paper. Mark four dots in the middle of the paper. Join them up to make a quadrilateral. This is the starting shape. Roll the die to decide who starts.

How to play

Take turns to roll the die.

- If you roll a **3**, you have to make a **triangle**, a **5** means you have to make a **pentagon**, and so on. If you roll 1 or 2 you miss a go. It helps if you each use a different colour.
- You must always **use** at least two dots that are already marked on the paper.
- You can only **add** two new dots at the most.
- You can only join onto the edges of your **own** shapes or the starting shape.
- If you can't make your shape, you miss that turn.
- Score 3, 4, 5 or 6 if you make your shape.

How to win

When all the dots have been used or both players miss a turn, add up the scores. The player with the highest score wins.

Remember to write down all the scores as you play.

Learn More About It

Key Facts

Capital letters are used to **label** vertices. The triangle has three sides called **PQ**, **QR** and **RP**.
The triangle is called **PQR**.

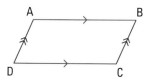

Parallel lines are always the same distance apart.
In this parallelogram, the side **AB** is parallel to the side **CD**.
Also **BC** is parallel to **DA**.

The parallel lines are marked with matching arrows.

Try It Out

Word Check

vertex a corner of a shape

side/edge part of the outside of a flat shape

label a name for a vertex

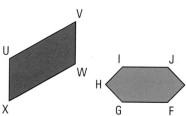

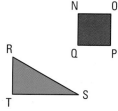

1 What is the name of each shape?

Example	ABCD
Answer	ABCD is a rectangle.

(a) EFGHIJ   (b) KLM   (c) NOPQ   (d) RST   (e) UVWX   (f) PQRST

2 Which vertices have a right angle?

Example	N has a right angle.

3 Name all the pairs of parallel lines you can find.

Example	IJ and GF are parallel.

Practice

F Write down the letter name of each shape. Then write down what type of shape it is.

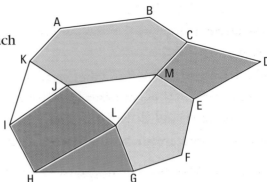

Example	a white shape
Answer	IJK, a triangle

1 the yellow shape

2 the pink shape

3 the grey shape

4 the other white shape

5 the blue shape

6 the green shape

G Copy the diagrams. Mark the parallel lines with arrows. Write down each pair of parallel lines using letters.

Example

Answer

EF and HG are parallel.
FG and EH are parallel.

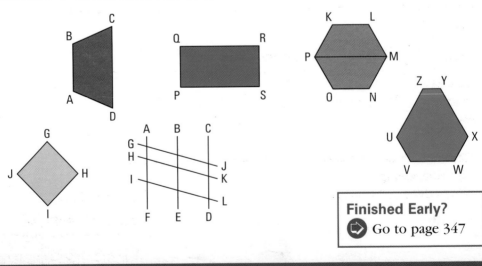

Finished Early?
Go to page 347

Further Practice

H Draw diagrams using these instructions.

1 two triangles joined along one edge

2 four quadrilaterals joined at one vertex

3 two concave hexagons joined along one side

4 four octagons that all touch each other along some of their sides

5 a convex pentagon with a quadrilateral stuck to each side

I **1** Copy this diagram. The long lines are parallel.

2 One new line adds a quadrilateral to the diagram.

3 Two new lines will add a pentagon to the diagram.

4 Now draw more lines to add a hexagon, heptagon, etc.

5 How·many new lines are there at each step? Record the results in a table like this.

Shape	Number of sides	New lines added
Quadrilateral	4	1
Pentagon	5	2
Hexagon	6	

6 How many new lines would there be if you were adding …
   (a) a decagon
   (b) a 20-sided polygon?

> **Finished Early?**
> ➡ Go to page 347

T 3 Three Dimensions

Learn About It

There are many different solid shapes.

Prisms have two ends the same. A slice through a prism always gives the same **cross-section**.

| triangular prism | cuboid | hexagonal prism | cylinder | prism |

Pyramids have a flat **base** and a pointed **apex**.

| square-based pyramid | tetrahedron | hexagonal pyramid | cone | pyramid |

There are lots of others.

| sphere | hemisphere | octahedron | frustums |

Any shape with straight **edges** and flat **faces** is called a **polyhedron**. Most of the shapes above are polyhedra. The round ones are not.

A **cube** is a polyhedron.
Here is some information about it.

6   faces (squares)
12   edges
8   vertices

Word Check

prism a 3D shape with the same cross-section all the way through

pyramid a 3D shape that comes to a point

face a flat part of the outside of a shape

edge where the faces of a shape join

vertex where edges join

polyhedron a 3D shape made up of flat faces and straight edges

Try It Out

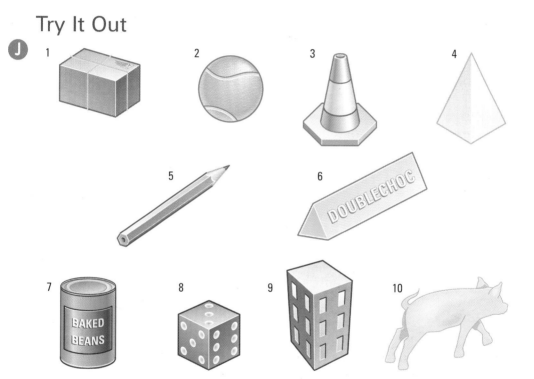

Here are some pictures of real objects. For each one …

(a) write its proper name

(b) write down if it is a prism, a pyramid, a polyhedron or none of these.

Practice

K Copy and complete the table for these shapes. Make a sketch of each one to help you.

Question	Name	Faces	Vertices	Edges
1	Cube	6	8	12

L Write the names of any shapes that fit the description.

1 6 faces **2** 8 vertices **3** 6 edges **4** 8 faces
5 18 edges **6** 7 faces **7** 12 vertices **8** 10 faces

Further Practice

Finished Early?
➡ Go to page 347

M Copy and complete the table for these prisms.
You may need to sketch them. They are all based on letters.

Question	Name	Faces	Vertices	Edges
1	L-shaped prism	8	12	18

Finished Early?
➡ Go to page 347

7 Symmetry

In this chapter you will learn about ...
1. line symmetry
2. rotational symmetry
3. making things symmetrical

1 Line Symmetry

Scrap paper, scissors, glue, triangular dot grid paper

Learn About It

This doll is **symmetrical**.

The dotted line is her **line of symmetry** or **mirror line**.

One half is a **mirror image** or **reflection** of the other half. The two halves are not the same. If they were, she would look something like this ...

Her line of symmetry is **vertical**, not **horizontal**. If it were horizontal, she would look something like this ...

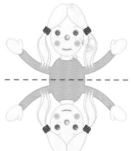

A shape can have **two** lines of symmetry.

Some shapes have **more than two** lines of symmetry.

Word Check

line of symmetry a line that divides half of a shape from its mirror image

mirror line line of symmetry

vertical top to bottom

horizontal left to right

reflection mirror image

Try It Out

A Look at these pictures. For each one, answer these questions.

(a) Does it have a **vertical** line of symmetry?

(b) Does it have a **horizontal** line of symmetry?

(c) How **many** lines of symmetry does it have?

1

2

3

4

5
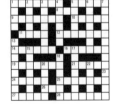

6

Practice

 B Some letters and numbers have symmetry.

1 Write out the alphabet in large capital letters, then mark on all the lines of symmetry. Use dotted lines. **A** has been done for you.

A B C D E F G H I J K L M N O P Q
R S T U V W X Y Z

2 Do the same thing with the numbers.

1 2 3 4 5 6 7 8 9 0

C

Squared paper

Copy each grid and mark on its lines of symmetry.

1 (a) 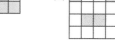 (b) (c) (d) (e) (f)

(g) (h)

Triangle grid paper

2 (a) (b) (c) (d)

(e) 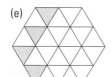 (f) 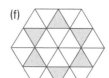 (g) 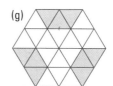 (h)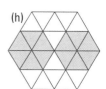

Finished Early?
➡ Go to page 348

Further Practice

 Some letters and numbers have symmetry.

1 Write out the alphabet in small letters, then mark on all the lines of symmetry. Use dotted lines. **a** has been done for you.

a b c d e f g h i j k l m n o p q r s t
u v w x y z

2 Do the same thing with these Greek letters.

Δ Φ Γ Λ Π Θ Σ Ω Ξ Ψ

Squared paper

E Copy each grid and mark on its lines of symmetry.

1 (a)   (b)   (c)   (d)   (e)

(f)   (g) 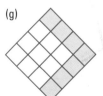 (h)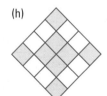

Finished Early?
 Go to page 348

❷ Rotational Symmetry

Learn About It

This galaxy is symmetrical, but it doesn't have any **lines** of symmetry.

This kind of symmetry is about turning.
It is called **rotational** symmetry. Watch as the galaxy turns round.

The last picture looks the same as the first, but it isn't. Look at the numbers on the arms. They are different.

There are **2** different positions where the galaxy looks the same.

So it has **order 2** rotational symmetry. The galaxies rotate around the **centre of rotation**. This is the red dot in the middle.

These two galaxies are order 3 and order 4. They do not have any line symmetry.

This picture **doesn't** have rotational symmetry.
You have to turn it **all the way round** before it looks the same again.

Word Check

rotate to turn round

rotational symmetry as you rotate something, there is more than one position where it looks the same

order of rotational symmetry the number of positions where it looks the same (always 2 or more)

centre of rotation the place you turn it around

Try It Out

You might need tracing paper

 For each picture, answer these questions.

(a) Does it have rotational symmetry?

(b) If it does, what is the order?

You can trace parts of the shapes if you like.

1  2  3

4  5  6

Practice

 Find the order of rotational symmetry in these diagrams. If there is no rotational symmetry, write *none*.

1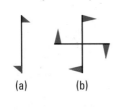

(a)   (b)   (c)   (d)   (e)   (f)

(g)   (h)   (i)   (j)   (k)   (l)

2

(a) (b) (c) (d)

(e) (f) (g) (h)

3 Draw all the different triangles and quadrilaterals you can think of. Find the order of rotational symmetry for each of them.

> **Finished Early?**
> ➲ Go to page 348

Further Practice

Ⓗ Find the order of rotational symmetry in these diagrams. If there is no rotational symmetry, write *none*.

1 (a) (b) (c) (d) (e) (f)

(g) (h) (i) (j) (k)

(l)

2 (a) (b) (c) (d)

(e) 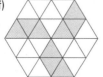 (f)  (g) 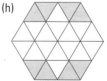 (h)

> **Finished Early?**
> ➲ Go to page 348

T3 Making Things Symmetrical

Learn About It

Any shape or design can be made symmetrical.

Word Check

reflect use a mirror line to give something symmetry

rotate to turn round

symmetrical having repeated parts which make a clear pattern

To give it line symmetry, **reflect** it in a mirror line.

 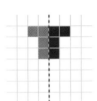

You can use two mirror lines.

 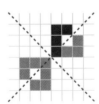

To give it rotational symmetry, **rotate** it.

order 2   order 4   order 3   order 6

Try It Out

Squared paper, triangle grid paper

 1 Copy each grid. Add more squares so that the red dotted lines are lines of symmetry.

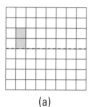
(a)

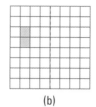
(b)

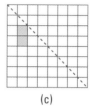
(c)

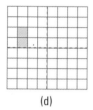
(d)

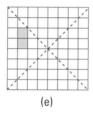
(e)

J 1 Copy the grid twice. Add to each one so that it has …

(a) order 2 rotational symmetry

(b) order 4 rotational symmetry.

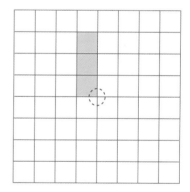

2 Copy the grid three times. Add to each one so that it has …

(a) order 2 rotational symmetry

(b) order 3 rotational symmetry

(c) order 6 rotational symmetry.

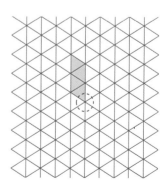

Practice

Squared paper

K Here are five sets of symmetry lines to use in each question.

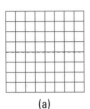 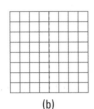 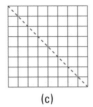 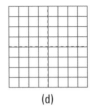 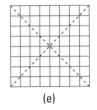

(a)　　　　　(b)　　　　　(c)　　　　　(d)　　　　　(e)

Make **five** copies of **each grid**. Use **all five** sets of lines with **each** starting pattern.

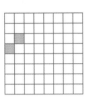 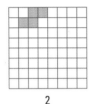 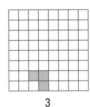 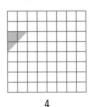 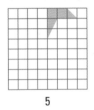

1　　　　　2　　　　　3　　　　　4　　　　　5

Add reflections so the dotted lines are lines of symmetry.

Squared paper

L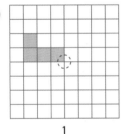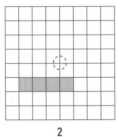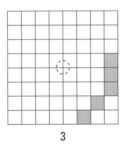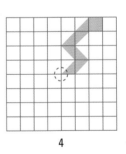

1　　　　　2　　　　　3　　　　　4

For each starting shape, copy the grid twice. Add to each one so that it has …
(a) order 2 rotational symmetry
(b) order 4 rotational symmetry.

Triangle grid paper

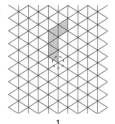 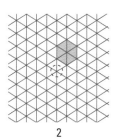 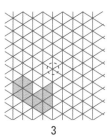 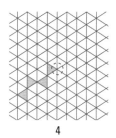

1　　　　　　　　　2　　　　　　　　　3　　　　　　　　　4

For each starting shape, copy the grid three times. Add to each one so that it has …

(a) order 2 rotational symmetry
(b) order 3 rotational symmetry
(c) order 6 rotational symmetry.

Finished Early?
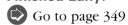 Go to page 349

Further Practice

Squared paper

1 Draw your initial in squares on a piece of squared paper. My initial is R. I would draw it like this.

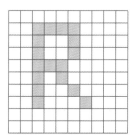

2 Add a vertical mirror line. Add squares so the picture is symmetrical.

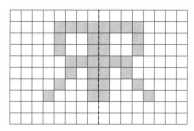

3 Start again. Draw two diagrams. Use a mirror line that is …
(a) horizontal　　　　　　　　　(b) diagonal.
(Look at Practice **M** to remind you.)

4 Start again. Draw two diagrams. Use two mirror lines that are …
(a) horizontal and vertical　　　　(b) diagonal.
(Look at Practice **M** to remind you.)

5 Start again. Draw two diagrams. Mark a centre of rotation.

Add squares so that the pattern has:
(a) order 2 rotational symmetry　　(b) order 4 rotational symmetry.

6 Try questions 1–5 with your other initials.

Finished Early?
 Go to page 349

Unit 3 *Properties of Shapes*
Summary of Chapters 6 and 7

- Shapes can be flat (2D) or solid (3D).
- Polygons are flat shapes with straight sides. They include triangles (3 sides), quadrilaterals (4 sides), pentagons (5 sides), hexagons (6 sides) and octagons (8 sides).
- Special quadrilaterals include square, rectangle, parallelogram, rhombus, trapezium and kite.
- Convex shapes always point outwards. Concave shapes point back into themselves.
- Vertices (corners) of shapes are labelled with capital letters (A, B, C, etc.). Lines use two letters (DE, EF, etc.).
  The name for a shape will use more letters. A triangle might be called PQR.
- Parallel lines never meet. On diagrams they are shown with arrows.
- Prisms have the same shape at both ends.
- Pyramids have a flat base and a pointed apex.
- Polyhedra have faces, edges and vertices.
- Shapes with line symmetry have one or more mirror lines. If you reflect the shape in one of these lines, it doesn't change.
- Shapes with rotational symmetry are made of equal parts turned through equal angles.
- Any shape can be made symmetrical. You need to add reflections or rotations to it.

Negative Numbers

In this chapter you will learn about …
1. numbers below zero
2. number lines
3. adding negative numbers
4. subtracting negative numbers.

1 Below Zero

Learn About It

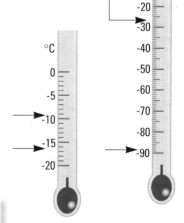

Water freezes at zero degrees Celsius (0 °C). **Temperature** is measured from this point using a **thermometer**. The height of the liquid shows the temperature.

The hottest temperature ever recorded on earth was 58 °C. This was at Al'Aziziyah in the Sahara desert.

On a very hot summer's day in this country the temperature could be 32 °C.

Temperatures below zero are written as **negative numbers**, using a minus sign. The lowest temperature recorded in Britain was 27 °C below zero at Braemar in Scotland. This is written −27 °C.

The lowest temperature ever recorded on earth was −89 °C at Vostok in Antarctica.

The higher up the scale the higher the temperature.
The lower down the scale the lower the temperature.

Sea water freezes at −9 °C and vinegar freezes at −17 °C.

So sea water freezes at a higher temperature than vinegar.

Word Check

thermometer used to measure temperature
negative below zero

Try It Out

A Write down the temperatures shown on each of these thermometers.

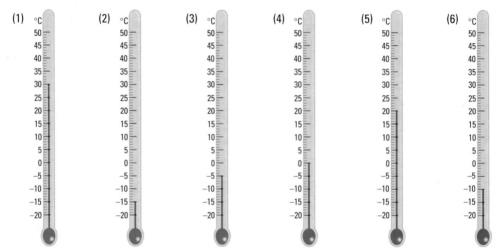

Learn More About It

You can find how far apart two temperatures are by counting.
The difference between –3 °C and 4 °C is 7 °C.

A temperature **increase** is found by counting upwards.
A temperature **decrease** is found by counting downwards.

If the temperature is –3 °C and it falls by 5 °C, then you count 5 down. The new temperature is –8 °C.

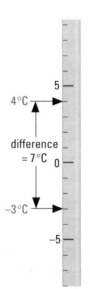

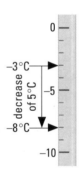

Word Check
increase count upwards
decrease count downwards

Try It Out

B Draw a temperature scale from –10 °C to 10 °C.

1 Find the difference between these temperatures.
   (a) 10 °C and 4 °C   **(b)** –2 °C and 4 °C
   (c) –5 °C and –1 °C   **(d)** 7 °C and –7 °C

2 Find the new temperature when …
   (a) 4 °C is increased by 3 °C   **(b)** –2 °C falls by 5 °C
   (c) –6 °C is increased by 4 °C   **(d)** –3 °C falls by 2 °C.

Practice

 The temperatures of these places are given for one day in January.

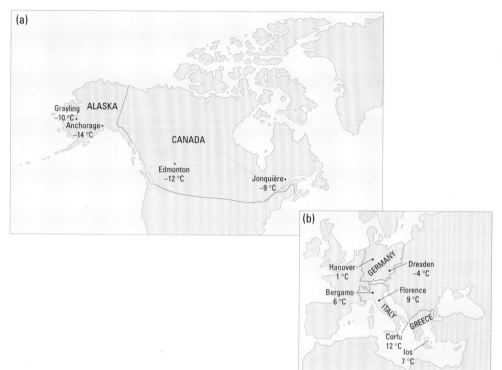

1 Mark them on a temperature scale. You can use the first letter of each name. (H for Hanover, and so on).

2 Name the place which is …
- **(a)** the coldest
- **(b)** the hottest in Canada
- **(c)** the coldest in Germany
- **(d)** the hottest in Alaska
- **(e)** 2 °C colder than Grayling
- **(f)** 5 °C colder than Bergamo
- **(g)** 5 °C colder than Hanover
- **(h)** 8 °C colder than Dresden.

3 What is the difference in temperature between …
- **(a)** Florence and Ios
- **(b)** Bergamo and Dresden
- **(c)** Hanover and Grayling
- **(d)** Edmonton and Anchorage
- **(e)** Dresden and Jonquière
- **(f)** Edmonton and Dresden
- **(g)** Grayling and Ios
- **(h)** Anchorage and Bergamo
- **(i)** Florence and Edmonton
- **(j)** Corfu and Grayling?

Finished Early?

➡ Go to page 349

Further Practice

D

P	Q	R	S	T	U	V	W	X	Y
0	0	10	10	5	5	0	−5	10	0
−5	−5	5	5						
−10	−10	0	0	−5	−5	−10	−15	0	−10

1 Draw one thermometer scale from −10 °C to 10 °C and mark these temperatures.

2 List the temperatures in order, coldest first.

3 Which temperature is …

    (a) 1 °C hotter than T   **(b)** 2 °C colder than Q

    (c) 3 °C hotter than W   **(d)** 3 °C hotter than V

    (e) 4 °C colder than R   **(f)** 5 °C colder than Q

    (g) 10 °C hotter than P   **(h)** 7 °C colder than U?

4 What is the difference in temperature between …

    (a) X and U   **(b)** T and Y   **(c)** V and P   **(d)** W and Q   **(e)** R and S

    (f) P and S   **(g)** Y and U   **(h)** X and V   **(i)** P and R   **(j)** W and S?

T 2 # Number Lines

Learn About It

Temperatures can be positive (above zero) or negative (below zero).

Positive and negative numbers are shown on a number line.

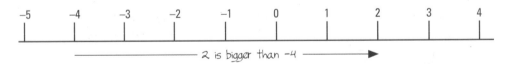

2 is bigger than −4

As you move to the right, the numbers get bigger, so 2 is bigger than −4.

You can find the difference between numbers by counting the gaps on a number line.

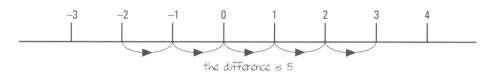

The difference between –2 and 3 is **5**.

Try It Out

E

1 Write down the numbers shown by arrows.

2 Write down the numbers which are ...
(a) more than zero   (b) bigger than 2
(c) less than –1   (d) more than –1.

F How much bigger is the first number than the second?
1 8 and 3   **2** 1 and –2   **3** 5 and –4
4 –2 and –7   **5** 4 and –3   **6** 2 and –5

Practice

G **1** Draw a number line from –10 to 10 and circle these numbers.

5,   –3,   –5,   9,   –7,   10,   –8,   2,   –1,   4

2 From these numbers write down ...
(a) the positive numbers   (b) the negative numbers
(c) the numbers more than –3   (d) the numbers less than 2
(e) the numbers less than –1   (f) the numbers less than –5
(g) the numbers more than –4   (h) the numbers less than –4.

3 How much bigger is the first number than the second?
(a) 2 and –1   (b) –3 and –5   (c) –7 and –8
(d) –5 and –8   (e) 4 and –5   (f) 2 and –7
(g) 10 and –5   (h) 5 and –5   (i) 10 and –8.

H **1** What number do you get when you ...
(a) increase –2 by 4   (b) increase –1 by 6   (c) increase –3 by 5
(d) increase –6 by 4   (e) increase –7 by 3   (f) decrease 5 by 7?

Finished Early?
➡ Go to page 350

Further Practice

1 These are names in code.

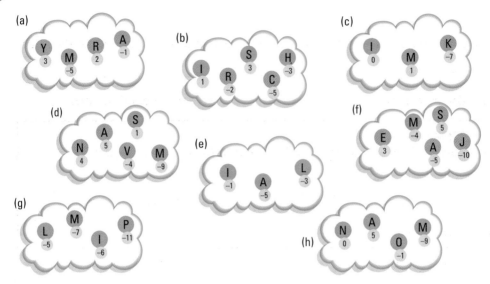

1 For each one, write the letters in order, smallest first. Use number lines to help you.

2 Find the difference between the numbers of the first and last letters of each name.

3 The number for each letter is increased by 3 in clouds **(a)** to **(d)**. Find the new numbers.

4 The number for each letter is decreased by 2 in clouds **(e)** to **(h)**. Find the new numbers.

T 3 Adding Negative Numbers

Learn About It

If you start with **5** and add **3** the answer is **8**. On a number line you move 3 places to the right.

When you add a positive number the answer is bigger. You move to the right.

If you start with **5** and add **–3** you move in the opposite direction. The answer is **2**.

When you add a negative number the answer is smaller. You move to the left.

Try It Out

J Mark the first number on a number line. Then add the second number.

> **Example** 2, –6
> **Working** Here we move 6 to the left and the answer is negative.
>
>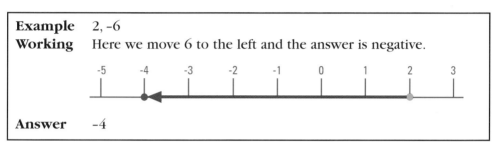
>
> **Answer** –4

1 2, 5 **2** 7, 2 **3** 8, –4 **4** 7, –5
5 8, –3 **6** 9, –4 **7** 2, –5 **8** 3, –4

Key Facts

Adding a positive number makes the answer bigger. Adding a negative number makes the answer smaller.

Practice

K Add these pairs of numbers.

1 9, –4	**2** 12, –6	**3** 13, –4	**4** 11, –7	**5** 10, –3
6 14, –7	**7** 17, –9	**8** 19, –11	**9** 20, –17	**10** 18, –16
11 9, –12	**12** 7, –11	**13** 5, –13	**14** 3, –14	**15** 12, –19

L Add these pairs of numbers.

1 –17, 5	**2** –11, 7	**3** –15, 10	**4** –12, 10	**5** –13, 13
6 –9, 12	**7** –10, 17	**8** –15, 18	**9** –14, 19	**10** –11, 20
11 –8, –9	**12** –13, –5	**13** –16, –12		
14 –18, –11	**15** –8, –17			

> **Finished Early?**
> ➡ Go to page 350

Further Practice

M Add these pairs of numbers.

1 10, –4	**2** 9, –3	**3** 7, –2	**4** 12, –5	**5** 7, –10
6 8, –12	**7** 5, –10	**8** 10, –14	**9** –9, 5	**10** –12, 6
11 –15, 10	**12** –16, 8	**13** –8, 10	**14** –10, 15	**15** –12, 16
16 –16, 20	**17** –4, –6	**18** –5, –10	**19** –8, –8	**20** –10, –2

T 4 Subtracting Negative Numbers

Learn About It

If you start with **5** and subtract **3** the answer is **2**. When you subtract a positive number the answer is smaller. The number is shifted to the left on the line.

If you start with **5** and subtract **− 3** the number moves the opposite way. The answer is larger. The number is shifted 3 places to the right and the answer is **8**.

Try It Out

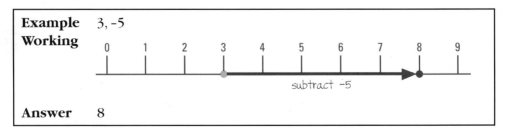 Subtract the second number from the first.

Example	3, −5
Working	

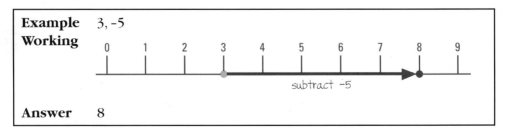

Answer	8

1 7, 2   **2** 8, 3
3 5, −4   **4** 6, −2
5 7, −3   **6** 4, −2
7 5, −4   **8** 6, −1

Key Fact

Subtracting a positive number makes the answer smaller.

Subtracting a negative number makes the answer larger.

Practice

Subtract the second number from the first.

Example	7, –4
Working	Starting at 7 you move 4 places to the right along the number line.
Answer	11

1 12, 4   **2** 13, 6   **3** 14, 10   **4** 10, 15
5 12, 17   **6** 13, 19   **7** 14, 16   **8** 17, 20
9 3, –7   **10** 4, –8   **11** 7, –12   **12** 5, –15
13 4, –14   **14** 8, –11   **15** 7, –13

Subtract the second number from the first.

1 –7, 2   **2** –13, 7   **3** –12, 8   **4** –11, 9   **5** –6, 13
6 –12, –9   **7** –17, –11   **8** –14, –13   **9** –16, –12   **10** –17, –11
11 –13, –16 **12** –11, –17 **13** –12, –18 **14** –14, –19 **15** –12, –20

Finished Early?
Go to page 351

Further Practice

Subtract the second number from the first.

1 10, 4   **2** 4, 10   **3** 6, 12   **4** 10, 15   **5** 6, –5
6 8, –5   **7** 5, –12   **8** 7, –13   **9** –6, 4   **10** –10, 3
11 –5, 10   **12** –7, 13   **13** –12, –8   **14** –14, –7   **15** –15, –10
16 –16, –8   **17** –8, –12   **18** –5, –10   **19** –12, –16 **20** –13, –15
21 3, 19   **22** 4, 16   **23** 5, 11   **24** 4, 7   **25** 12, 16
26 14, 17   **27** 10, –3   **28** 15, –7   **29** 18, –2   **30** –2, 5
31 –3, 7   **32** –5, 11   **33** –4, 6   **34** –2, –3   **35** –7, –4
36 –8, –2   **37** –9, –7   **38** –12, –3   **39** –2, –5   **40** –7, –9

Unit 4 *Negative Numbers*

Summary of Chapter 8

- A thermometer shows temperatures.
- Temperatures can be below zero.
- Negative numbers are numbers below zero.
- A number line is a line with numbers in order.
- A number line is like a horizontal thermometer scale.
- Negative numbers are to the left, positive numbers are to the right.
- You can draw part of a number line.
- Adding a positive number makes the answer bigger.
- Adding a negative number makes the answer smaller.
- Subtracting a positive number makes the answer smaller.
- Subtracting a negative number makes the answer larger.

Coordinates

In this chapter you will learn ...

1 how to read coordinates

2 how to plot points

1 Reading Coordinates

Learn About It

You can describe the position of the black dot like this.

Start from 0.

The black dot is 3 squares across and 2 squares up.

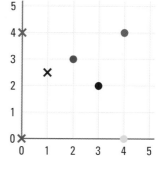

The numbers 3 and 2 are called **coordinates**.

They are written like this: (3, 2).

So, the black dot has coordinates (3, 2).

The first number tells you how far across, the second number tells you how far up.

Word Check

point same as a dot

coordinates a pair of numbers that give the position of a point

Try It Out

A Write down the coordinates of these **points**.

1 red dot   **2** blue dot   **3** yellow dot

4 black cross   **5** red cross   **6** blue cross

Learn More About It

The dark blue lines are called **axes**.

They meet at a point called the **origin**, in the corner.

The axis going across is called the **x-axis** or **horizontal** axis. So, the x-coordinate of point A is 3.

The axis going up is called the **y-axis** or **vertical** axis.

So, the y-coordinate of point A is 2.

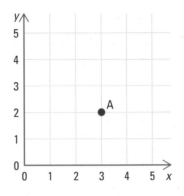

Word Check

x-axis the axis that runs across the page; the horizontal axis

y-axis the axis that runs up the page; the vertical axis

origin where the axes meet; it has coordinates (0, 0)

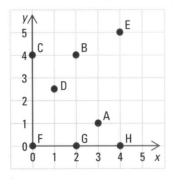

Try It Out

B **1** Write down the ...

(a) x-coordinate of A

(b) x-coordinate of B

(c) y-coordinate of C

(d) y-coordinate of D

(e) x-coordinate of E

(f) y-coordinate of F

(g) x-coordinate of G

(h) y-coordinate of H.

2 Write down the points with these coordinates.

(a) (2, 1)   (b) (3, 3)

(c) (1, 4)   (d) (0, 3)

(e) (1, 0)

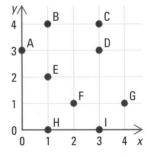

Practice

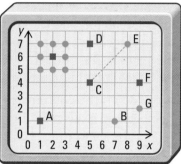

C **1** Write down the coordinates of all the corners of these shapes.

(**a**) triangle

(**b**) rectangle

(**c**) parallelogram

(**d**) trapezium

(**e**) square

(**f**) kite

2 ■ is an Alliance spacecraft.

● is an Empire spacecraft.

(**a**) One of the Alliance spacecraft is surrounded by Empire spacecraft.

    (i) Write down its coordinates.

    (ii) Write down the coordinates of all the surrounding Empire spacecraft.

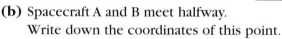

(**b**) Spacecraft A and B meet halfway. Write down the coordinates of this point.

(**c**) Spacecraft C is firing a laser at spacecraft E. Write down the coordinates of the points it passes through (write down the whole number coordinates only).

(**d**) An Alliance spacecraft at (5, 1) needs **rescuing**.

    (i) Which Alliance spacecraft is nearest?

    (ii) What are its coordinates?

(**e**) An explosion destroys all spacecraft with y-coordinates below 4. Which spacecraft are destroyed?

Word Check

rescuing saving

Finished Early?

Go to page 352

Further Practice

D **1** The coordinates of the red circle are $(2, 3)$.
Write down the coordinates of these.

(a) red square   (e) blue cross
(b) red cross   (f) black circle
(c) blue circle   (g) black square
(d) blue square   (h) black cross

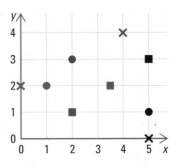

2 (a) Puddleton has coordinates $(3, 4)$.
Warmley has coordinates $(12, 4)$. A road
joins Puddleton and Warmley. Write
down the coordinates of all the points
the road passes through. (Write down
the whole number coordinates only.)

(b) Write down the coordinates of all the
points these roads pass through.

(i) Warmley to Chean

(ii) Chean to Puddleton

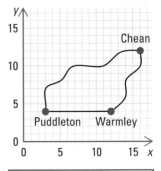

Finished Early?
Go to page 352

 2 **Plotting Points**

Learn About It

Squared paper

1 Plotter is a robot that **plots points**
(draws dots).
Plotter needs to be told
the coordinates of the points.

Here are the coordinates of Plotter's first
program: $(2, 1)$ $(4, 4)$ $(4, 2)$ $(0, 4)$ $(2, 5)$
$(1, 3)$ $(3, 0)$.

Plotter drew the first two points and
then broke down.

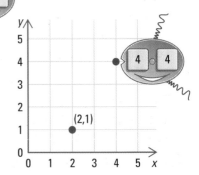

2 Carefully copy the diagram onto squared paper.

Draw the axes first. Use 1 cm for 1 unit.

Number the axes. Don't forget to write the
x and y at the ends. Plot the points.

Write the coordinates next to the points.

Now finish Plotter's program. Start with $(4, 2)$.

Word Check

dot same as a point

plot draw

point same as a dot

3 Plotter needs to be more **accurate** with this new program:

$(2\frac{1}{2}, 1)$ $(1\frac{1}{2}, 3)$ $(1, 1\frac{1}{2})$ $(3, 3\frac{1}{2})$ $(\frac{1}{2}, 4)$ $(3\frac{1}{2}, 2\frac{1}{2})$

Copy the axes onto squared paper.

The first point is $2\frac{1}{2}$ squares across and 1 square up.

Plot it as accurately as you can.

Finish Plotter's program. Write the coordinates next to the points.

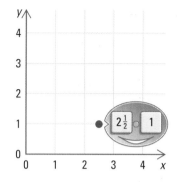

Try It Out

Squared paper

E Here is another Plotter program:

$(3\frac{1}{2}, 2)$ $(1, 2\frac{1}{2})$ $(2\frac{1}{2}, 3\frac{1}{2})$ $(2\frac{1}{2}, 0)$ $(\frac{1}{2}, \frac{1}{2})$ $(0, 1\frac{1}{2})$

Draw the same axes as above.

Number them in the same way.

Run through the program.

Write the coordinates next to the points.

Word Check
accurate exact

Practice

Squared paper

1 Plotter II can join up the points to make shapes.

Copy these axes. Run each of these programs, joining the points.

Use the *same* axes for all the programs.

Write down the name of each shape.

Plotter has started the first program for you.

(a) $(1, 3)$ $(2, 3)$ $(2, 5)$ $(1, 3)$

(b) $(2\frac{1}{2}, 4)$ $(4\frac{1}{2}, 4)$ $(5, 5)$ $(3, 5)$ $(2\frac{1}{2}, 4)$

(c) $(3, 1)$ $(5, 1)$ $(3, 0)$ $(3, 1)$

(d) $(3, 2)$ $(4\frac{1}{2}, 2)$ $(4\frac{1}{2}, 3\frac{1}{2})$ $(3, 3\frac{1}{2})$ $(3, 2)$

(e) $(2, 1)$ $(0, 1)$ $(2\frac{1}{2}, 2)$ $(2, 1)$

2 Draw your own axes and run through this program, joining the points.

$(2, 4)$ $(2\frac{1}{2}, 2\frac{1}{2})$ $(4, 2)$ $(2\frac{1}{2}, 1\frac{1}{2})$ $(2, 0)$ $(1\frac{1}{2}, 1\frac{1}{2})$ $(0, 2)$ $(1\frac{1}{2}, 2\frac{1}{2})$ $(2, 4)$

What shape have you made?

Finished Early?
➡ Go to page 352

Further Practice

G Plotter III programs are written in a table.

This program is the same as: (1, 7) (2, 5) (3, 3) (4, 1).

x	1	2	3	4
y	7	5	3	1

1 Draw your own axes and run this program.
What do you notice about the points?

Run these programs. Draw new axes for each program.
What do you notice about the points?

2

x	1	2	3	4
y	3	3	3	3

3

x	1	2	3	4
y	1	2	3	4

Plotter has a message for you.

Squared paper

H **1** Copy these axes onto squared paper and
number them as shown.

2 Join the points in these programs to discover
the message.

(a) (1, 2) (1, 7) (4, 7) (4, 2)
(b) (5, 2) (5, 7)
(c) (5, 4) (8, 7)
(d) (5, 4) (8, 2)

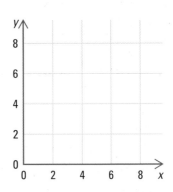

Graph paper

I Copy these axes onto graph paper.
Run through each of these programs,
joining up the points.
Use the *same* axes for all the programs.

1 (15, 5) (20, 10) (20, 20) (4, 20) (4, 10)
(9, 5) (15, 5)

2 (7, 16) (10, 18)

3 (17, 16) (14, 18)

4 (9, 15) Make a big dot on its own.

5 (15, 15) Make a big dot on its own.

6 (12, 8) (16, 11) (12, 10) (8, 11) (12, 8)
Describe the picture you have drawn.

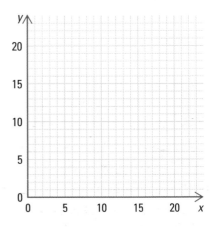

Finished Early?
➡ Go to page 352

NUMBER SKILLS **Find the mean of two U**

10 Line Graphs

In this chapter you will learn about …
1. reading graphs
2. drawing graphs
3. conversion graphs

1 Reading Graphs

Learn About It

1. Every 2 hours, Jan records the temperature outside. He joins up the points to make a **line graph**.

2. The —∧∨— sign breaks the temperature axis. This is because the temperatures don't start at 0.

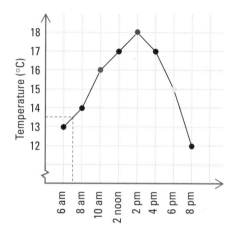

3. Put your finger on the blue point.

   Move down to the time axis. It is 10.00am.

   Put your finger back on the blue point.

   Move left to the temperature axis. It is 16 °C.

   So, the temperature was 16 °C at 10.00am.

   (a) Read the time and temperature for the yellow point.

   (b) What is the temperature at 8.00am?

   (c) At what time was the temperature 13 °C?

   (d) What was the temperature at 12 noon? At what other time was the temperature the same?

4. The red point is at the highest temperature.

   (a) What is the highest temperature?

   (b) At what time of day was it hottest?

   (c) At what time of day was it coldest?

Word Check

line graph a graph with the points joined up

5 The temperature at 8.00am was 14 °C. At 10.00am it was 16 °C.
The temperature **increased** by 2 °C.

  (a) The temperature increased between 6.00am and 7.00am.
   By how much?

  (b) The temperature **decreased** between 6.00pm and 8.00pm.
   By how much?

  (c) The temperature increased between 8.00am and 2.00pm.
   By how much?

6 Jan did not record the temperature at 7.00am.

  He **estimates** that the temperature was $13\frac{1}{2}$°C, using the dotted line.

  (a) Estimate the temperature at 9.00am. Use a ruler to help you.

  (b) Estimate the temperature at 3.00pm.

  (c) Estimate the temperature at 7.00pm.

  (d) Estimate when the temperature
   was $16\frac{1}{2}$°C.

> ### Word Check
> **increase** get bigger
> **decrease** get smaller
> **estimate** your best guess

Try It Out

A Leena weighs herself each birthday. She drew this graph.

1 What was her lowest weight? How old
   was she then?

2 What was Leena's highest weight?
   How old was she then?

3 How much did Leena weigh when
   she was 18 years old?

4 At which ages did she weigh the same?
   How much did she weigh?

5 Leena's weight decreased between
   16 and 17 years of age. By how much?

6 How much weight did Leena put on
   between the ages of 17 and 20?

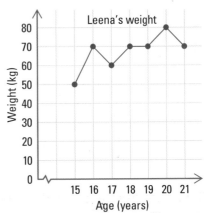

Practice

B The graph shows the price of an ounce of gold every 2 years.
Prices are in US Dollars ($).

1 What was the price of gold in …
   (a) 1980
   (b) 1982?

2 When was the price of gold …
   (a) $450
   (b) $350 (there are several answers)?

3 Estimate the price of gold in …
   (a) 1981
   (b) 1987.

4 (a) When was gold the most expensive?
       What was the price?
   (b) When was gold the cheapest?
       What was the price?

5 (a) What was the biggest price increase over 2 years?
   (b) Between which years did this happen?

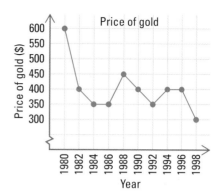

C The graph shows Yee Man's journey.

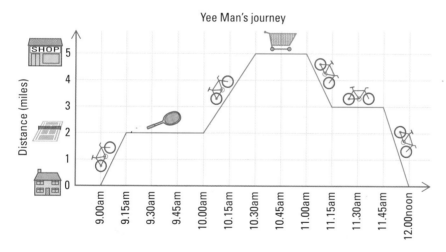

He cycled from home to the park, played tennis, cycled to the shop,
did some shopping and cycled home.

   1 What time did Yee Man leave home?
   2 When did he arrive at the park?
   3 How far is the park from home?
   4 How long did he spend playing tennis?
   5 When did he leave the park?
   6 How long did he take to cycle to the shop?
   7 How long did he spend shopping?

Yee Man had a puncture on the way home.

8 What time was this?

9 How far from home was he?

10 How long did he take to mend the puncture?

11 When did he arrive home?

12 How long was his journey altogether?

Finished Early?

Go to page 353

Further Practice

D Lola bought a motor bike in 1950 for £200. The graph shows its value over the years.

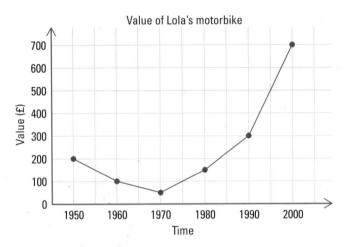

Value of Lola's motorbike

1 What was its value in …

    (a) 1960   **(b)** 1980?

2 When was its value …

    (a) £50   **(b)** £300?

3 **(a)** When did the value of the motor bike begin to increase?

    (b) How much did the value increase between 1970 and 1980?

    (c) How much did the value decrease between 1950 and 1970?

4 Estimate the value in …

    (a) 1975   **(b)** 1995.

5 Lola sold the motor bike in 2000. She got more than she paid for it. How much more?

Finished Early?

Go to page 353

2 Drawing Graphs

Learn About It

Squared paper, graph paper

Each birthday, Morgan records his height in a table.
Copy his table of **data**.

Age (years)	10	11	12	13	14	15	16
Height (cm)	135	140	150	160	170	175	180

Word Check

data information

scale tells you what
1 cm stands for

Drawing a line graph makes the data easier
to understand.

Copy these axes onto squared paper. Start
at the bottom left corner. But leave some
spaces for the numbers and words.

Use these **scales** for the axes:

Horizontal axis 1 cm for 1 year (written
1 cm : 1 year)

Vertical axis 1 cm for 10 cm (written
1 cm : 10 cm)

Carefully plot the points. Use crosses
instead of dots: they are more accurate.

Now join up the points with straight lines. Give your graph the title 'Morgan's
height'.

There is a problem with your graph.
Most of the space is wasted.

Let's start again.

Use a new side of squared paper.

Copy these new axes.

The ⟋⟍ sign breaks the axes.
This is because the heights and ages
don't start at 0.

Plot the points and join them up.

Your new graph is much clearer.

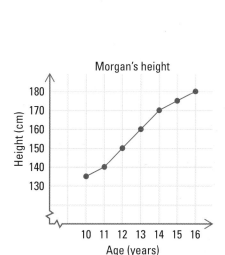

Try It Out

Squared paper

E Leena weighs herself each birthday.
She records her weight in a table.

Age (years)	15	16	17	18	19	20	21
Weight (kg)	50	70	60	70	70	80	70

1 Copy the table.

2 Copy the axes onto squared paper.
Use these scales:
Horizontal axis 1 cm : 1 year
Vertical axis 1 cm : 5 kg

3 Plot the points using crosses.

4 Join the points using straight lines.

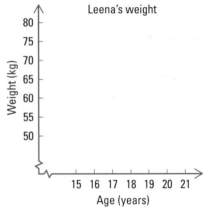

Practice

Squared paper

F Hoda and Dale are doing an experiment. Hoda drops the ball and Dale measures how high it bounces. The table shows their results.

Drop (cm)	100	140	180	220	260	300
Bounce (cm)	60	75	90	105	115	125

1 Copy the table.

2 Copy the axes onto squared paper.
Use these scales:
Horizontal axis 1 cm : 40 cm
Vertical axis 1 cm : 10 cm

3 Plot the points using crosses.

4 Join the points using straight lines.

5 Estimate the bounce when the drop is 240 cm.

6 Estimate the drop when the bounce is 120 cm.

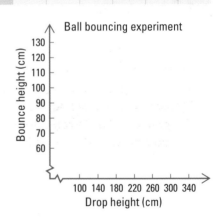

7 Make your graph a bit longer using a dotted line. Then estimate the bounce when the drop is 340 cm. Do you think this is a good estimate? Explain why.

Finished Early?
⮞ Go to page 353

Further Practice

Squared paper

G Wai Keen did an experiment. She timed how long a pendulum takes to swing back and forth twenty times. She did this for pendulums of different length. The table shows her results.

Length (cm)	100	120	140	160	180
Time (seconds)	42	46	50	53	56

1 Copy the table.

2 Copy the axes onto squared paper.
Use these scales:
Horizontal axis 1 cm : 20 cm
Vertical axis 1 cm : 2 seconds

3 Plot the points using crosses.

4 Join the points using straight lines.

5 Estimate the time when the length is 110 cm.

6 Estimate the length when the time is 48 seconds.

7 Make your graph a bit longer using a dotted line. Then estimate the time when the pendulum is 200 cm. Do you think this is a good estimate? Explain why.

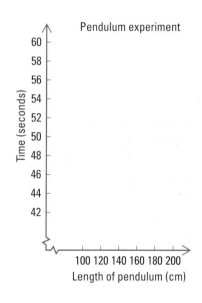

Pendulum experiment

Finished Early?
⮞ Go to page 353

P 3 Conversion Graphs

Learn About It

Squared paper

1 Didar is going on holiday to France. She wants to **convert** £50 to French Francs (FFr) for spending money.

Her holiday brochure contains a **currency conversion graph**.

How many French Francs can Didar buy for £50? Write FFr before your answer.

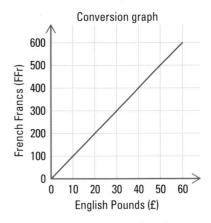

Conversion graph

2 When Didar returns from France, she has FFr 150 left.
How many pounds does she get at the bank?

3 You can make your own currency conversion graph for travelling to Germany.

You need to know how many German Marks (DM) you can buy for £1.
This is called the **exchange rate**.

The exchange rate for German Marks at this bank is: £1 buys DM 3.

So £10 buys 10 × 3 = DM 30
£20 buys 20 × 3 = DM 60

and so on.

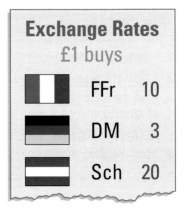

Exchange Rates
£1 buys

	FFr	10
	DM	3
	Sch	20

4 Copy and complete this table.

English Pounds (£)	0	10	20	30	40	50
German Marks (DM)	0	30	60			

5 Copy these axes onto squared paper. Complete the numbering.

6 Plot the points and join them with a straight line.

7 Use your graph to convert …

   (a) £35 to DM
   (b) DM 75 to £
   (c) DM 180 to £ (you may need to make your line longer).

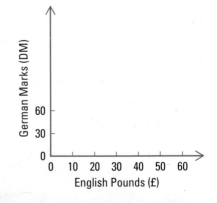

Word Check

convert change

conversion graph a graph that changes one quantity into another

currency the kind of money used in a country, e.g. US Dollars ($)

currency conversion graph a graph that changes one currency into another

exchange rate tells you how much foreign currency can be bought for £1

Try It Out

Squared paper

Charlotte is travelling to Austria on holiday. She wants to convert English Pounds to Austrian Schillings (Sch). The exchange rate at the bank is: £1 buys Sch 20.

1 Copy and complete this table.

English Pounds (£)	0	10	20	30	40	50
Austrian Schillings (Sch)	0	200	400			

2 Copy these axes onto squared paper. Complete the numbering.

3 Carefully plot the points using crosses.

4 Join the points using a straight line.

5 How many Austrian Schillings does Charlotte get for £45?

6 Charlotte returns with Sch 100. How many pounds can she buy?

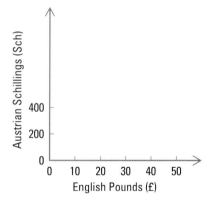

Practice

Graph paper

The counter on this Walkman shows where you are on the tape.

The table shows the counter reading for various playing times.

1 Copy the table.

Playing time (minutes)	20	40	60
Counter reading	30	60	90

2 Copy the axes onto graph paper.
Number the Playing time axis up to
80 minutes. Number the Counter
reading axis up to 100.

3 Plot the points and join them with
your ruler.

4 If the tape plays for 36 minutes,
what is the counter reading?

5 If the counter reading is 72, how
long has the tape been playing?

6 If the tape plays for 70 minutes, what is the
counter reading?
(You may need to make your line longer.)

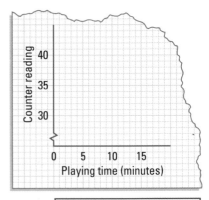

Finished Early?
➡ Go to page 354

Further Practice

Squared paper

J The table shows the sizes of women's dresses in England and France.

1 Copy the table.

English dress size	8	12	20
French dress size	36	40	48

2 Copy the axes onto squared paper.
Use these scales:
Horizontal axis 1 cm : 2 sizes
Vertical axis 1 cm : 2 sizes
Complete the numbering.

3 Carefully plot the points using crosses.

4 Join the points using a straight line.

5 A dress in England is size 10.
What is its size in France?

6 Antoinette is size 46 in France.
What size is she in England?

7 Nadine is size 24 in England.
What size is she in France?
(You may need to make your line longer.)

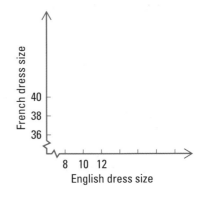

Finished Early?
➡ Go to page 354

Unit 5 *Coordinates and Graphs*

Summary of Chapters 9 and 10

- A graph has a pair of axes.
  They meet at the origin, in the corner.
- The *x*-coordinate of A is 3.
  The *y*-coordinate of A is 6.
  Point A has coordinates (3, 6).
  The origin has coordinates (0, 0).
- Plotter is a robot that plots points
  (draws dots).

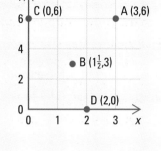

- The line graph shows that …
  At 6 years of age, the cactus was 13 cm high.
  The cactus was 16 cm high when it was
  7 years old.
- The sign —$\wedge\!\!\vee$— shows the numbers on the
  axes don't start at 0.

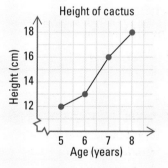

- The conversion graph shows that …
  £20 is worth €30
  €60 is worth £40
- The exchange rate is: £1 buys €1.50
  So £10 buys €15.

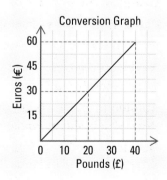

11 Using Tables and Charts

In this chapter you will learn about …
1. reading tables
2. pictograms and bar charts
3. reading two-way tables

Tables contain information. Information is sometimes called **data**.

Charts make the data look more interesting and easier to understand.

T 1 Tables

Learn About It

Class 7B are having their first PE lesson.

The PE teacher asks the pupils which sport they like best.

His table shows that …

- football is the most popular sport
- only 2 pupils like tennis best
- swimming is twice as popular as hockey.

Sport	Number of pupils
Gymnastics	4
Swimming	6
Hockey	3
Football	11
Tennis	2

You can find the size of class 7B by adding up the numbers of pupils:

$4 + 6 + 3 + 11 + 2 = 26$

There are 26 pupils in 7B.

Try It Out

A Lydia recorded the colours of the cars in her school car park.

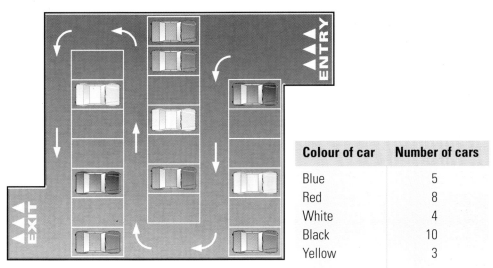

Colour of car	Number of cars
Blue	5
Red	8
White	4
Black	10
Yellow	3

1 How many cars are red?

2 What is the **most common** car colour?

3 How many cars have this colour?

4 Calculate the number of cars in the car park.

5 How many cars are **not** red?

Word Check

data information

most common happens the most

Practice

B **1** The table shows the GCSE grades in mathematics obtained by the pupils of Summerdown School.

GCSE grade	A*	A	B	C	D	E	F	G	U	Total
Number of pupils	3	6	19	18	11	4		0	1	66

(a) How many pupils got a grade E?

(b) How many pupils got a grade C or higher?

(c) The number of F grades is missing. Calculate this number.

2 Mr Scramble runs a chicken farm. The table shows how many eggs his chickens laid last week.

A chicken can lay one egg a day, at most.

Number of eggs	Number of chickens
0	5
1	8
2	12
3	20
4	25
5	40
6	60
7	50

(a) How many chickens laid 6 eggs last week?

(b) How many chickens laid an egg every day last week?

(c) How many chickens laid less than 3 eggs?

(d) How many chickens are on the farm?

3 The school shop is collecting money for new computers.

Jay empties the money box and records the coins collected today.

Coin	Number
1p	35
2p	15
5p	12
10p	4
20p	2
50p	1
£1	0

Total value

$35 \times 1p = 35p$

$15 \times 2p = 30p$

(a) How many 10p coins are there?

(b) How many coins were in the box?

(c) Copy the table.

(d) Calculate the missing totals.

(e) Add up the totals to find the amount collected today.

> **Finished Early?**
> ➡ Go to page 355

Further Practice

C Mr Chong refills chocolate machines. The table shows the bars he finds in a machine.

1 Which chocolate bar has sold out?

2 How many chocolate bars are in the machine altogether?

3 When full, the machine contains 20 of each chocolate bar. How many hazelnut bars does Mr Chong need to put in the machine?

Chocolate	Number left in machine
Plain	14
Milk	0
Hazelnut	12
Fruit & Nut	6
White	16

> **Finished Early?**
> ➡ Go to page 355

② Pictograms and Bar Charts

Learn About It

Sean's CD collection

Sean has drawn a **pictogram** of his CD collection.

He used this picture to stand for 4 CDs.

This is the **key** to understanding his pictogram.

He chose a square because it can be split into 4 equal parts.

 Rock

 Pop

 Soul

Reggae

 stands for 4 CDs

 stands for 3 CDs

 stands for 2 CDs

stands for 1 CD

We can now read Sean's pictogram.

Rock means 4 + 4 = 8 CDs

Pop means 4 + 4 + 3 = 11 CDs

Soul means 4 + 2 = 6 CDs

Reggae means 4 + 4 + 4 + 1 = 13 CDs

Word Check

pictogram a diagram that uses pictures to stand for data

key this tells you what one picture is worth

Try It Out

Ⓓ Jenny, Patrick and Chantal sold red noses for Comic Relief Day.
How many did each pupil sell?

Red noses sold

Jenny

Patrick

Chantal

 KEY ◯ stands for 4 noses

Learn More About It

Fyzah runs the school shop. She has drawn a bar chart to show the drinks sold this lunchtime.

The first bar shows she sold 8 cans of cola.

The second bar is halfway between 4 and 6. That's 5 cans high. So, she sold 5 cans of orange juice.

She did not sell any ginger beer. The bar has no height.

She sold 3 cans of lemonade.

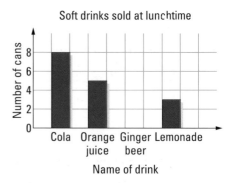
Soft drinks sold at lunchtime

Word Check

bar chart a diagram that uses bars to stand for data

Try It Out

E The bar chart shows how the pupils of 7A travel to school.

Copy and complete the table.

Transport	Number of pupils
Bus	
Car	
Walk	
Cycle	

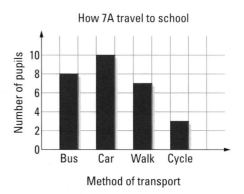
How 7A travel to school

Practice

F **1** The bar chart shows the fuel customers bought at a petrol station in one day. Copy and complete the table.

Fuel	Number of customers
Diesel	
Four star	
Unleaded	
Super unleaded	

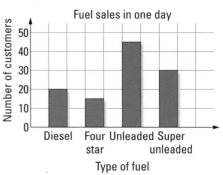
Fuel sales in one day

2 If stands for 16 books, what do these pictures stand for?

(a)   (b)   (c)   (d)

3 If 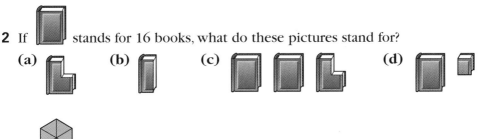 stands for 12 sweets, what do these pictures stand for?

(a)   (b)   (c)   (d)

4 If stands for 10 bicycles, estimate the number of bicycles these pictures stand for.

(a)   (b)   (c)

G **1** The bar chart shows the number of Easter eggs the pupils of 7A received.

Number of Easter eggs received by 7A

(a) How many pupils received 2 Easter eggs?

(b) How many pupils received 4 Easter eggs?

(c) Copy and complete this table.

Number of Easter eggs	Number of pupils
1	
2	
3	
4	
5	

(d) Calculate the number of pupils in class 7A.

Finished Early?
Go to page 355

Further Practice

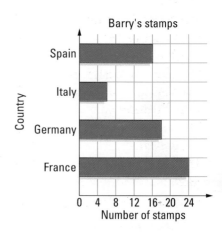

Barry's stamps

H **1** Barry collects foreign stamps.
He has made a horizontal bar chart.

   (a) How many French stamps
does he have?

   (b) He has more French than German
stamps. How many more?

   (c) Calculate how many stamps in
his collection.

2 The pictogram shows the numbers
of burgers sold in three popular
restaurants one evening.

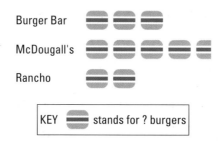

Burgers sold in one evening

Burger Bar

McDougall's

Rancho

KEY ▬ stands for ? burgers

   (a) The key to the pictogram is missing. Burger Bar sold 60 burgers.
Find the key.

   (b) How many burgers did Rancho sell?

   (c) Estimate how many burgers McDougall's sold.

> **Finished Early?**
> ➭ Go to page 355

❸ Two-way Tables

Learn About It

1 Mrs Jones is planning a trip to
Disneyland® Paris with her son Daniel.

They are flying from Edinburgh to
Paris this summer.

Mrs Jones looks up the ticket prices in this table.
She reads across from **Edinburgh** and down from **Summer**.
The air tickets cost £150 each.
The cost for both of them is 2 × £150 = £300

Air fares to Paris (£)		
	Winter	**Summer**
Birmingham	£118	£128
Edinburgh	£130	£150
London	£108	£134
Manchester	£118	£130
Newcastle	£150	£175

2 Find the cost of these air tickets.

(a) London in summer
(b) Manchester in winter
(c) Newcastle in summer (two tickets)

3 The Jones family live in Newcastle. Mr Jones will be driving his wife and Daniel to Edinburgh. He reads across from **Newcastle** and down from **Edinburgh**. He has to drive 107 miles.

Road distances (miles)

Birmingham

293	Edinburgh
118	405	London
88	218	199	Manchester
198	107	280	141	Newcastle

4 Find these distances.

(a) Birmingham to London
(b) Manchester to Edinburgh
(c) Newcastle to Manchester

5 Mrs Jones and Daniel want to spend 3 days in the Disneyland® theme park. Daniel's **3 day child pass** in **summer** costs £44. Mrs Jones' **3 day adult pass** in **summer** costs £58.

Disneyland® theme park passes						
	Child			Adult		
	1 Day	2 Day	3 Day	1 Day	2 Day	3 Day
Winter	£14	£28	£38	£18	£35	£47
Summer	£16	£32	£44	£21	£41	£58

6 How much do these passes cost?

(a) 1 day child pass in winter.
(b) 3 day adult pass in winter.
(c) 1 day passes in summer for two children and one adult.

Try It Out

1 Mr Richards is planning a trip to Disneyland® with his 10-year-old daughter Maria.

(a) They are flying from Birmingham in winter. How much will their air fares cost?

(b) They live in Manchester. How far is Manchester from Birmingham?

(c) They want to spend 2 days in Disneyland®. How much will their theme park passes cost?

Practice

J 1 Mr Richards wants to hire a saloon car for a week on his winter holiday. How much will this cost him?

2 Mrs Jones and Daniel will be spending 3 nights of their summer holiday in Hotel France. How much will this cost them?

Car hire (per week)		
	Winter	**Summer**
Small hatchback	£139	£149
Saloon	£169	£179
Estate car	£205	£229
Four-wheel drive	£219	£249

Hotel France						Prices per person
Number of nights	2	3	4	5	6	7
Winter	£37	£62	£81	£100	£121	£144
Summer	£47	£74	£96	£117	£141	£166
Children FREE						

3 Mr and Mrs Walters live in London with their two children. They will be flying to Paris in the summer and spending one day at the Disneyland® theme park. They will stay 2 nights at Hotel France and hire an estate car for 2 weeks.

(a) Copy and complete the table for the Walters family.

(b) Calculate the total cost.

(c) Aunt Flo is travelling from Newcastle to London, to look after the house. How far does she have to drive? See the road distances table on p. 113.

Holiday costs	
Air fares	£
Disneyland® theme park passes	£
Car hire	£
Hotel France	£

4 Plan a holiday to Disneyland® for you and your family. You will need to decide …
- which airport to fly from
- how far you need to travel to the airport
- whether you will go in winter or summer
- how many days you will spend in the theme park
- how many nights you will spend in Hotel France
- how long you want to hire a car for and which model.

(a) Copy and complete the table like the one in question 3.

(b) Calculate the total cost of your holiday.

> **Finished Early?**
> 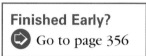 Go to page 356

Further Practice

K **1** Use the tables on pages 113 and 114 to answer these questions.

(a) What is the distance from London to Edinburgh?

(b) How much does a 1 day pass cost for a child in summer?

(c) How much does it cost to hire an estate car for 1 week in summer?

(d) How much does it cost for 2 adults to spend 3 nights in Hotel France in winter?

2 Mr and Mrs Weatherspoon are planning a trip to Disneyland® with their daughter Maureen.

(a) They are flying from Manchester in winter. How much will their air fares cost altogether?

(b) They live in Newcastle. How far is Newcastle from Birmingham?

(c) They want to spend 2 days in Disneyland®. How much will their theme park passes cost?

(d) They are going to hire a saloon car for a week. How much will it cost?

(e) They want to stay in Hotel France for 6 nights. How much will the hotel bill be?

Holiday costs	
Air fares	£
Disneyland® theme park passes	£
Car hire	£
Hotel France	£

(f) Copy and complete the table.

(g) Calculate the total cost of their holiday.

> **Finished Early?**
> Go to page 356

12 Making Tables and Charts

In this chapter you will learn about …
1. tallying data
2. drawing bar charts
3. drawing pictograms

1 Tallying Data

Learn About It

1 Here are the letters of the alphabet:

a b c d e f g h i j k l m n o p q r s t u v w x y z.

Some letters happen more often than others:

The letter **t** happens seven times in this sentence.

The letter **m** happens only once in this sentence.

2 The most common letters are: **t n e a i**.

Which letter do you think happens the most in the English language?

Let's investigate.

3 Copy this **tally chart**.

Letter	Tally	Total
t		
n		
e		
a		
i		

4 Now slowly read this sentence from *Alice's Adventures in Wonderland*:

'When I used to read fairy tales,
I fancied that kind of thing never happened,
and now here I am in the middle of one!'

Each time you spot one of the letters **t, n, e, a, i**, make a **tally mark** |
in your tally chart. Include capital letters in your tally.

Group five tally marks together like this instead of writing
This makes them easier to count later on.

5 Add up the tally marks for each letter and write the totals in your chart.

6 Look at your results.

   (a) Which is the most common letter?

   (b) Which is the least common letter?

   (c) Write the letters in order, from most common to least common.

Word Check

tally mark a mark that records a single thing

tally chart a table for tally marks

Try It Out

 Investigate this passage from *Star Wars*:

> *'This is our most desperate hour. Help me, Obi-Wan Kenobi, you're my only hope.'*

1 Make a tally chart like the one above.

2 Carefully read through the passage, looking for the letters **t**, **n**, **e**, **a**, **i**.

3 Make a tally mark for each letter you spot. Don't forget to group them in fives ||||| .

4 Add up the tally marks and write the totals in your chart.

5 Write down the letter that happens the most often.

6 Write down the letter that happens the least often.

7 Write the letters in order, from most often to least often.

8 Write a sentence comparing the passages from *Star Wars* and *Alice's Adventures in Wonderland*. Describe at least two differences.

Practice

 A coin to toss

B **1** Toss a coin 50 times. Keep count of the tosses up to 50. Record your results in a tally chart like this.

	Tally	Total
Heads		
Tails		

2 Alex cycles to school. Each day she records the number of minutes her journeys take. Here are her times over a four-week period:

10	12	15	12	11	14	14	12	13	13
13	12	12	12	14	13	11	10	15	11
13	13	11	12	14	13	12	11	11	13
10	12	13	11	14	12	15	11	12	14

(a) What is her shortest journey time?
(b) What is her longest journey time?
(c) Copy and complete the table.
(d) What is Alex's most common journey time?

Journey time (minutes)	Tally	Total
10		
11		

Finished Early?
➡ Go to page 356

Further Practice

A die

One person rolls an ordinary six-sided die 60 times. Keep count of the rolls up to 60. The other records the results in a tally chart like this.

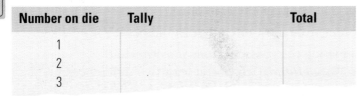

Number on die	Tally	Total
1		
2		
3		

1 Are the results as you expected? Explain your answer.

2 Swap around and repeat the experiment. Are the results about the same?

Finished Early?
➡ Go to page 356

2 Drawing Bar Charts

Learn About It

Squared paper

Joanne asks her classmates which fruit they like best.

She makes a table of her results and decides to draw a bar chart.

Fruit	Number of pupils
Orange	4
Pear	0
Banana	8
Apple	6

First she draws a pair of axes on squared paper.
Joanne is investigating fruit. Fruit goes along the horizontal axis.
There are 4 kinds of fruit. She will need space for 4 bars.

Bananas are the most popular fruit, chosen by 8 pupils. Joanne numbers the vertical axis from 0 to 8.

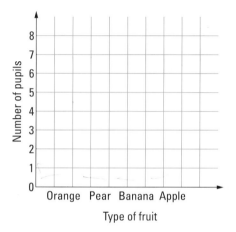

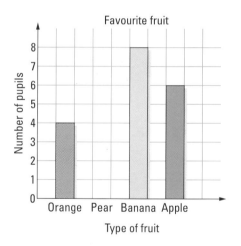

She leaves one square of space between bars.
Joanne draws the top of each bar first.
None of her classmates liked pears.
So the bar for pears has no height.

Key Fact

Rules for drawing bar charts

- Use squared paper
- Draw a pair of axes
- Give each axis a name
- Number the vertical axis, starting at 0 (use a scale if needed)
- Put names of bars on the horizontal axis
- Make the bars equally wide
- Put a space between the bars
- Draw the top of each bar first
- Give your chart a title

Try It Out

Squared paper

D 1 Copy Joanne's table.

2 Copy her bar chart onto squared paper.

3 Check that you have followed the rules for drawing a bar chart.

Learn More About It

Darryl works in a children's shoe shop. He recorded the sizes of all the pairs of shoes sold during the week. The manageress wants a bar chart to hang up.

Shoe size	Number of pairs
8	9
$8\frac{1}{2}$	4
9	8
$9\frac{1}{2}$	14
10	9
$10\frac{1}{2}$	5

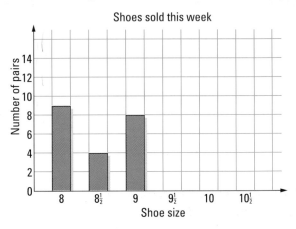

The number of pairs goes up the vertical axis.

The largest number of pairs is 14.

Darryl uses 1 cm for every 2 pairs. This is the **scale** for the axis.

This way his bars won't be too tall.

The first bar is 9 pairs tall.

That's halfway between 8 and 10.

> **Word Check**
>
> **scale** tells you how to number the axes

Try It Out

Squared paper

E 1 Copy Darryl's table.

2 Copy his bar chart onto squared paper.

3 Complete his bar chart.

4 Check that you have followed the rules for drawing a bar chart.

Practice

Squared paper

1 Franz asked each of his classmates 'How many children are there in your family'? Here are the data he collected:

3	3	2	1	4	3	2	2	6	3	6	3
1	3	2	2	2	6	4	1	3	2	4	4
2	2	1	1	4	3						

(a) Copy and complete the tally chart.

Children in family	Tally	Number of families
1		
2		
3		
4		
5		
6		

(b) Draw a bar chart on squared paper. Use a scale of 1 cm to 2 families.

2 Maureen counted the passengers in cars passing her school.

Draw a bar chart using squared paper. Use a scale of 1 cm to 4 cars.

Passengers	Number of cars
1	12
2	26
3	20
4	14
5	3
6	1

Further Practice

Squared paper

G **1** The table to the right shows the number of times needed to start Mr Moore's old car in the morning.

Number of times needed to start car	Number of mornings
1	8
2	5
3	5
4	3
5	2

Finished Early?

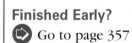

Go to page 357

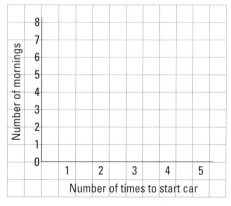

(a) Copy these axes onto squared paper. **(b)** Draw a bar chart.

Graph paper

2 Warton Girls' School has four sports clubs: Football, Netball, Tennis and Cricket. The table shows how many pupils belong to each club.

Use graph paper to draw a bar chart.

Number the vertical axis from 0 to 50.
Use a scale of 1 cm to 5 pupils.
Each small square stands for 1 pupil.

Sports club	Number of pupils
Football	23
Netball	35
Tennis	49
Cricket	42

Finished Early?
➡ Go to page 357

❸ Drawing Pictograms

Learn About It

Arup, Brid, Glenda and Peter race electric cars.

The winner of each race draws a wheel next to their name on the scoreboard. This makes a simple pictogram.

This week, Arup has won 7 races, Brid 3, Glenda 4 and Peter 5.

Arup wins another race but there is no space for another wheel.

He solves the problem by using one wheel to stand for 2 wins. This is the **key** to his pictogram.

Arup used the rules in the Key Fact box to draw his new pictogram.

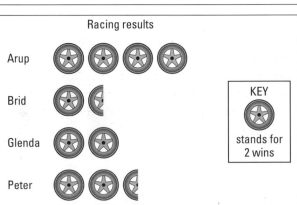

NUMBER SKILLS **Count in twos**

Key Fact

Rules for drawing pictograms
- Use lined or squared paper
- Choose a simple picture
- Choose a **key** so that there are not more than 7 pictures in a row
- Make the pictures the same size, shape and colour
- Equally space the pictures
- Put the key in the pictogram
- Give the pictogram a title

Try It Out

H The table shows the racing results for Arup, Brid, Glenda and Peter over a two-week period.

Draw a pictogram using the key: stands for 2 wins. Use the rules for drawing a pictogram.

Driver	Number of races won
Arup	12
Brid	7
Glenda	9
Peter	8

Practice

1 The table shows the racing results for Arup, Brid, Glenda and Peter over a month.

Draw a pictogram using the key: stands for 4 wins. Answer questions (a), (b) and (c) to help you draw it.

Driver	Number of races won
Arup	20
Brid	15
Glenda	10
Peter	17

(a) How will you draw 2 wins?

(b) How will you draw 1 win?

(c) How will you draw 3 wins?

(d) Draw the pictogram using the rules in the Key Fact box at the top of this page.

2 This week, Arup won 7 races, Brid 3, Glenda 4 and Peter 5. Brid wants to make her results look better. She has drawn her own pictogram. What is wrong with her pictogram? Describe as many things as you can.

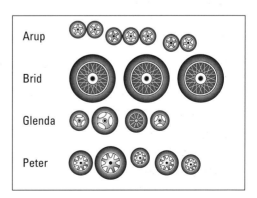

J Write down the key you would use to draw pictograms for these tables of data. Choose your own pictures. Remember: there must not be more than 7 pictures in a row. Draw pictograms for each.

1

Colour	Number of Smarties
Red	20
Green	15
Blue	12
Pink	17
Yellow	11

2

Sports club	Number of pupils
Football	23
Netball	35
Tennis	49
Cricket	42

Finished Early?
➡ Go to page 357

Further Practice

K **1** Murray is an airline pilot. This month he made 6 flights to Spain, 8 flights to France and 4 flights to Germany. Copy and complete the pictogram.

Murray's flights

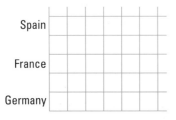

KEY stands for 3 flights

2 This table shows how many programmes were on television one day.

Draw a pictogram. Choose your own picture to stand for 4 programmes.

Channel	Number of programmes
BBC1	12
BBC2	15
ITV	25
Channel 4	22

Graph paper

3 Rachna lives in Amsterdam. She recorded the first 125 vehicles to pass her school.

  (a) Draw a pictogram for her data. Choose your own picture. Find the correct key to use. Remember: there must not be more than 7 pictures in a row.

  (b) Draw a bar chart for her data. Use graph paper.

Vehicle	Total
Car	55
Tram	24
Bicycle	33
Motorcycle	13

Finished Early?
➡ Go to page 357

Unit 6 *Statistical Diagrams*

Summary of Chapters 11 and 12

- You can record data (information) in tables.
- You can record data in bar charts and pictograms.

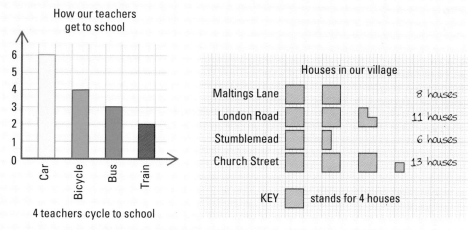

How our teachers get to school

4 teachers cycle to school

Houses in our village

Maltings Lane			8 houses
London Road			11 houses
Stumblemead			6 houses
Church Street			13 houses

KEY □ stands for 4 houses

- These are the rules for drawing bar charts.

Use squared paper	Put names of bars on the
Draw a pair of axes	horizontal axis
Give each axis a name	Make the bars equally wide
Number the vertical axis,	Put a space between the bars
starting at 0 (use a scale	Draw the top of each bar first
if needed)	Give your chart a title

- These are the rules for drawing pictograms.

Use lined or squared paper	Make the pictures the same size,
Choose a simple picture	shape and colour
Choose a **key** so that there are	Equally space the pictures
not more than 7 pictures in a	Put the key in the pictogram
row	Give the pictogram a title

- You can record data using tally marks.

  Use |||| to record five objects.

13 Calculating with Confidence

In this chapter you will learn about ...
1. shortcuts
2. mixed operations
3. brackets
4. checking your answer

1 Shortcuts

Learn About It

1 Write these numbers in a line across the page.

23   56   160   239

Add 10 and 9 to each one. Write your answers below the numbers and find the difference between them.

	23	56	160	239
Add 10	33			
Add 9	32			
Difference	1			

Write down a shortcut for adding 9 from the answers for adding 10.
Test your shortcut with other numbers.

2 Add 100 and 99 to 23, 56, 160 and 239.

What is the difference between adding 100 and adding 99? Write down a shortcut for adding 99 from the answers for adding 100. Test your shortcut with other numbers.

	23	56	160	239
Add 100	123			
Add 99	122			
Difference	1			

3 Subtract 10 and 9 from 23, 56, 160 and 239.

What is the difference between subtracting 10 and subtracting 9?
Write down a rule for subtracting 9. Test your rule with other numbers.

4 Subtract 100 and 99 from 120, 240, 339 and 489. What is the difference between subtracting 100 and subtracting 99?
Write down a shortcut for subtracting 99. Test your shortcut with other numbers.

5 Multiply 3, 5, 16 and 25
by 10 and then by 9.
Find the difference
between multiplying by
10 and multiplying by 9.
Write down a shortcut
for multiplying by 9.
Test your shortcut with other numbers.

		3	5	16	25
Multiply by 10		30			
Multiply by 9		27			
Difference		3			

6 Multiply 3, 5, 16 and 25 by 100 and then by 99. What is the difference
between multiplying by 100 and multiplying by 99? Write down a shortcut
for multiplying by 99. Test your shortcut with other numbers.

Try It Out

 Work out:

1 $43 + 9$ **2** $75 + 99$ **3** $45 - 9$ **4** $254 - 99$

Example	24×9
Working	$24 \times 10 = 240$
	$24 \times 9 = 240 - 24$
Answer	216

5 13×9 **6** 15×9 **7** 9×22 **8** 99×4

9 $62 + 9$ **10** $64 + 99$ **11** $72 - 9$ **12** $128 - 99$

13 16×9 **14** 18×9 **15** 9×21 **16** 99×3

Key Facts

Shortcut: a quick way of working out
Add 9: Add 10 and subtract 1.
Add 99: Add 100 and subtract 1.
Subtract 9: Subtract 10 and add 1.
Subtract 99: Subtract 100 and add 1.
Multiply a number by 9: Multiply by 10 and subtract the number.
Multiply a number by 99: Multiply by 100 and subtract the number.

Practice

B Work out:

1 9 + 37	**2** 39 + 99	**3** 45 + 99	**4** 155 + 199
5 246 + 299	**6** 65 – 9	**7** 43 – 9	**8** 167 – 99
9 276 – 99	**10** 494 – 99	**11** 576 – 299	**12** 247 – 199
13 14 × 9	**14** 17 × 9	**15** 9 × 34	**16** 9 × 26

C **1** Darren has 99 tapes at the start of the year and during the year he buys 23 more. How many tapes does he have at the end of the year?

2 Diana had collected 143 cans for recycling and Indira had collected 99. How many had they collected altogether?

3 In a school with 395 children there are 199 boys. How many girls are there?

4 Craig is washing up after his birthday party. If there were 44 dirty plates to start with and he has washed 9 of them how many are still dirty?

5 A school has a delivery of new chairs. There are 29 chairs for each classroom and there are 9 classrooms. How many chairs are there altogether?

6 How much would you pay for 17 tickets costing £9 each?

7 A teacher is organising a school trip. Each ticket costs £8 and 99 pupils are going. How much will the trip cost?

8 What number is 67 more than 99?

> **Finished Early?**
> ⇨ Go to page 358

Further Practice

D Find the answers to these.

1 37 + 9	**2** 42 + 9	**3** 9 + 245	**4** 74 + 99
5 66 + 99	**6** 99 + 156	**7** 99 + 243	**8** 55 – 9
9 75 – 9	**10** 162 – 9	**11** 277 – 99	**12** 383 – 99

E **1** Jim has collected 78 coins in a jar. If his mother gives him 99 coins how many will he have altogether?

2 A bus with 43 passengers on it arrives at a stop. No one gets off, but 19 new passengers get on. How many passengers are now on the bus?

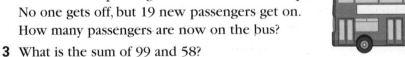

3 What is the sum of 99 and 58?

4 Mira picked 67 kg of plums one day and 99 kg the next. How much did she pick altogether?

5 139 schoolchildren go on a trip in four coaches. If there are 99 children on three of the coaches, how many are on the other one?

6 A pencil costs 9p. How much change do you get from 50p if you buy one pencil?

7 A carpenter saws 99 cm off a piece of wood of length 160 cm. What length of wood does he have left?

8 A rope is 135 m long. If 99 m is cut off how much is left?

❷ Mixed Operations

Learn About It

Ben and Bella both work out $9 + 6 \times 4$.

Ben does $9 + 6 \times 4 = 15 \times 4 = 60$.

Bella does $9 + 6 \times 4 = 9 + 24 = 33$

The answers are different. They cannot both be right.

They did the addition and multiplication in different orders. This makes the answers different.

If you have a mixture of operations $(+, -, \times, \div)$ then the order is …

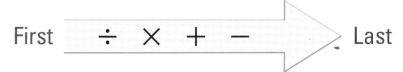

First $\div$ $\times$ $+$ $-$ Last

So Bella is correct. She multiplied before adding.

You do **not** work out operations as you come to them.

Try It Out

Work out these. Write down the stages in your calculations.

1 $12 + 5 - 9$ **2** $3 \times 4 + 5$ **3** $6 + 4 \times 5$ **4** $9 \times 5 - 12$ **5** $50 - 6 \times 3$

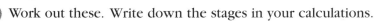

Example	$7 + 15 \div 5$
Working	$7 + 15 \div 5 = 7 + 3$
Answer	10

6 $9 + 45 \div 15$

7 $18 - 42 \div 14$

8 $30 \div 5 \times 4$

Key Fact

The order of operation is …

1 Division
2 Multiplication
3 Addition
4 Subtraction.

Practice

G Work out these. Write down the stages in your calculations.

1 $25 + 10 - 12$	**2** $33 + 19 - 10$	**3** $3 \times 12 + 10$	**4** $12 + 4 \times 9$
5 $12 \times 3 + 24$	**6** $15 + 10 \times 5$	**7** $12 \times 4 - 19$	**8** $72 - 18 \times 2$
9 $48 \div 4 + 50$	**10** $66 + 55 \div 5$	**11** $84 - 72 \div 3$	**12** $92 - 60 \div 12$
13 $67 - 121 \div 11$	**14** $36 \div 4 \times 5$	**15** $6 \times 30 \div 5$	**16** $12 \times 48 \div 4$

H Work out the answers to these.

1 There are 13 people in a school hall. Four classes each of 25 pupils join them. How many people are now in the hall?

2 There are 12 bars of chocolate left in a shop. Seven boxes each containing 24 bars are delivered. How many bars of chocolate are in the shop?

3 In the maths book cupboard there are 5 shelves each holding 18 books and 1 shelf holding 13 books. How many books are there altogether?

4 Kim stores her CDs in boxes which can each hold 15 CDs. There are 6 full boxes and one box contains 9 CDs. How many CDs does Kim have?

5 A tray in a garden centre holds 18 plants. There are 6 full trays and one tray with 13 plants in it. How many plants are there altogether?

6 Mrs Pearce stores pens in packets of 32. She has 5 full packets and 7 pens left over. How many pens does she have altogether?

Finished Early?
→ Go to page 358

Further Practice

I This is Dave's homework. He has made some mistakes!

Write out the questions. Tick the correct answers and correct the wrong ones.

1. $12 + 39 - 7 = 44$	2. $20 + 5 \times 3 = 75$
3. $24 - 6 \times 3 = 6$	4. $18 + 4 \times 9 = 54$
5. $70 - 5 \times 8 = 30$	6. $72 \div 3 \times 4 = 6$
7. $84 \div 12 \times 2 = 14$	8. $60 + 6 \times 5 = 330$

J Work out these, writing down the stages in your calculations.

1 $10 + 15 - 8$	**2** $24 + 12 - 20$	**3** $4 \times 11 + 20$	**4** $24 + 5 \times 6$
5 $4 \times 12 + 14$	**6** $14 + 10 \times 4$	**7** $10 \times 3 - 26$	**8** $80 - 20 \times 3$
9 $60 - 10 \times 3$	**10** $75 - 3 \times 15$	**11** $40 - 3 \times 12$	**12** $20 \times 3 - 25$
13 $15 + 40 \div 20$	**14** $49 + 30 \div 10$	**15** $60 \div 12 + 40$	**16** $16 + 45 \div 5$

❸ Brackets

Learn About It

Donna writes instructions to subtract 6 from 15 and multiply the answer by 2.

But $15 - 6 \times 2 = 15 - 12$
$= 3$

This is not what Donna wants to do.
She wants to subtract **before** multiplying.

To write it correctly Donna must use **brackets**.

$(15 - 6) \times 2 = 9 \times 2$
$= 18$

Parts of a calculation **in brackets** are worked out **first**.

> ### Key Fact
> Always work out the brackets first.

Example	$12 \times (6 - 4)$
Working	$12 \times (6 - 4) = 12 \times 2$
Answer	24

Try It Out

Ⓚ Work out these.

1 $(12 + 8) \times 3$ **2** $(18 - 6) \times 7$ **3** $12 \times (15 - 8)$ **4** $9 \times (12 + 8)$
5 $(25 + 35) \div 12$ **6** $72 \div (15 - 9)$ **7** $(12 \times 3) \div 4$ **8** $(9 \times 4) \div 3$

Practice

Ⓛ Find the answers to these.

1 $(23 + 37) \times 3$ **2** $(14 + 21) \times 2$ **3** $(24 + 17) \times 4$
4 $12 \times (13 + 7)$ **5** $15 \times (14 + 16)$ **6** $20 \times (42 - 32)$
7 $10 \times (81 - 19)$ **8** $20 \times (56 - 48)$ **9** $(72 - 27) \div 9$
10 $(96 + 24) \div 12$ **11** $(12 \times 5) \div 3$ **12** $(14 \times 10) \div 7$
13 $(21 + 15) \times 4$ **14** $(23 + 17) \times 3$ **15** $(61 - 43) \times 5$
16 $9 \times (121 - 49)$ **17** $(84 - 61) \times 7$ **18** $(95 + 13) \div 12$

Work out these.

Example	**(a)** $8 + 5 \times 3$	**(b)** $(8 + 5) \times 3$
Working	$8 + 15$	13×3
Answer	23	39

1 (a) $12 + 7 \times 3$ **(b)** $(12 + 7) \times 3$

2 (a) $26 - 2 \times 10$ **(b)** $(26 - 2) \times 10$

3 (a) $24 + 6 \times 3$ **(b)** $(24 + 6) \times 3$

4 (a) $14 \times 5 + 15$ **(b)** $14 \times (5 + 15)$

5 (a) $21 \times (20 - 8)$ **(b)** $21 \times 20 - 8$

6 (a) $30 \times 24 - 16$ **(b)** $30 \times (24 - 16)$

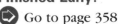

Finished Early?
Go to page 358

Further Practice

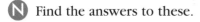 Find the answers to these.

1 $(17 + 3) \times 2$ **2** $(24 + 16) \times 3$ **3** $(12 + 18) \times 5$

4 $12 \times (12 + 8)$ **5** $10 \times (12 + 18)$ **6** $5 \times (40 - 30)$

7 $8 \times (71 - 56)$ **8** $10 \times (71 - 59)$ **9** $(98 - 28) \div 14$

10 $(45 + 32) \div 11$ **11** $(16 \times 3) \div 12$ **12** $(8 \times 9) \div 6$

Write out these questions. Tick the ones that are correct. Write the correct answers for the ones that are wrong.

1. $(23 + 17) \times 3 = 120$ 2. $4 \times (15 + 13) = 73$

3. $15 \times (12 - 9) = 171$ 4. $(32 + 18) \times 4 = 200$

5. $32 + 18 \times 4 = 200$ 6. $(20 + 3) \times 5 = 115$

7. $20 + 3 \times 5 = 115$ 8. $(125 - 5) \times 6 = 85$

9. $(24 + 16) \times 4 = 160$ 10. $24 + 16 \times 4 = 160$

11. $(36 + 48) \div 12 = 7$ 12. $36 + 48 \div 12 = 7$

13. $65 - 21 \times 2 = 88$ 14. $(65 - 21) \times 2 = 88$

15. $(112 + 38) \div 25 = 5$ 16. $164 - 72 \div 2 = 47$

4 Checking Your Answer

Learn About It

To check a calculation numbers are rounded to **one significant figure**. They are rounded so that only the first digit is not zero.

Single-digit numbers stay the same. So 3 stays as 3.

Two-digit numbers are rounded to the nearest 10. So 26 is rounded to 30.

Three-digit numbers are rounded to the nearest 100. So 234 is rounded to 200.

Try It Out

P Round these numbers to one significant figure.

1 76　　　**2** 389　　　**3** 7　　　**4** 84　　　**5** 67　　　**6** 749

Learn More About It

Roland does this calculation.

He wants to check the calculation. Rounding the numbers makes it easier to spot mistakes.

This answer is close to the original answer. So 301 **looks** correct.

You cannot be **certain** that an answer is correct by checking. But if one answer is two or more times the size of the other, your calculation is probably wrong.

$48 + 11 \times 23$

$= 48 + 253$

$= 301$

48 to one significant figure is 50

11 to one significant figure is 10

23 to one significant figure is 20

$50 + 10 \times 20$

$= 50 + 200$

$= 250$

Word Check

one significant figure one non-zero digit

checking an answer repeating the calculation with numbers rounded to one significant figure

Try It Out

Q Work out these and check your answers by rounding.

Example	43×22
Working	$43 \times 22 = 946$
	$40 \times 20 = 800$
Answer	So 946 looks correct

1 $23 + 69$　　**2** $47 + 38$　　**3** $98 - 43$　　**4** $87 - 32$　　**5** 32×18　　**6** 81×59

Practice

R Copy out these calculations. Check each of them by rounding.

Work out correct answers for those that are wrong.

1 $36 - 21 + 11 = 46$

2 $105 - 25 \times 3 = 240$

3 $280 + 9 \times 25 = 505$

4 $72 - 3 \times 18 = 920$

5 $25 + 150 \times 6 = 925$

6 $66 - 3 \times 12 = 792$

7 $90 \div 5 \times 2 = 36$

8 $90 \div (5 \times 2) = 9$

9 $(64 - 24) \times 2 = 16$

S Work out and check your answers.

1 $25 \times 9 + 75$
2 $31 + 23 \times 2$
3 $48 \times 3 + 5$
4 $176 \div 16 - 4$
5 $23 + 134 \times 5$
6 $24 + 156 \times 6$
7 $238 - 13 \times 14$
8 $251 \times 4 - 93$
9 $321 \times 3 + 7$
10 $63 + 27 \times 16$
11 $79 + 21 \times 11$
12 $19 \times 5 - 29$
13 $(34 + 21) \times 7$
14 $23 \times (44 - 19)$
15 $42 \times (75 - 33)$

Finished Early?
➪ Go to page 359

Further Practice

T Work out these and check your answers.

1 27×3
2 49×5
3 208×3
4 29×19
5 139×8
6 $87 + 99$
7 $489 + 234$
8 $232 + 299$
9 $476 - 199$
10 $523 - 99$
11 $354 - 199$
12 $361 \div 19$
13 $462 \div 21$
14 $23 + 42 \times 2$
15 $294 - 34 \times 3$
16 $(78 - 43) \times 4$
17 $67 + 23 \times 6$
18 $(67 + 23) \times 6$
19 $220 - 24 \times 5$
20 $(220 - 24) \times 5$

14 Powers and Roots

In this chapter you will learn about ...
1. squaring
2. cubing
3. square roots

① Squaring

Learn About It

Yasmin arranges tiles in squares.

←1→   ←—2—→   ←——3——→

The numbers of tiles in the squares are 1, 4 and 9. The number of tiles on one side multiplied by itself gives 1, 4 and 9. Multiplying a number by itself is called **squaring**. The numbers 1, 4 and 9 are **square numbers**.

7 squared is $7 \times 7 = 49$.

7^2 means square 7. So $7^2 = 49$.

 Squaring is **not** the same as multiplying the number by 2.

7^2 does **not** mean 7×2.

 There is also a button on your calculator that will square a number. $\boxed{x^2}$

If you put in 3.5 and then press $\boxed{x^2}$ the answer will be 12.25.

Try It Out

 1 Copy and complete this table.

The second and third rows are the squares of the first row.

1	2	3	4	5	6	7	8	9	10
1^2	2^2	3^2							
1	4								

> **Key Fact**
>
> To square a number, multiply it by itself.
>
> Squaring is raising a number to the power of 2.

2 Which of these are squares of
whole numbers?

16   24,   30,

36, 5^2, 3^2

48,   12, 15^2 1

3 Find …

(**a**) 16^2 (**b**) 3.5^2 (**c**) 2.4^2 (**d**) 7.5^2 (**e**) 75^2 (**f**) 50^2 (**g**) 100^2.

Practice

B **1** Charlotte thinks these are square numbers. Write them out, mark them with
ticks if they are square numbers or crosses if not.

25, 4^2, 49, 88, 2×5, 6^2

17^2, 32, 8×8, 50

2 Find …

(**a**) the square of 14   (**b**) 3.2^2
(**c**) 4.5 squared   (**d**) 10.6^2
(**e**) 62^2 (**f**) the square of 78
(**g**) the square of 82.5   (**h**) 12.5^2
(**i**) 80^2 (**j**) 90^2.

C Find the missing numbers.

1 The square of 6 is …   **2** The square of 8 is …
3 10 squared is …   **4** 15 squared is …
5 13^2 is …   **6** If you square 100 you get …

D **1** Draw a number line from 0 to 100. Make your line 10 cm long.

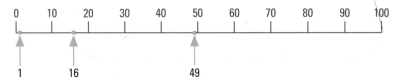

Mark the square numbers on the line. Three have been done for you.

2 Draw a line for numbers 100 to 200 and mark in the square numbers.

3 Draw a line for numbers 200 to 300 and mark in the square numbers.

4 What happens to the spaces between the squares as the numbers get larger?

Finished Early?
 Go to page 359

Further Practice

E **1** Write down the numbers which are square numbers.

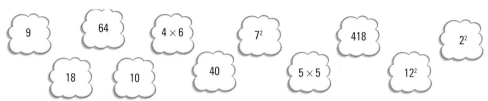

9   64 4×6 7^2 418 2^2

18   10   40 5×5 12^2

 2 Find …

    (a) 16^2 **(b)** 1.5^2 **(c)** 2.4^2 **(d)** 5.5^2 **(e)** 45^2

    (f) 70^2 **(g)** 60^2 **(h)** 25^2 **(i)** 28^2 **(j)** 2.8^2.

F Find the missing numbers.

  1 5^2 is …   **2** The square of 11 is …

  3 Square 13 and you get …   **4** 5 squared equals …

  5 … is the square of 6   **6** 7^2 is …

  7 If you square 4 you get …   **8** … equals 20 squared.

  9 $2^2 \times 5^2 = \dots$

❷ Cubing

Learn About It

Roy arranges building blocks to make cubes.

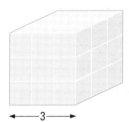

←1→   ←2→   ←3→

The numbers of blocks in these cubes are 1, 8 and 27.

These numbers are called **cubes**. They are the cubes of 1, 2 and 3.

2 cubed means $2 \times 2 \times 2 = 8$.

2^3 means 2 cubed.

2^3 means $2 \times 2 \times 2$.

2^3 does **not** mean 2×3.

> ## Key Fact
> The cube of a number is given by three of the numbers multiplied together.
> Cubing is raising a number to the power of 3.

Try It Out

 **1** Find ...

(a) 4^3 (b) 3^3 (c) 5^3 (d) 6^3.

2 Copy and complete this table.

The second and third rows are the cubes of the first row.

1	2	3	4	5	6	7	8	9	10
1^3	2^3								
1	8								

Practice

(H) **1** Pick out the cube numbers from these and write them out.

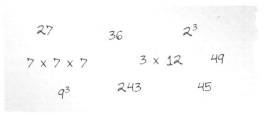

27   36 2^3

7 × 7 × 7   3 × 12   49

9^3 243   45

2 Find ...

(a) the cube of 9   (b) the cube of 10   (c) 20^3 (d) 12^3
(e) 5^3 (f) 50^3 (g) the cube of 25   (h) 32^3
(i) 28^3 (j) 17^3.

(I) You have this number of small cubes. Would they make a big cube with none left over?

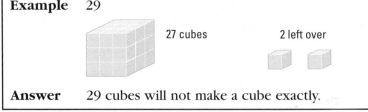

Example   29

27 cubes   2 left over

Answer   29 cubes will not make a cube exactly.

(a) 10   (b) 16   (c) 3^3 (d) 2^2 (e) 3 × 6
(f) 64   (g) 5^3 (h) 6 × 6 × 6   (i) 72

Finished Early?
Go to page 359

Further Practice

J This is a page from Kay's book. She has been working out cubes. Copy these out and mark them. Correct any that are wrong.

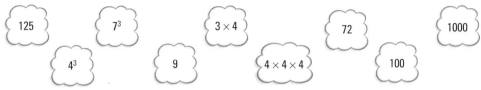

1. $4^3 = 54$
2. $6^3 = 36$
3. $5^3 = 125$
4. $10^3 = 100$
5. $8^3 = 24$
6. $12^3 = 36$
7. $7^3 = 240$
8. $9^3 = 729$
9. $13^3 = 39$
10. $14^3 = 2744$

K **1** Pick out the cube numbers from these and write them out.

125   7^3 3×4 72   1000

4^3 9 $4 \times 4 \times 4$ 100

2 Find the cubes of these numbers.

(**a**) 15   (**b**) 20   (**c**) 60   (**d**) 4   (**e**) 40
(**f**) 3   (**g**) 30   (**h**) 70   (**i**) 80   (**j**) 120

L Find the missing numbers.

1 The cube of 2 is ...
2 3^3 equals ...
3 When you cube 4 you get ...
4 $9 \times 9 \times 9$ is ... cubed.
5 10 cubed is ...
6 The cube of 20 equals ...

3 # Square Roots

Learn About It

Squared paper

1 Copy these number lines using squared paper.

Use 2 cm for 10 on the top line. 1 cm for each number on the bottom line.

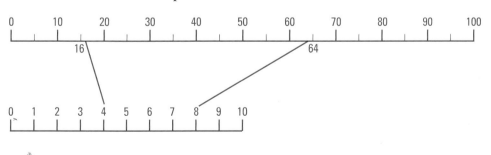

Work out the squares of the numbers 1 to 10. Mark them on the top line.

Connect the numbers 1 to 10 on the bottom line with their squares on the top line.

Two have been done for you.

2 You can work back from the squares to the original numbers.

Starting with 64 you can see that $64 = 8^2$.

Finding the original number in this way is called finding the **square root**. The symbol for this is $\sqrt{}$.

$\sqrt{64}$ means the square root of 64.

$\sqrt{64} = 8$.

Finding the square root and squaring are **inverses** of each other.

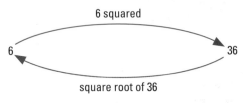

6 squared

6 _____→ 36

square root of 36

3 Write out the connections between the numbers you have marked using the $\sqrt{}$ symbol.

$\sqrt{1} = 1$

$\sqrt{4} = 2$

etc.

> **Word Check**
>
> **inverse** the opposite of an operation

4 You can find a square root by trying numbers.

To find $\sqrt{169}$, try the number 12.

$12 \times 12 = 144$ so 12 is smaller than $\sqrt{169}$.

Try a larger number.

$13 \times 13 = 169$ so $\sqrt{169} = 13$.

5 You can use a calculator to find a square root.

Put in the number then press $\boxed{\sqrt{x}}$.

Try this with the numbers on your top number line.

> ## Key Fact
>
> The square root of a number, multiplied by itself, equals the number.

Try It Out

 See how many of the **red** numbers you can write as a square root of one of the **blue** numbers.

There will be some left over.

2, 4, 6, 8, 11, 9, 5, 7, 3

4, 25, 12, 16, 36, 48, 49, 121, 27, 81

N Find these square roots.

1 $\sqrt{49}$	**2** $\sqrt{144}$	**3** $\sqrt{81}$	**4** $\sqrt{64}$
5 $\sqrt{225}$	**6** $\sqrt{121}$	**7** $\sqrt{400}$	**8** $\sqrt{900}$

Practice

O Find the missing numbers.

1 ... is the square root of 256.

2 $\sqrt{196} = ...$

3 If $325^2 = 105\,625$ then $\sqrt{105\,625} = ...$

4 20 is the square root of ...

5 $\sqrt{441} = 21$ so $21^2 = ...$

6 $\sqrt{7} \times \sqrt{7} = ...$

P Find a whole number above and below these square roots.

Example	$\sqrt{40}$
Working	$\sqrt{36}$ is 6 and $\sqrt{49}$ is 7
Answer	$\sqrt{40}$ is between 6 and 7

1 $\sqrt{77}$	**2** $\sqrt{54}$	**3** $\sqrt{89}$	**4** $\sqrt{99}$	**5** $\sqrt{111}$
6 $\sqrt{84}$	**7** $\sqrt{180}$	**8** $\sqrt{240}$	**9** $\sqrt{620}$	**10** $\sqrt{823}$

Q Rajnesh and his class are going to put tiles in a garden at their school.

They are given tiles by a local builder. They make a square. How long will the sides be if they have the following number of tiles?

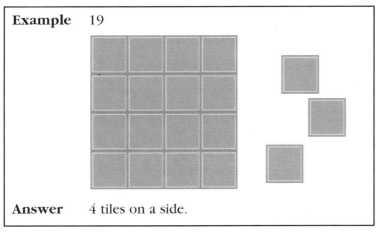

Example 19

Answer 4 tiles on a side.

1 36   **2** 50   **3** 65   **4** 120   **5** 170   **6** 190   **7** 250   **8** 200

Further Practice

R Find the missing numbers.

1 The square root of 225 is ...

2 $\sqrt{36} = ...$

3 $39 \times 39 = 1521$ so $\sqrt{1521} = ...$

4 12 is the square root of ...

5 $\sqrt{256} = 16$ so $16^2 = ...$

6 $\sqrt{8} \times \sqrt{8} = ...$

S Some of these statements are true and some are false.

List them in two columns headed **true** and **false**.

The square root of 36 is 6.
The square root of 256 is 16.
The square root of 12 is 24.
As $27^2 = 729$ then $\sqrt{27} = 729$.
11 is the square root of 121.
The square root of 14 is 7.
The square root of 81 is 9.
18 is the square root of 36.
The square root of 27 is 3.
The square root of 144 is 12.
As $30 \times 30 = 900$ then $\sqrt{900} = 30$.
The square root of 400 is 20.

T Find a whole number above and below these.

1 $\sqrt{45}$ **2** $\sqrt{30}$ **3** $\sqrt{24}$ **4** $\sqrt{80}$ **5** $\sqrt{72}$

6 $\sqrt{60}$ **7** $\sqrt{115}$ **8** $\sqrt{160}$ **9** $\sqrt{420}$ **10** $\sqrt{500}$

Finished Early?
➡ Go to page 360

Unit 7 *Computation*

Review of Chapters 13 and 14

Shortcut: a quick way of working out.

- To add 9 or 99 to a number, add 10 or 100 and subtract 1.
- To subtract 9 or 99 from a number, subtract 10 or 100 and add 1.
- To multiply a number by 9 or 99, multiply by 10 or 100 and subtract the number.
- The order of operations is:
  1 divide
  2 multiply
  3 add
  4 subtract.
- Work out the inside of brackets first.
- One significant figure means one non-zero digit.
- To square a number, multiply the number by itself.
- The cube of a number is given by three of the numbers multiplied together. So $2^3 = 2 \times 2 \times 2 = 8$.
- Finding the square root is the opposite of squaring.

15 Fractions

In this chapter you will learn about ...
1 fraction diagrams
2 equivalent fractions and lowest terms
3 fractions of an amount
4 calculating with fractions

P 1 Fraction Diagrams

Learn About It

1 These pictures all show **one-half** of something.

One-half is written $\frac{1}{2}$.

$$\frac{1}{2}$$
1 ← one thing ...
— ← ... divided ...
2 ← ... into two equal parts

Draw two different pictures of your own that show $\frac{1}{2}$.

2 These pictures all show **one-third** of something.

One-third is written $\frac{1}{3}$.

1 ← one thing ...
— ← ... divided ...
3 ← ... into three equal parts

Draw two different pictures of your own that show $\frac{1}{3}$.

3 These pictures all show **one-quarter** of something.

One-quarter is written $\frac{1}{4}$.

1 ◄──── one thing ...
── ◄──── ... divided ...
4 ◄──── ... into four equal parts

Draw two different pictures of your own that show $\frac{1}{4}$.

4 There are lots of other kinds of fractions. Here are a few of them.

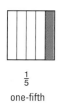 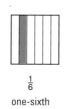 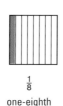  

| $\frac{1}{5}$ | $\frac{1}{6}$ | $\frac{1}{8}$ | $\frac{1}{10}$ | $\frac{1}{12}$ |
| one-fifth | one-sixth | one-eighth | one-tenth | one-twelfth |

5 The number on the bottom of the fraction is called its **denominator**.

Key Fact

The denominator tells you how many equal pieces your shape is divided into.

$$\frac{1}{12} \longleftarrow \text{denominator}$$

Word Check

fraction a part of something

denominator the number on the bottom of a fraction; it tells you how many parts to divide a shape into

one-half one of two equal parts of something

one-third one of three equal parts of something

one-quarter one of four equal parts of something

Try It Out

(A) Each diagram shows a fraction. Write the fraction down in numbers **and** in words.

1   2   3   4   5   6

7   8   9   10   11   12

(B) Draw a fraction diagram for each question.

1 one-quarter	**2** $\frac{1}{6}$	**3** $\frac{1}{8}$	**4** one-fifth
5 one-third	**6** $\frac{1}{2}$	**7** $\frac{1}{10}$	**8** one-twelfth
9 $\frac{1}{3}$	**10** $\frac{1}{7}$	**11** $\frac{1}{4}$	**12** one-sixteenth

Learn More About It

1 This picture shows a circle divided into quarters.

One-quarter ($\frac{1}{4}$) is coloured in.

Two-quarters ($\frac{2}{4}$) are coloured in.

Three-quarters ($\frac{3}{4}$).

Four-quarters ($\frac{4}{4}$). The whole circle is now coloured in.

2 Draw four copies of this rectangle.

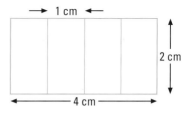

   (a) On the first one, colour in $\frac{1}{4}$.

      Write $\frac{1}{4}$ and *one-quarter* next to it.

   (b) On the next one, colour in $\frac{2}{4}$.

      Write $\frac{2}{4}$ and *two-quarters* next to it.

   (c) On the next one, colour in $\frac{3}{4}$.

      Write $\frac{3}{4}$ and *three-quarters* next to it.

   (d) On the next one, colour in $\frac{4}{4}$.

      Write $\frac{4}{4}$ and *four-quarters or one whole* next to it.

3 Draw six copies of this rectangle.

Colour the rectangles to show $\frac{1}{6}$, $\frac{2}{6}, \frac{3}{6}, \frac{4}{6}, \frac{5}{6}$ and $\frac{6}{6}$. Label them in numbers and in words.

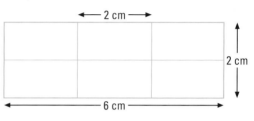

4 The denominator of the fraction tells you how many parts there are altogether. The top number is called the **numerator**.

Key Fact

The numerator tells you how many of the fraction parts you need.

numerator ⟶ **5** ⟵ five parts …
⟵ … out of …
denominator ⟶ **12** ⟵ … twelve parts altogether

5 Alia has stuck the labels on the wrong diagrams. Each diagram should match one of the fractions.

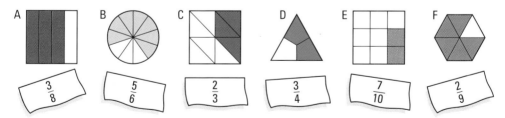

A   B   C   D   E   F

$\frac{3}{8}$ $\frac{5}{6}$ $\frac{2}{3}$ $\frac{3}{4}$ $\frac{7}{10}$ $\frac{2}{9}$

Count the number of parts to find the denominator. Count the number coloured in to find the numerator.

Example If you think fraction C is $\frac{2}{3}$, write $C = \frac{2}{3}$.

Word Check

numerator how many of the parts are needed for the fraction

Try It Out

C Each diagram shows a fraction. Write the fraction down in numbers **and** in words.

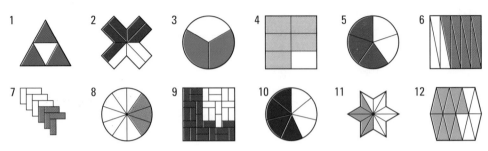

D Draw a fraction diagram for each question.

1 $\frac{3}{4}$ **2** $\frac{5}{8}$ **3** $\frac{2}{5}$ **4** $\frac{3}{10}$ **5** $\frac{5}{6}$ **6** $\frac{2}{3}$ **7** $\frac{7}{8}$ **8** $\frac{5}{12}$ **9** $\frac{7}{10}$ **10** $\frac{3}{16}$ **11** $\frac{3}{5}$ **12** $\frac{2}{7}$

Practice

Centimetre squared paper

E Each rectangle is made up of 1 cm squares. Copy each rectangle twice and colour the fractions shown.

1 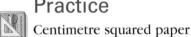 **(a)** $\frac{1}{4}$ **(b)** $\frac{3}{4}$

2 **(a)** $\frac{1}{6}$ **(b)** $\frac{5}{6}$

3 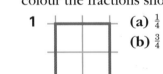 **(a)** $\frac{7}{8}$ **(b)** $\frac{3}{8}$

4 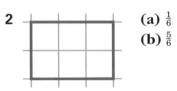 **(a)** $\frac{2}{5}$ **(b)** $\frac{4}{5}$

5 **(a)** $\frac{1}{10}$ **(b)** $\frac{3}{10}$

6  **(a)** $\frac{1}{3}$ **(b)** $\frac{3}{3}$

7  **(a)** $\frac{2}{9}$ **(b)** $\frac{5}{9}$

8  **(a)** $\frac{7}{12}$ **(b)** $\frac{1}{12}$

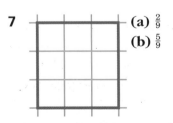

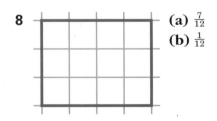

9 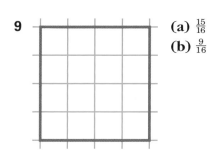 **(a)** $\frac{15}{16}$
(b) $\frac{9}{16}$

10 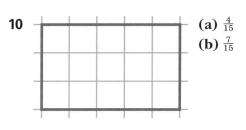 **(a)** $\frac{4}{15}$
(b) $\frac{7}{15}$

Finished Early?
Go to page 360

Further Practice

F Each diagram shows a fraction. Write the fraction down in numbers **and** in words.

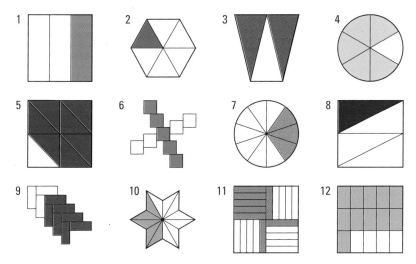

G This diagram shows that $\frac{3}{4}$ of the counters are coloured.
Draw a diagram like this for each question.
Use any colour you like.

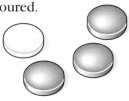

1 $\frac{1}{4}$ **2** $\frac{3}{8}$ **3** $\frac{2}{5}$ **4** $\frac{7}{10}$ **5** $\frac{5}{12}$ **6** $\frac{2}{6}$ **7** $\frac{3}{16}$ **8** $\frac{2}{3}$ **9** $\frac{1}{2}$ **10** $\frac{19}{20}$ **11** $\frac{4}{9}$ **12** $\frac{3}{7}$

Finished Early?
Go to page 360

T 2 Equivalence: Lowest Terms

Learn About It

Fractions that look different but mean the same thing are called **equivalent**.

These fractions are equivalent to $\frac{1}{2}$.

$\frac{1}{2} = \frac{2}{4} = \frac{3}{6} = \frac{4}{8} = \frac{5}{10} = \frac{6}{12} = \dots$

This goes on forever!

You can make equivalent fractions easily. Multiply the numerator and denominator by the same number.

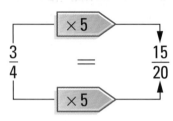

You can also divide.

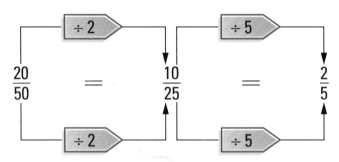

After $\frac{2}{5}$, you can't go any further. This fraction is in **lowest terms**. There are no equivalent fractions with smaller numbers.

Making the numbers in a fraction smaller is called **cancelling**.

Word Check

equivalent fractions fractions that contain different numbers but mean the same thing

cancel find an equivalent fraction with smaller numbers, by dividing top and bottom

lowest terms the equivalent fraction with the smallest possible numbers; completely cancelled.

Try It Out

H In each cloud …

(a) Find any fractions that are in lowest terms. Write each on a separate line.

(b) Find other fractions that are equivalent to these. Write them on the same lines as their lowest terms fractions.

(c) There should be one fraction left over – an 'odd one out'. Write it on a separate line. Cancel it to lowest terms.

Example

$\frac{2}{4}$ $\frac{1}{3}$ $\frac{3}{6}$ $\frac{5}{15}$ $\frac{1}{2}$ $\frac{2}{6}$ $\frac{3}{9}$ $\frac{4}{14}$ $\frac{7}{14}$

Working (a) $\frac{1}{2}$

$\frac{1}{3}$ (Find lowest terms.)

Answer (b) $\frac{1}{2} = \frac{2}{4} = \frac{3}{6} = \frac{7}{14}$.

$\frac{1}{3} = \frac{2}{6} = \frac{3}{9} = \frac{5}{15}$ (Find equivalent fractions.)

(c) $\frac{4}{14} = \frac{2}{7}$ (odd one out)

1

$\frac{1}{4}$ $\frac{4}{20}$ $\frac{1}{5}$ $\frac{2}{10}$ $\frac{3}{12}$ $\frac{10}{40}$ $\frac{4}{6}$ $\frac{3}{15}$ $\frac{2}{8}$

2

$\frac{8}{20}$ $\frac{2}{5}$ $\frac{8}{12}$ $\frac{2}{3}$ $\frac{6}{15}$ $\frac{4}{8}$ $\frac{12}{18}$ $\frac{4}{10}$ $\frac{4}{6}$

3

$\frac{6}{30}$ $\frac{10}{20}$ $\frac{5}{10}$ $\frac{1}{5}$ $\frac{1}{2}$ $\frac{15}{30}$ $\frac{2}{10}$ $\frac{5}{25}$ $\frac{3}{9}$

4

$\frac{8}{14}$ $\frac{5}{8}$ $\frac{12}{21}$ $\frac{15}{24}$ $\frac{25}{40}$ $\frac{10}{16}$ $\frac{4}{7}$ $\frac{16}{28}$ $\frac{15}{21}$

5

$\frac{4}{10}$ $\frac{3}{10}$ $\frac{15}{60}$ $\frac{1}{4}$ $\frac{15}{50}$ $\frac{24}{80}$ $\frac{7}{28}$ $\frac{6}{24}$ $\frac{9}{30}$

6

$\frac{18}{21}$ $\frac{2}{18}$ $\frac{54}{63}$ $\frac{35}{45}$ $\frac{1}{9}$ $\frac{7}{63}$ $\frac{6}{7}$ $\frac{12}{14}$ $\frac{3}{27}$

Practice

I Copy and complete these equivalent fraction chains.

1 $\frac{1}{2} = \frac{3}{*} = \frac{5}{*} = \frac{*}{12} = \frac{*}{16} = \frac{10}{*}$

2 $\frac{1}{3} = \frac{*}{6} = \frac{*}{12} = \frac{5}{*} = \frac{8}{*} = \frac{*}{30}$

3 $\frac{2}{3} = \frac{4}{*} = \frac{6}{21} = \frac{*}{30} = \frac{*}{*} = \frac{24}{*}$

4 $\frac{7}{10} = \frac{*}{20} = \frac{*}{50} = \frac{49}{*} = \frac{63}{*} = \frac{*}{100}$

5 $\frac{*}{5} = \frac{*}{10} = \frac{6}{*} = \frac{*}{20} = \frac{*}{40}$

6 $\frac{1}{*} = \frac{*}{12} = \frac{3}{*} = \frac{5}{30} = \frac{10}{*}$

7 $\frac{1}{20} = \frac{5}{*} = \frac{10}{*} = \frac{12}{*} = \frac{*}{300}$

8 $\frac{*}{*} = \frac{*}{16} = \frac{9}{24} = \frac{15}{*} = \frac{*}{72}$

J Cancel these fractions to their lowest terms.

1 $\frac{3}{9}$ **2** $\frac{6}{12}$ **3** $\frac{2}{8}$ **4** $\frac{15}{20}$ **5** $\frac{12}{18}$ **6** $\frac{12}{20}$

7 $\frac{2}{18}$ **8** $\frac{21}{24}$ **9** $\frac{12}{14}$ **10** $\frac{6}{30}$ **11** $\frac{90}{100}$ **12** $\frac{4}{64}$

Further Practice

K For each question, write down (a) the fraction shown in the diagram, (b) the fraction in lowest terms. Copy the diagram if it helps.

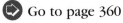

Finished Early?
➡ Go to page 360

Example

Answer   (a) $\frac{4}{8}$ (b) $\frac{1}{2}$

---

1   2   3   4   5   6

7   8   9   10   11   12

L In each question, two of the fractions are equivalent and one is different. Write down the two equivalent fractions together. Write the odd one out separately.

Example   (a) $\frac{2}{5}$ (b) $\frac{1}{3}$ (c) $\frac{2}{6}$

Working $\frac{1}{3}$ and $\frac{2}{6}$ are equivalent.

Answer $\frac{1}{3} = \frac{2}{6}$. $\frac{2}{5}$ is the odd one out.

---

1 (a) $\frac{2}{4}$ (b) $\frac{1}{4}$ (c) $\frac{4}{8}$ **2** (a) $\frac{6}{16}$ (b) $\frac{2}{5}$ (c) $\frac{3}{8}$

3 (a) $\frac{4}{8}$ (b) $\frac{10}{14}$ (c) $\frac{20}{28}$ **4** (a) $\frac{2}{3}$ (b) $\frac{14}{21}$ (c) $\frac{12}{16}$

5 (a) $\frac{10}{12}$ (b) $\frac{8}{10}$ (c) $\frac{15}{18}$ **6** (a) $\frac{2}{3}$ (b) $\frac{6}{9}$ (c) $\frac{5}{15}$

7 (a) $\frac{9}{12}$ (b) $\frac{15}{24}$ (c) $\frac{30}{48}$ **8** (a) $\frac{56}{63}$ (b) $\frac{64}{72}$ (c) $\frac{56}{64}$

9 (a) $\frac{12}{18}$ (b) $\frac{8}{16}$ (c) $\frac{11}{22}$ **10** (a) $\frac{18}{21}$ (b) $\frac{10}{12}$ (c) $\frac{12}{14}$

❸ Fractions of an Amount

Finished Early?
➲ Go to page 360

Learn About It

Here are 60 pound coins.

What is $\frac{1}{2}$ of £60?

$\frac{1}{2}$ of £60 is £30. This is because
$60 \div 2 = 30$.

$\frac{1}{3}$ of £60 = £60 ÷ 3 = £20.

$\frac{1}{4}$ of £60 = £60 ÷ 4 = £15.

Key Fact
To find $\frac{1}{*}$ of something, divide
by *.

Try It Out

Ⓜ Adnan makes special drinks by mixing things.

Here are some of his recipes.

Drink	Ingredients
Tropical Cooler	$\frac{1}{2}$ orange juice, $\frac{1}{4}$ pineapple juice, $\frac{1}{4}$ mango juice
Long Fizz	$\frac{1}{2}$ lemonade, $\frac{1}{3}$ orange juice, $\frac{1}{6}$ lime cordial
Ruff Stuff	$\frac{1}{2}$ cola, $\frac{1}{5}$ cherryade, $\frac{1}{10}$ lemon juice, $\frac{1}{10}$ raspberry syrup
Adnan's Dare	$\frac{1}{3}$ soda water, $\frac{1}{4}$ cream soda, $\frac{1}{6}$ ginger beer, $\frac{1}{8}$ cold tea, $\frac{1}{8}$ tomato juice

Work out how much of each ingredient Adnan needs for these.

1 20 cl of Tropical Cooler   **2** 30 cl of Long Fizz

3 48 cl of Adnan's Dare   **4** 20 cl of Ruff Stuff

5 72 cl of Long Fizz   **6** 50 cl of Ruff Stuff

7 80 cl of Tropical Cooler   **8** 96 cl of Adnan's Dare

Learn More About It

What is $\frac{2}{5}$ of £60?

$\frac{1}{5}$ of £60 = £60 ÷ 5 = £12.

Two-fifths is two times this.

So $\frac{2}{5}$ of £60 = 2 × £12 = £24.

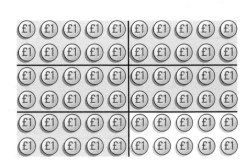

What is $\frac{5}{6}$ of £60?

$\frac{1}{6}$ of £60 = £60 ÷ 6 = £10.

Five-sixths is five times this.

So $\frac{5}{6}$ of £60 = 5 × £10 = £50.

Key Fact

To find any fraction of something:

1 Divide by the denominator to find $\frac{1}{*}$.

2 Multiply this answer by the numerator.

Try It Out

(N) Helena mixes up things to fill pies.

Here are some of her recipes.

Pie	Filling
Chickpot	$\frac{1}{2}$ potato, $\frac{2}{5}$ chicken, $\frac{1}{10}$ gravy
Fishnut	$\frac{1}{3}$ haddock, $\frac{5}{12}$ hazelnuts, $\frac{1}{4}$ tomato
All Day Breakfast	$\frac{3}{8}$ egg, $\frac{1}{4}$ bacon, $\frac{1}{4}$ baked beans, $\frac{1}{8}$ brown sauce
Betcha Can't	$\frac{2}{5}$ kippers, $\frac{3}{8}$ milk chocolate, $\frac{3}{20}$ plain crisps, $\frac{3}{40}$ chutney

Work out how much of each ingredient Helena needs for these.

1 A 250 g Chickpot

2 A 360 g Fishnut

3 A 320 g All Day Breakfast

4 A 440 g Chickpot

5 A 400 g Betcha Can't

6 A 960 g All Day Breakfast

7 A 540 g Fishnut

8 A 960 g Betcha Can't

Practice

(◉) Work these out. Two answers are the same. The other is the odd one out.

> **Example**   **(a)** $\frac{1}{3}$ of 24   **(b)** $\frac{1}{4}$ of 36   **(c)** $\frac{1}{2}$ of 16
> **Working**   **(a)** $\frac{1}{3}$ of 24 = 24 ÷ 3 = 8.
>   **(b)** $\frac{1}{4}$ of 36 = 36 ÷ 4 = 9.
>   **(c)** $\frac{1}{2}$ of 16 = 16 ÷ 2 = 8.
> **Answer**   **(a)** 8   **(b)** 9   **(c)** 8
>   **(b)** is the odd one out.

1 (a) $\frac{1}{2}$ of 12 pence   **(b)** $\frac{1}{5}$ of 30 pence   **(c)** $\frac{1}{4}$ of 32 pence

2 (a) $\frac{1}{4}$ of 20 cm   **(b)** $\frac{1}{2}$ of 40 cm   **(c)** $\frac{1}{5}$ of 25 cm

3 (a) $\frac{3}{4}$ of £24   **(b)** $\frac{1}{8}$ of £48   **(c)** $\frac{1}{2}$ of £36

4 (a) $\frac{2}{3}$ of 21 kg   **(b)** $\frac{1}{4}$ of 60 kg   **(c)** $\frac{1}{3}$ of 45 kg

5 (a) $\frac{4}{8}$ of 48 cars   **(b)** $\frac{3}{4}$ of 40 cars   **(c)** $\frac{3}{8}$ of 64 cars

6 (a) $\frac{3}{10}$ of 30 books   **(b)** $\frac{2}{5}$ of 25 books   **(c)** $\frac{1}{2}$ of 20 books

7 (a) $\frac{4}{9}$ of 27 hours   **(b)** $\frac{2}{5}$ of 25 hours   **(c)** $\frac{1}{3}$ of 36 hours

8 (a) $\frac{9}{20}$ of 80 km   **(b)** $\frac{1}{4}$ of 140 km   **(c)** $\frac{7}{10}$ of 50 km

P You can make these easier to do. Cancel the fractions to lowest terms first.

Example $\frac{12}{16}$ of £20

Working and answer (hard way) £20 ÷ 16 × 12 = £1.25 × 12 = £15.

Working and answer (easy way) $\frac{12}{16}$ in lowest terms is $\frac{3}{4}$.

$$£20 ÷ 4 × 3 = £5 × 3 = £15.$$

---

1 $\frac{5}{10}$ of 18 pence   **2** $\frac{3}{9}$ of 12 km   **3** $\frac{10}{16}$ of 24 hours

4 $\frac{7}{14}$ of £46   **5** $\frac{9}{12}$ of 20 CDs   **6** $\frac{10}{15}$ of 27 people

7 $\frac{8}{10}$ of 35 pages   **8** $\frac{12}{20}$ of 90 minutes   **9** $\frac{28}{35}$ of 30 days

10 $\frac{3}{30}$ of 140 g   **11** $\frac{8}{12}$ of 6 cm   **12** $\frac{10}{25}$ of 55 weeks

Further Practice

> **Finished Early?**
> ➡ Go to page 361

Q **1** Find these fractions.

    (a) $\frac{1}{2}$ of £30   **(b)** $\frac{1}{3}$ of £30   **(c)** $\frac{1}{5}$ of £30

    (d) $\frac{1}{2}$ of 24 hours   **(e)** $\frac{1}{4}$ of 24 hours   **(f)** $\frac{1}{4}$ of 48 km

    (g) $\frac{1}{3}$ of 48 km   **(h)** $\frac{1}{6}$ of 48 km   **(i)** $\frac{1}{8}$ of 40 pence

    (j) $\frac{1}{10}$ of 40 pence

2 These need to be cancelled first.

    (a) £36 $\boxed{\frac{2}{4} \text{ of}}$ **(b)** £36 $\boxed{\frac{2}{6} \text{ of}}$ **(c)** 20 cm $\boxed{\frac{3}{15} \text{ of}}$

    (d) 20 cm $\boxed{\frac{2}{8} \text{ of}}$ **(e)** 42 litres $\boxed{\frac{4}{24} \text{ of}}$

> **Finished Early?**
> ➡ Go to page 361

T ④ # Adding and Subtracting with Fractions

Learn About It

Fractions can be added together. To do this, they must have the same denominator.
$\frac{1}{8} + \frac{5}{8} = \frac{6}{8}$. This cancels down to $\frac{3}{4}$.

The strips show this is right.

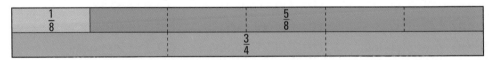

Key Fact

You can only add or subtract fractions if they have the same denominator (bottom number).

If they do, add or subtract the numerators (top numbers) only.

Sometimes, the answer can be bigger than a whole.

$\frac{5}{6} + \frac{5}{6} = \frac{10}{6}$.

This is called a top-heavy or **improper** fraction.

$\frac{10}{6}$ is $\frac{6}{6} + \frac{4}{6}$. $\frac{6}{6}$ is a whole one. $\frac{4}{6}$ cancels down to $\frac{2}{3}$.

The answer is $1\frac{2}{3}$. Anything with a whole number and a fraction part is called a **mixed fraction**.

The strips show this is right.

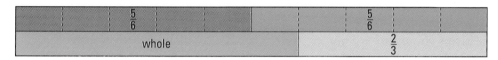

Subtraction works the same way.

$\frac{9}{10} - \frac{3}{10} = \frac{6}{10} = \frac{3}{5}$

Turn a mixed fraction into an improper fraction first.

$2\frac{1}{8} - \frac{7}{8}$.

A whole is $\frac{8}{8}$. Two wholes are $\frac{16}{8}$.

So $2\frac{1}{8}$ is $\frac{17}{8}$ altogether.

So work out $\frac{17}{8} - \frac{7}{8} = \frac{10}{8} = 1\frac{2}{8} = 1\frac{1}{4}$.

Word Check

improper fraction a fraction which has a numerator bigger than the denominator

mixed fraction anything with a whole number part and a fraction part

Try It Out

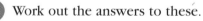 Work out the answers to these.

1 $\frac{1}{5} + \frac{3}{5}$ **2** $\frac{1}{8} + \frac{3}{8}$ **3** $\frac{2}{7} + \frac{2}{7}$ **4** $\frac{3}{5} + \frac{4}{5}$ **5** $\frac{7}{11} + \frac{7}{11}$ **6** $\frac{5}{8} + \frac{7}{8}$

7 $\frac{5}{6} - \frac{1}{6}$ **8** $\frac{8}{9} - \frac{2}{9}$ **9** $\frac{11}{16} - \frac{9}{16}$ **10** $1\frac{3}{7} - \frac{6}{7}$ **11** $1\frac{1}{6} - \frac{5}{6}$ **12** $1\frac{1}{4} - \frac{3}{4}$

Learn More About It

Sometimes the fractions have different denominators.

You have to make them all into the same type first. Then you can add or subtract.

To do $\frac{1}{2} + \frac{1}{10}$, find the fraction $\overset{*}{10}$ equivalent to $\frac{1}{2}$. It is $\frac{5}{10}$.

So $\frac{1}{2} + \frac{1}{10} = \frac{5}{10} + \frac{1}{10}$ (*Change to equivalent fractions*)

$\qquad = \frac{6}{10}$ (*Add them*)

$\qquad = \frac{3}{5}$.   (*Cancel to lowest terms*)

The strips show this is right.

Subtracting works the same way.

$1\frac{1}{3} - \frac{5}{6} = \frac{4}{3} - \frac{5}{6}$ (*Change mixed fraction to improper*)

$\qquad = \frac{8}{6} - \frac{5}{6}$ (*Change to equivalent fractions*)

$\qquad = \frac{3}{6}$ \quad (*Subtract them*)

$\qquad = \frac{1}{2}.$ \quad (*Cancel to lowest terms*)

Sometimes you have to change **both** fractions.

$\frac{1}{2} + \frac{1}{3}$ can be done if you change to sixths.

$\frac{1}{2} + \frac{1}{3} = \frac{3}{6} + \frac{2}{6}$ (*Change to equivalent fractions.*)

$\qquad = \frac{5}{6}.$ \quad (*Add them.*)

The strips show this is right.

$\frac{1}{2}$		$\frac{1}{3}$
	$\frac{5}{6}$	

Key Fact

When you add or subtract fractions with different denominators, change them all to the same type first.

Try It Out

(S) Change the fractions to the type in brackets, then answer the questions.

> **Example** $\frac{1}{4} + \frac{1}{8} \left(\frac{*}{8}\right)$
>
> **Working** $\frac{1}{4} + \frac{1}{8} = \frac{2}{8} + \frac{1}{8}$ (*Change to eighths*)
>
> **Answer** $= \frac{3}{8}$

1 $\frac{1}{3} + \frac{1}{6} \left(\frac{*}{6}\right)$ **2** $\frac{1}{2} + \frac{1}{8} \left(\frac{*}{8}\right)$ **3** $\frac{2}{5} + \frac{7}{10} \left(\frac{*}{10}\right)$ **4** $\frac{7}{8} - \frac{3}{4} \left(\frac{*}{8}\right)$

5 $\frac{5}{6} - \frac{7}{12} \left(\frac{*}{12}\right)$ **6** $1\frac{1}{2} - \frac{5}{14} \left(\frac{*}{14}\right)$ **7** $\frac{1}{5} + \frac{1}{2} \left(\frac{*}{10}\right)$ **8** $\frac{3}{4} + \frac{1}{6} \left(\frac{*}{12}\right)$

9 $\frac{2}{3} + \frac{2}{5} \left(\frac{*}{15}\right)$ **10** $\frac{9}{10} - \frac{3}{4} \left(\frac{*}{20}\right)$ **11** $\frac{3}{10} - \frac{1}{12} \left(\frac{*}{60}\right)$ **12** $1\frac{5}{8} - \frac{5}{6} \left(\frac{*}{24}\right)$

T Practice

Work these out. Write *same* if the two answers are the same. Write different if they are not. There are some hints for which type of fraction to change to.

Example	(a) $\frac{1}{3} + \frac{1}{6}$ (b) $\frac{3}{4} - \frac{1}{4}$
Working	(a) $\frac{1}{3} + \frac{1}{6} = \frac{2}{6} + \frac{1}{6} = \frac{3}{6} = \frac{1}{2}$
	(b) $\frac{3}{4} - \frac{1}{4} = \frac{2}{4} = \frac{1}{2}$
Answer	(a) $\frac{1}{2}$ (b) $\frac{1}{2}$ same

1 (a) $\frac{1}{4} + \frac{1}{4}$ (b) $\frac{2}{3} - \frac{1}{6}$ **2** (a) $\frac{1}{6} + \frac{2}{3}$ (b) $1\frac{1}{4} - \frac{5}{12}$

3 (a) $\frac{5}{8} + \frac{1}{2}$ (b) $\frac{4}{5} + \frac{3}{10}$ **4** (a) $\frac{1}{12} + \frac{1}{4}$ (b) $\frac{2}{5} - \frac{1}{15}$

5 (a) $\frac{3}{10} + \frac{2}{5}$ (b) $\frac{5}{6} - \frac{1}{8} \left(\frac{*}{24}\right)$ **6** (a) $2\frac{1}{7} - \frac{9}{14}$ (b) $\frac{11}{16} + \frac{13}{16}$

7 (a) $1\frac{1}{2} - \frac{1}{10}$ (b) $\frac{2}{3} + \frac{7}{9}$ **8** (a) $\frac{3}{20} + \frac{9}{10}$ (b) $\frac{7}{12} + \frac{1}{2}$

9 (a) $\frac{29}{40} - \frac{5}{8}$ (b) $\frac{5}{6} - \frac{3}{4} \left(\frac{*}{12}\right)$ **10** (a) $1\frac{1}{2} + \frac{13}{7} \left(\frac{*}{14}\right)$ (b) $2 - \frac{1}{14}$

> **Finished Early?**
> Go to page 361

Further Practice

U Work out the answers to these.

1 $\frac{1}{5} + \frac{3}{5}$ **2** $\frac{1}{10} + \frac{3}{10}$ **3** $\frac{2}{9} + \frac{2}{9}$ **4** $\frac{2}{3} + \frac{2}{3}$ **5** $\frac{11}{12} + \frac{11}{12}$ **6** $\frac{6}{9} + \frac{7}{9}$

7 $\frac{5}{8} - \frac{1}{8}$ **8** $\frac{8}{11} - \frac{2}{11}$ **9** $\frac{11}{12} - \frac{7}{12}$ **10** $1\frac{3}{8} - \frac{5}{8}$ **11** $2\frac{1}{3} - \frac{2}{3}$ **12** $1\frac{2}{7} - \frac{5}{7}$

V Work these out. Change the fractions to the type in brackets.

Example	$\frac{1}{3} + \frac{1}{12} \left(\frac{*}{12}\right)$
Working	$\frac{1}{3} + \frac{1}{12} = \frac{4}{12} + \frac{1}{12}$ (Change to twelfths.)
Answer	$\frac{5}{12}$

1 $\frac{1}{4} + \frac{1}{8} \left(\frac{*}{8}\right)$ **2** $\frac{1}{2} + \frac{3}{8} \left(\frac{*}{8}\right)$ **3** $\frac{3}{5} + \frac{3}{10} \left(\frac{*}{10}\right)$ **4** $\frac{7}{12} - \frac{1}{4} \left(\frac{*}{12}\right)$

5 $\frac{1}{6} - \frac{1}{24} \left(\frac{*}{24}\right)$ **6** $1\frac{1}{3} - \frac{5}{18} \left(\frac{*}{18}\right)$ **7** $\frac{1}{4} + \frac{1}{6} \left(\frac{*}{12}\right)$ **8** $\frac{3}{5} + \frac{1}{6} \left(\frac{*}{30}\right)$

9 $\frac{2}{9} + \frac{5}{6} \left(\frac{*}{18}\right)$ **10** $\frac{11}{12} - \frac{5}{8} \left(\frac{*}{60}\right)$ **11** $\frac{3}{8} - \frac{1}{12} \left(\frac{*}{24}\right)$ **12** $1\frac{3}{4} - \frac{9}{14} \left(\frac{*}{28}\right)$

> **Finished Early?**
> Go to page 361

16 Decimals

In this chapter you will learn about ...
1. numbers with one decimal place
2. numbers with two decimal places
3. adding and subtracting decimals
4. multiplying and dividing decimals
5. decimals and place value

P1 One Decimal Place

2 mm graph paper

Learn About It

1   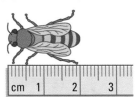   The bee is 2 cm or 20 mm long.

2 The caterpillar is longer than 3 cm and shorter than 4 cm.

It is 3 cm and 7 mm long.
It is 37 mm long.
It is 3.7 cm long.

3 The dot is called a **decimal point**. It comes after the number of whole centimetres (3). Then come the **tenths** of centimetres (7).

Three point seven centimetres means 3 cm and 7 tenths of a centimetre.
$3.7 = 3\frac{7}{10}$.
A **decimal** is any number written with a decimal point.
3.7 has **one decimal place**.

4 Look at the bee again. It is 2 cm and 0 tenths of a centimetre. So you can say it is 2.0 cm long.

2.0 means the same as 2.

5 Look at this number line. The arrows point to numbers. Write them down.

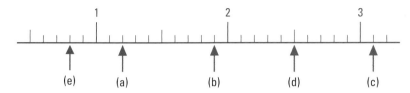

6 Draw a number line like the one in step 5.

Mark arrows for these numbers.

(a) 1.4 **(b)** 2.2 **(c)** 3.0 **(d)** 1.7 **(e)** 0.6

7 Here is another way to show decimals.
Use a large square to
stand for a unit.

Then a strip like
this can stand
for a tenth.

You could draw the number **3.7** like this.

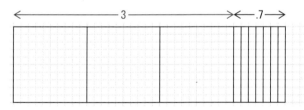

8 Draw squares and strips for the numbers in step 6.

Word Check

decimal point a dot
between the units and
tenths

decimal any number that
uses a decimal point

one decimal place a
number with tenths
written after the decimal
point

1 d.p. one decimal place

Try It Out

A Measure the minibeasts.

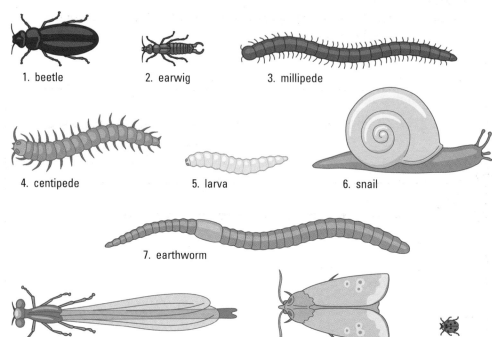

1. beetle   2. earwig   3. millipede

4. centipede   5. larva   6. snail

7. earthworm

8. dragonfly   9. moth   10. ladybird

Practice

B **1** Change these measurements in mm to cm.

Example	37 mm
Answer	3.7 cm

   (a) 26 mm **(b)** 71 mm   **(c)** 49 mm   **(d)** 64 mm   **(e)** 9 mm
   (f) 28 mm **(g)** 105 mm **(h)** 216 mm **(i)** 711 mm **(j)** 1056 mm

C In each question, draw a number line like this.

Copy this example.

Example 4 and 5.
Working Find the two large marks on the number line. Label them with the given numbers.

Write the one decimal place (1 d.p.) numbers in between.

Write the 1 d.p. numbers at the right-hand end.

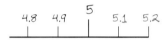

Write the 1 d.p. numbers at the left-hand end.

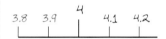

Answer

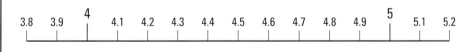

1 1 and 2   **2** 7 and 8   **3** 0 and 1   **4** 9 and 10   **5** 20 and 21
6 –3 and –2   **7** –1 and 0

D For each question on page 164:

(a) to **(e)** write down the numbers with arrows.
(f) write down the gap between marks.

Example Look at question 1.
Answers **(a)** 5.1   **(b)** … (*Write your answers for parts (b) to (e).*)
(f) The gap between each mark is 0.1.

1

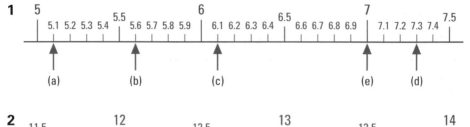

2

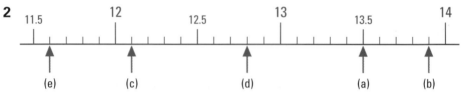

3 **4** **5**

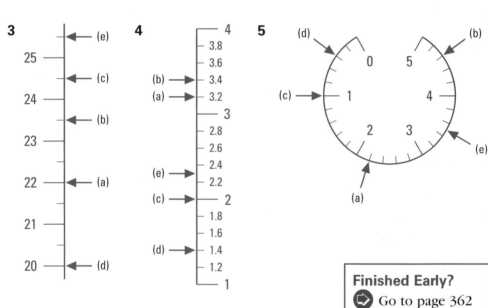

Finished Early?
➡ Go to page 362

Further Practice

E Change these measurements in mm to cm.

Example	37 mm
Answer	37 mm = 3.7 cm

1 21 mm	**2** 33 mm	**3** 14 mm	**4** 62 mm	**5** 40 mm
6 6 mm	**7** 8 mm	**8** 36 mm	**9** 93 mm	**10** 70 mm
11 100 mm	**12** 105 mm	**13** 111 mm	**14** 120 mm	**15** 255 mm
16 681 mm	**17** 404 mm	**18** 1338 mm	**19** 1004 mm	**20** 1 mm

2 mm graph paper

F Draw squares and strips to show these decimals.

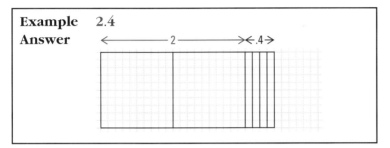

Example 2.4

1 1.6   **2** 6.1   **3** 2.8   **4** 4.4   **5** 3.0   **6** 0.3   **7** 0.7   **8** 2.5

> **Finished Early?**
> Go to page 362

Go to page 362

❷ Two Decimal Places

2 mm graph paper

Learn About It

1 In between the 1 d.p. numbers are more numbers.
These numbers need a second decimal place.

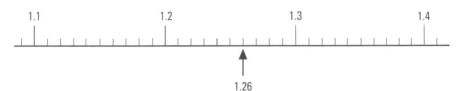

Draw a copy of this number line.

2 The second decimal place is for **hundredths**. Look at the decimal **1.26**.
You say this '**one** point **two six**' – not 'one point twenty-six'.
It means **one** whole, **two** tenths and **six** hundredths.
1.26 = $1 + \frac{2}{10} + \frac{6}{100}$.

3 Look at 1.3 on the number line. It has **no** hundredths. You can write it as
1.30.
1.30 means the same as 1.3.
2.00 means the same as 2.0 and 2.

NUMBER SKILLS Use tenths and hundredths, order whole numbers

4 Look at this number line. The arrows point to numbers. Write them down.

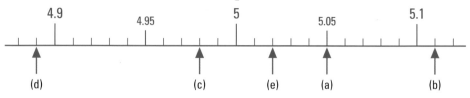

5 Draw a number line like the one in step 4.

Mark arrows for these numbers.

(a) 4.95   (b) 5.01   (c) 5.08   (d) 5.12   (e) 4.88

Try It Out

Ⓖ For each question …

(a) to (e) write down the numbers with arrows

(f) write down the gap between marks.

Example	Look at question 1.
Answers	(a) 1.09 (b) … (*Write your answers for parts (b) to (e).*)
	(f) The gap between each mark is 0.01.

1
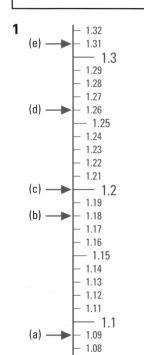

2
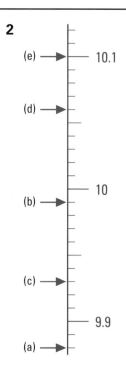

3

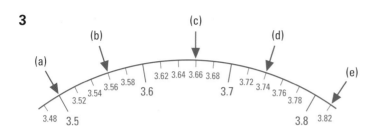

4

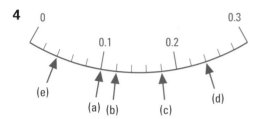

5

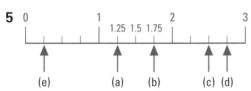

Learn More About It

1 It is important to know when one decimal is bigger than another.

You look at each digit in turn.
Which is bigger, 1.4 or 1.38?
Write them one above the other.

> 1 . 4
> 1 . 3 8

Look at the units.

> 1 . 4
> 1 . 3 8

They are the same. That doesn't help.
Look at the first decimal place.
1.4 has more tenths than 1.38.
So 1.4 is bigger.

> 1 . 4
> 1 . 3 8

Word Check

second decimal place the place for hundredths in a decimal

two decimal places a number with tenths and hundredths written after the decimal point

2 d.p. two decimal places

Try It Out

H **1** Do the same thing with these.

    1 2.3 and 2.7   **2** 5.61 and 4.62

    3 3.14 and 3.3   **4** 1.28 and 1.25

    5 10.1 and 10.01

Practice

I Write down all the two decimal place (2 d.p.) numbers from …

> **Example**   1.6 to 1.7
>
> **Answer**   1.61, 1.62, 1.63, 1.64, 1.65, 1.66, 1.67, 1.68, 1.69

  1 1.3 to 1.4   **2** 2.5 to 2.6   **3** 0.9 to 1   **4** 3 to 3.1   **5** 0 to 0.1

J For each question …

    (a) write down the biggest number

    (b) write down the smallest number

    (c) put the **rest** of the numbers into order, smallest first.

1
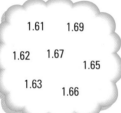

2

3

4

> **Finished Early?**
> Go to page 362

Further Practice

K Copy the number lines. Label all the marks on each line.

1

2

3

4

5

6

L For each question …

(a) write down the biggest number

(b) write down the smallest number

(c) put the **rest** of the numbers into order, smallest first.

1

2

3

4

Finished Early?
Go to page 362

T③ Adding and Subtracting Decimals

Learn About It

Adding and subtracting decimals is just like working with whole numbers.

Compare these.

```
  1 2 5        1 2.5        1.2 5
+ 2 5 8      + 2 5.8      + 2.5 8
-------      -------      -------
  3 8 3        3 8.3        3.8 3
    1            1            1
```

To subtract, e.g. 2.5 – 1.66, set it out like this.

```
  2.5 0
+ 1.6 6
-------
```

Try It Out

Ⓜ Gerald has three pieces of fencing.

 A

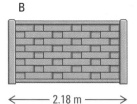 B

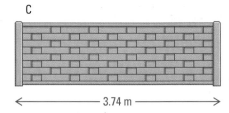 C

←— 1.3 m —→   ←——— 2.18 m ———→   ←——————— 3.74 m ———————→

1 Work out the different lengths of fence Gerald can make.

(a) A + B   (b) A + C   (c) B + C   (d) A + B + C

2 Work out the difference between these pieces of fencing.

(a) B – A   (b) C – A   (c) C – B

Practice

Ⓝ What change would you get from £5?

1 £4.92   2 £4.18   3 £2.55   4 £1.99

5 £1.67   6 £3.02   7 £0.75

> **Word Check**
> ....
> **sum** answer you get when numbers are added
> **difference** answer you get when one number is subtracted from another

◉ Find the sum and difference of these decimals.

Example   1.54 and 3.7
Working

```
  1.5 4            3.⁶7.¹0
+ 3.7 0          - 1.5 4
-------          -------
  5.2 4            2.1 6
    ̄1
```

Answer   Sum = 5.24, difference = 2.16.

1 1.3 and 4.6   **2** 6.5 and 2.9
3 3.11 and 4.25   **4** 7.06 and 2.58
5 10.5 and 6.86   **6** 21.61 and 13.8

Finished Early?
 Go to page 363

Ⓟ Work these out. Write *same* if the two answers are the same. Write *different* if they are not.

Example   (a) 2.8 + 3.7   (b) 8.32 − 1.62
Working

```
    2.8              ⁷8.¹3 2
  + 3.7            - 1.6 2
  -----            -------
    6.5              6.7 0
     ̄1
```

Answer   (a) **6.5**   (b) **6.7** *different*

1 (a) 2.6 + 3.1   (b) 4.3 + 1.4
2 (a) 5.24 + 4.63   (b) 3.32 + 6.55
3 (a) 4.1 − 2.8   (b) 6.34 − 5.04
4 (a) 6 + 1.05   (b) 10.05 − 3.5
5 (a) 8 − 2.22   (b) 7.7 − 1.92
6 (a) 2 + 2   (b) 2.44 + 1.56
7 (a) 14.33 − 1.42   (b) 6.48 + 6.45
8 (a) 10.01 − 5.05   (b) 2.48 + 2.48

Finished Early?
 Go to page 363

T 4 Multiplying and Dividing Decimals

Learn About It

You can multiply a decimal by a whole number. Use the same methods as for whole numbers.

Example 4.3×2

$$\begin{array}{r} 4.3 \\ \times 2 \\ \hline 8.6 \\ \hline \end{array}$$

Example 2.94×8

$$\begin{array}{r} 2.94 \\ \times 8 \\ \hline 23.52 \\ \hline \end{array}$$

Example 6.3×32

$$\begin{array}{r} 6.3 \\ \times 32 \\ \hline 12.6 \\ 189.0 \\ \hline 201.6 \\ \hline 11 \end{array}$$

Try It Out

Q Joshua is ordering stock for his bookshop. Copy and fill in his order form.

Question number	Book	Price	Quantity	Total
1	Puzzle World	£3.50	× 3	
2	Record Breakers	£12.25	× 4	
3	Animal Stories	£4.99	× 7	
4	Space Rangers	£6.99	× 5	
5	Crafts and Hobbies	£13.65	× 2	
6	Hot Website Guide	£8.95	× 12	
7	The Human Body	£10.24	× 16	
8	Cartoon Collection	£5.88	× 24	
			TOTAL	

Learn More About It

Dividing decimals is similar to dividing whole numbers.

> *Hint: remember you need to write out the 28× table.*

Example 21.5 ÷ 5

$$5\overline{)2\ 1.^{1}5} \quad = 4.3$$

Example 74.48 ÷ 28

$$28\overline{)7\ 4.4\ 8} \quad = 2.6\ 6$$
$$\frac{5\ 6}{1\ 8\ 4}$$
$$\frac{1\ 6\ 8}{1\ 6\ 8}$$
$$\frac{1\ 6\ 8}{0}$$

This one was done by long division. You can do it by short division if you like.

Example 2.9 ÷ 2

$$2\overline{)2.9^{1}0} \quad = 1.4\ 5$$

you need to add a 0 here so the remainder can be put with it

Key Fact

Sometimes you need to add extra decimal places to the number being divided.

Try It Out

R Share these amounts of money out equally.

1 £3.62 between 2 people
2 £15.24 between 3 people
3 £2.65 between 5 people
4 £34.72 between 8 people
·5 £125.58 between 6 people
6 £22.23 between 9 people
7 £35.28 between 12 people
8 £171.75 between 15 people
9 £1664.40 between 24 people
10 £6.75 between 45 people

Practice

S Copy and complete this multiplication square. One has been done for you.

	3.7	12.4	7.75	20.68
× 2		24.8		
× 6				
× 13				
× 25·				

T Divide these amounts.

1 12.96 m (a) into 3 equal parts (b) into 2 equal parts
2 £12.80 (a) into 4 equal parts (b) into 5 equal parts
3 7.32 tonnes (a) into 3 equal parts (b) into 6 equal parts
4 104.76 km (a) into 9 equal parts (b) into 12 equal parts
5 £132 (a) into 8 equal parts (b) into 15 equal parts
6 128 cm² (a) into 16 equal parts (b) into 25 equal parts

> **Finished Early?**
> 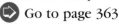 Go to page 363

Further Practice

U In each question, two of the answers are the same and one is different.
Work out the answers. Find the odd one out.

Example (a) 1.2×4 (b) 1.6×3 (c) $9.8 \div 2$	

Working (a) $\begin{array}{r} 1.2 \\ + \ \ 4 \\ \hline 4.8 \end{array}$ (b) $\begin{array}{r} 1.6 \\ + \ \ 3 \\ \hline 4.8 \\ \scriptstyle 1 \end{array}$ (c) $\begin{array}{r} 4.9 \\ 2\overline{)9.^18} \end{array}$

Answer (c) is the odd one out.

1 (a) 1.5×3 (b) 2.6×2 (c) 0.9×5
2 (a) $5.4 \div 3$ (b) $9.5 \div 5$ (c) $3.6 \div 2$
3 (a) $9.93 \div 3$ (b) $16.6 \div 5$ (c) $29.88 \div 9$
4 (a) 12.1×7 (b) $169 \div 2$ (c) 42.35×2
5 (a) $3.6 \div 5$ (b) 0.12×6 (c) $5.84 \div 8$
6 (a) 1.62×13 (b) 1.17×18 (c) 1.41×15

> **Finished Early?**
> 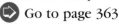 Go to page 363

P⑤ Decimals and Place Value

Learn About It

1 When you multiply a whole number by 10, its digits move **one place** to the left. You fill the empty column with a 0.

So $123 \times 10 = 1230$.

This works with decimals, too.

So $1.23 \times 10 = 12.3$.

When you multiply by 100, you move **two places** to the left.

So $1.23 \times 100 = 123$.

2 Multiply these numbers (i) by 10, (ii) by 100.

  (a) 4.67   **(b)** 3.5   **(c)** 0.22   **(d)** 0.3   **(e)** 0.07

3 Dividing by 10 or 100 is similar to multiplying. You have to move the digits one or two places to the **right**.

So $45.6 \div 10 = 4.56$.

$789 \div 100 = 7.89$.

Sometimes you need to 'tidy up' the answer.

tens	units	.	tenths	hundredths
2	0			

÷ 100

tens	units	.	tenths	hundredths
		.	2	0

=

units	.	tenths
0	.	2

$20 \div 100 = .20$. The last 0 is not needed because there are no hundredths. The units column is blank, so you put a 0 there. The answer is $20 \div 100 = 0.2$.

4 Divide these numbers (i) by 10, (ii) by 100.

  (a) 731 **(b)** 32 **(c)** 70 **(d)** 6 **(e)** 101

5 To multiply or divide by 1000, move the digits **three places**.

So $1.42 \times 1000 = 1420$ and $300 \div 1000 = 0.3$.

For larger numbers, move more places.

Try It Out

 Work out what is in each number machine. It could be ×10, ×100, ×1000, ÷10, ÷100 or ÷1000.

Example   4.14 [**?**] 414

Working   The digits have moved two places to the left. ×100 does this.

Answer   4.14 [**× 100**] 414

---

1 1.2 [**?**] 12   **2** 62 [**?**] 6.2   **3** 0.5 [**?**] 50

4 1.78 [**?**] 178   **5** 32 [**?**] 0.32   **6** 0.05 [**?**] 0.5

7 0.3 [**?**] 30   **8** 250 [**?**] 2.5   **9** 164 [**?**] 16.4

10 40.04 [**?**] 400.4   **11** 1.66 [**?**] 1660   **12** 4150 [**?**] 4.15

Learn More About It

If you can multiply and divide by 10 and 100, there are lots of other things you can do.

1 You can work out 3.1×20, because 20 is 2×10.

$$3.1 \times 20$$

is the same as $3.1 \times 2 \quad \times 10$

is the same as $6.2 \qquad \times 10 = 62$.

2 Work out 2.4×20 yourself.

3 You can work out 22×0.4. Find 22×4 first, then divide by 10:
$$22 \times 0.4$$
is the same as $22 \times 4 \quad \div 10$
is the same as $88 \qquad \div 10 = 8.8$.

4 Work out 31×0.3 yourself.

5 You can divide 4.6 by 20. To divide by 20, divide by 2, then by 10.
$$4.6 \div 20$$
is the same as $4.6 \div 2 \quad \div 10$
is the same as $2.3 \qquad \div 10 = 0.23$.

6 Work out $3.6 \div 20$ yourself.

7 You can divide 1950 by 1300. To divide by 1300, divide by 13, then by 100.
$$1950 \div 1300$$
is the same as $1950 \div 13 \quad \div 100$
is the same as $150 \qquad\qquad \div 100 = 1.5$.

8 Work out $584 \div 800$ yourself.

Ⓦ Try It Out

Work out the answers to these.

1 3.7×30	**2** 4.16×20	**3** 27×0.2	**4** 1.3×0.5
5 $4.4 \div 40$	**6** $351 \div 90$	**7** $362 \div 200$	**8** $3661 \div 700$
9 5.5×140	**10** $700.8 \div 320$	**11** 1.8×2300	**12** $2445 \div 1500$

Practice

Ⓧ Copy and complete the table.

Question	Item	Cost of 1	Cost of 10	Cost of 100
1	Newspaper	£0.35		
2	Floppy disk			£17
3	Mountain bike	£154.99		
4	Pad of paper	£2.20		
5	CD		£139.50	
6	Coach ticket			£455
7	Hot meal		£65	
8	Video hire	£1.75		
9	Car			£925 595
10	Pen		£3.30	

Finished Early?
 Go to page 363

Work these out. Write *same* if the two answers are the same. Write *different* if they are not.

Example	**(a)** 0.05×10 **(b)** $50 \div 100$
Working	**(a)** $0.05 \times 10 = 0.5$ *(Move digits 1 place to the left)*
	(b) $50 \div 100 = 0.5$ *(Move digits 2 places to the right)*
Answer	**(a)** 0.5 **(b)** 0.5 *same*

1 (a) $1.2 \div 10$ **(b)** $12 \div 100$
2 (a) 0.08×10 **(b)** $80 \div 100$
3 (a) $541 \div 10$ **(b)** 5.41×100
4 (a) $32 \div 20$ **(b)** 0.8×20
5 (a) 0.03×50 **(b)** $450 \div 300$
6 (a) $36 \div 400$ **(b)** $81 \div 90$
7 (a) 0.6×100 **(b)** 0.15×40
8 (a) 4.28×30 **(b)** 3.21×40
9 (a) 0.55×4 **(b)** $22 \div 100$
10 (a) $17 \div 50$ **(b)** $68 \div 200$

Finished Early?
➡ Go to page 363

Further Practice

 Each number machine has six numbers that are fed into it. Copy the table, then fill in the output numbers. Write any working underneath the table.

Question	Input numbers	Number machine	Output numbers
1	1.6, 3.25, 12.6, 0.75, 0.05, 0.3	×10	
2	7.7, 2.46, 45.4, 0.23, 0.08, 0.6	×100	
3	23, 3.7, 65.2, 0.7, 10.7, 208	÷10	
4	46, 80, 150, 642, 3, 1253	÷100	
5	5.5, 13.61, 16.7, 0.8, 0.03, 0.57	×20	
6	345, 50.1, 6.9, 14.4, 645, 8952	÷30	
7	1.55, 6.8, 0.42, 0.8, 0.03, 12.76	×50	
8	49, 917, 34.3, 134.4, 2.1, 21.7	÷70	
9	0.56, 6.3, 2.52, 13.8, 0.05, 0.9	×400	
10	120, 126, 42, 1350, 84, 60	÷600	

17 Percentages

In this chapter you will learn about ...
1. percentages
2. percentages of an amount
3. fractions, decimals and percentages

1 Percentages

Learn About It

This rectangle has been divided into 100 squares.

21 of the squares are yellow.

$\frac{21}{100}$ of the rectangle is yellow.

A fraction out of 100 is called a **percentage**.

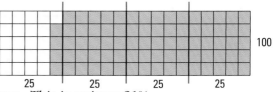

21 per cent of the rectangle is yellow. This is written 21%.

The whole rectangle is 100%.

100 − 21 = 79, so 79% of the rectangle is green.

$\frac{1}{2}$ of this rectangle is yellow.

That is 50 squares, $\frac{50}{100}$.

So 50% is yellow.

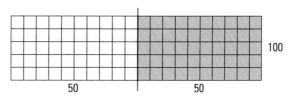

$\frac{1}{4}$ of this rectangle is yellow.

That is 25 squares, $\frac{25}{100}$.

So 25% is yellow.

$\frac{3}{4}$ is green. That is 75 squares, $\frac{75}{100}$.

So 75% is green.

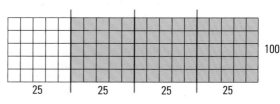

Word Check

percentage a fraction in hundredths (out of 100)

per cent 100 per cent make one whole

% per cent

Try It Out

A For each square, write

    (a) the percentage that is yellow

    (b) the percentage that is green .

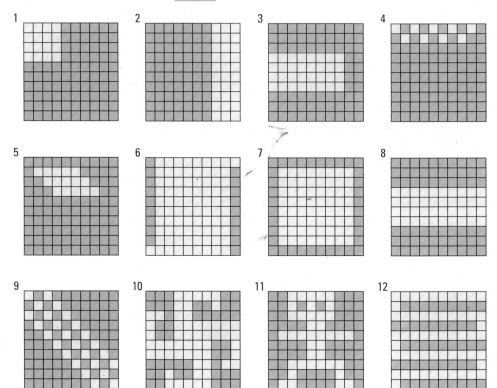

B On grids like the ones in Try It Out **A**, colour squares so that …

1 40% is coloured	**2** 17% is coloured
3 60% is coloured	**4** 78% is coloured
5 9% is coloured	**6** 30% is not coloured
7 26% is not coloured	**8** 70% is not coloured
9 85% is not coloured	**10** 4% is not coloured
11 93% is coloured	**12** 38% is not coloured.

Practice

1 Write these fractions as percentages.

Example	$\frac{37}{100}$
Answer	37%

(a) $\frac{56}{100}$ (b) $\frac{23}{100}$ (c) $\frac{77}{100}$ (d) $\frac{35}{100}$

(e) $\frac{94}{100}$ (f) $\frac{3}{100}$ (g) $\frac{16}{100}$ (h) $\frac{62}{100}$

2 Write these percentages as fractions over 100. Cancel the fraction to lowest terms if you can.

Example	30%
Working	$30\% = \frac{30}{100} = \frac{3}{10}$
Answer	$30\% = \frac{3}{10}$

(a) 37%   (b) 79%   (c) 25%   (d) 61%

(e) 60%   (f) 50%   (g) 13%   (h) 75%

D What percentage of each square is **(a)** yellow , **(b)** green ?

1
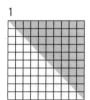
2

3

4

5
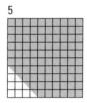

6
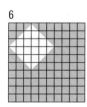
7
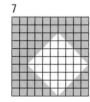
8

9

10
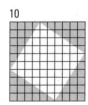

> **Finished Early?**
> ➡ Go to page 364

Further Practice

E What percentage of each square is **(a)** red , **(b)** blue ?

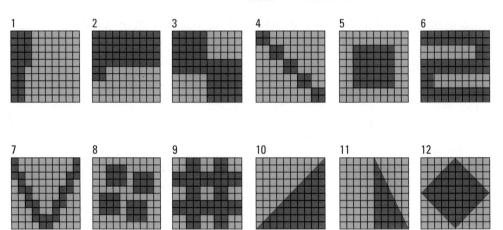

F On grids like the ones in Further Practice **F**, colour squares so that …

1 20% is coloured
3 80% is coloured
5 8% is coloured
7 46% is not coloured
9 95% is not coloured

2 57% is coloured
4 48% is coloured
6 10% is not coloured
8 60% is not coloured
10 14% is not coloured

Finished Early?
➡ Go to page 364

P 2 Percentages of an Amount

Learn About It

1 Yousif did a survey of his class. It was about how far they lived from school. These were his results.

Distance	Percentage of class
Less than 1 km	40%
1–2 km	20%
2–5 km	20%
5–10 km	10%
More than 10 km	10%

2 Yousif lost the piece of paper he used when he was doing the survey.
His teacher asked him how many pupils lived less than 1 km away.
He couldn't remember.

His teacher showed him how to work it out. There were 30 pupils
in Yousif's class.

40% of 30 pupils = $\frac{40}{100}$ of 30 pupils.

$$= 30 \times \frac{40}{100} \text{ (of always means multiply)}$$
$$= 30 \times 40 \div 100$$
$$= 1200 \div 100$$
$$= 12 \text{ pupils}$$

So 12 pupils lived less than 1 km away.

This is the rule. ⟶

> # Key Fact
> To work out a percentage
> of something, multiply by
> the number of per cent and
> divide by 100.

3 Work out the rest of the information for Yousif's survey. Copy Yousif's table.
Add a new column for **Number of pupils**.

4 Joanne earns £460 per month.

She gets a pay rise, 13% more.

She wants to know how much extra money she will get.

13% of £460 = $\frac{13}{100}$ of £460

£460 $\times \frac{13}{100}$ = £460 $\times$ 13 $\div$ 100
$$= \pounds5980 \div 100$$
$$= \pounds59.80$$

So she will get £59.80 extra each month.

```
  4 6 0          ×     400    60
×   1 3       ┌──────┬──────┐
─────────  10 │ 4000 │  600 │
1 3 8 0       ├──────┼──────┤
4 6 0 0   or   3 │ 1200 │  180 │
─────────     └──────┴──────┘
5 9 8 0
                  5200 +  780   = 5980
```

5 James works in the same office as
Joanne. James earns £720 per
month. He gets the same pay rise,
13%. Work out how much extra
money he will get.

Word Check
....
of when you see 'of' in a
  calculation, you have to multiply.
per month each month

NUMBER SKILLS Divide by 100; multiply any number by U or TU;
know percentage equivalents for $\frac{1}{2}$, and $\frac{1}{4}$, $\frac{1}{5}$, $\frac{1}{10}$

183

ıry It Out

G Copy and complete the table.

Amount (100%)	Percentage					
	50%	25%	10%	70%	41%	7%
£200	£100					
50 kg						
1300 l						
£255						

Practice

H **1** A supermarket asked **800 customers** what they liked best for breakfast.

a    b   c   d

cereals, 46%   toast, 37%   cooked breakfast, 12%   just tea or coffee, 5%

How many people said they liked each one?

2 This table shows the metals used to make some different metal objects.

Object	Made from	Weight
Pewter mug	73% tin, 27% lead	500 g
Brass plate	70% copper, 30% zinc	3150 g
Bronze figure	70% copper, 30% tin	2490 g
Roll of solder	50% tin, 50% lead	325 g

How much of each metal was used to make each object?

I **1** Don buys these things to sell in his hi-fi shop.
   (a) CD player, £120
   (b) Mini system, £150
   (c) Rack system, £499
   (d) Personal stereo, £55
He then **adds 25%** to these prices.

Work out **(i)** how much he adds on, **(ii)** what he sells each thing for.

2 A bookstore has a sale.

Work out **(i)** how much is taken off each book, **(ii)** what the sale price is.

(a) Graphic novel, was £11.00
(b) Dictionary, was £8.90
(c) Puzzle book, was £6.50
(d) Atlas, was £17.50

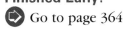

Book Sale

everything

30% off

Further Practice

Finished Early?
➡ Go to page 364

J Alex mixes paint in a DIY store.

His machine uses four colours: white, red, yellow and blue.

There are three tin sizes: large (5 litres), medium (2.5 litres) and small (750 ml).

He has to tell the machine how much of each colour to use.

He types the amounts into the machine's computer, in millilitres (ml).

Example	To make Orange Sunset, Alex needs 10% white, 40% red and 50% yellow. What does he type in to mix a large tin?
Working:	A large tin is 5 litres. That is 5000 ml. Work the percentages out from this. White: 10% of 5000 ml = $5000 \times \frac{10}{100}$ = 5000 × 10 ÷ 100 $\qquad\qquad\qquad\qquad$ = 50,000 ÷ 100 = 500 ml. Red: 40% of 5000 ml = $5000 \times \frac{40}{100}$ = 5000 × 40 ÷ 100 $\qquad\qquad\qquad\qquad$ = 2000 ml. Yellow: 50% of 5000 ml = $5000 \times \frac{50}{100}$ = 5000 × 50 ÷ 100 $\qquad\qquad\qquad\qquad$ = 250 000 ÷ 100 = 2500 ml
Answer:	Alex types in 500, 2000, 2500, 0. (Remember, he needs to tell the computer there's no blue!)

Work out what Alex types in to mix **(a)** a large tin, **(b)** a medium tin, **(c)** a small tin of these colours.

1 Mint Green: 70% white (no red), 15% yellow and 15% blue.
2 Purple Haze: 10% white, 60% red (no yellow), 30% blue.
3 Chestnut: 5% white, 43% red, 21% yellow, 31% blue.
4 Mustard: 38% white, 4% red, 46% yellow, 12% blue.

Finished Early?
➡ Go to page 364

T ③ Fractions, Decimals and Percentages

Learn About It

Any percentage is just a fraction in hundredths. For example, $21\% = \frac{21}{100}$.

Any fraction has a percentage that is **equivalent** to it. To work it out, find an equivalent fraction. This needs to have a **denominator** of 100.

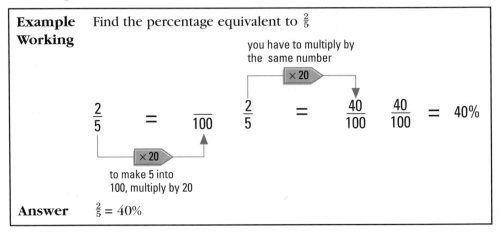

Example Find the percentage equivalent to $\frac{2}{5}$

Working

you have to multiply by the same number

$\times 20$

$$\frac{2}{5} = \frac{}{100} \qquad \frac{2}{5} = \frac{40}{100} \qquad \frac{40}{100} = 40\%$$

$\times 20$

to make 5 into 100, multiply by 20

Answer $\frac{2}{5} = 40\%$

Any decimal can be made into a percentage or a fraction.

Example Find the percentage equivalent to 0.32.

Working 0.32 means 3 tenths and 2 hundredths.

$$0.32 = \frac{3}{10} + \frac{2}{100} = \frac{30}{100} + \frac{2}{100} = \frac{32}{100} = 32\%$$

Answer $0.32 = 32\%$

$\frac{32}{100}$ in lowest terms is $\frac{8}{25}$.

So $0.32 = \frac{8}{25}$ as well.

$70\% = \frac{70}{100} = \frac{7}{10} = 0.7$.

$3\% = \frac{3}{100} = 0.03$.

Word Check

equivalent fractions, decimals or percentages that mean the same.

denominator the number below the line in a fraction.

Try It Out

K Change these fractions into (**a**) percentages, (**b**) decimals.

1 $\frac{7}{100}$	**2** $\frac{29}{100}$	**3** $\frac{61}{100}$	**4** $\frac{3}{10}$	**5** $\frac{3}{5}$	**6** $\frac{1}{20}$
7 $\frac{4}{50}$	**8** $\frac{12}{25}$	**9** $\frac{11}{20}$	**10** $\frac{39}{50}$	**11** $1\frac{3}{100}$	**12** $1\frac{7}{10}$

L Change these percentages into (**a**) fractions, (**b**) decimals.

1 31%	**2** 47%	**3** 93%	**4** 70%	**5** 40%	**6** 35%
7 14%	**8** 36%	**9** 95%	**10** 66%	**11** 109%	**12** 130%

Practice

(M) In each question, two of the numbers are equivalent and one is different.
Change them all to percentages. Write the equivalent ones together.
Write the 'odd one out' separately.

Example   **(a)** $\frac{2}{5}$ **(b)** 0.2   **(c)** 40%

Working   **(a)** $\frac{2}{5} = \frac{40}{100} = 40\%$

  (b) $0.2 = \frac{2}{10} = \frac{20}{100} = 20\%$

  (c) 40%

Answer $\frac{2}{5} = 40\%$. 0.2 is the odd one out.

---

1 (a) $\frac{3}{10}$ **(b)** 0.3 **(c)** 3% **2 (a)** $\frac{27}{100}$ **(b)** 27.100 **(c)** 27%

3 (a) $\frac{13}{50}$ **(b)** 0.26 **(c)** 13% **4 (a)** $\frac{24}{25}$ **(b)** 0.24 **(c)** 24%

5 (a) $\frac{4}{5}$ **(b)** 0.45 **(c)** 80% **6 (a)** $\frac{7}{10}$ **(b)** 0.07 **(c)** 7%

7 (a) $\frac{1}{2}$ **(b)** 1.2 **(c)** 50% **8 (a)** $\frac{41}{50}$ **(b)** 0.86 **(c)** 86%

9 (a) $\frac{17}{25}$ **(b)** 0.68 **(c)** 17% **10 (a)** $\frac{1}{25}$ **(b)** 0.25 **(c)** 25%

(N) On each screen are some fractions, decimals and percentages.

First change them all into percentages. Then write them out in order, smallest to largest.

Example

0.1   3/20

12%

0.16   17%

Working $0.1, \frac{3}{20}, 12\%, 17\%, 0.16$
  (*Write down the numbers on the screen*)
  $0.1 = 10\%, \frac{3}{20} = \frac{15}{100} = 15\%, 12\%, 17\%, 0.16 = 16\%.$
  (*Change into percentages*)
  10%, 12%, 15%, 16%, 17%
  (*Write the percentages in order*)

Answer $0.1, 12\%, \frac{3}{20}, 0.16, 17\%$
  (*Write the original numbers in order*)

Finished Early?
Go to page 364

Further Practice

Copy and complete the table. Write your working underneath the table.

Question	Fraction (hundredths)	Fraction (lowest terms)	Decimal	Percentage
1	$\frac{3}{100}$			
2		$\frac{1}{5}$		
3	$\frac{17}{100}$			
4			0.3	
5		$\frac{7}{20}$		
6				45%
7				48%
8			0.66	
9		$\frac{4}{5}$		
10	$\frac{98}{100}$			

Finished Early?
Go to page 364

Unit 8 *Fractional Parts*

Summary of Chapters 15, 16 and 17

- The **denominator** of a fraction is the number on the bottom.
- The **numerator** of a fraction is the number on the top.
- Fractions using different numbers can be **equivalent** to each other.
  To find an equivalent fraction, multiply or divide top and bottom by the
  same number. $\frac{2}{5} = \frac{4}{10} = \frac{6}{15} = \frac{14}{35} = \frac{200}{500}$.
- A fraction with the smallest possible numbers is in **lowest terms**.
- To work out any fraction of something …
  1 divide by the bottom number
  2 multiply by the top number.
- To add or subtract fractions …
  1 change all the fractions to the same type
  2 add the top numbers together
  3 cancel the answer to lowest terms.
- Mixed fractions have a whole number and a fraction part.
- The first place after the decimal point is for **tenths**. The second is for
  hundredths.
- To find the bigger of two decimals …
  1 compare the units. If they are the same …
  2 compare the tenths. If they are the same …
  3 compare the hundredths.
- To add and subtract decimals …
  1 set them out in columns. Line up all the decimal points.
  2 work as if they were whole numbers. Line up the decimal point
    in the answer with the rest.
- To multiply and divide decimals, work as if they were whole numbers.
  Line up the decimal point in the answer with the ones in the question.
- To multiply a decimal by 10 or 100, move the digits 1 or 2 places to the
  left. To divide, move the digits to the right.
- A percentage is a fraction in hundredths. $1\% = \frac{1}{100}$, $10\% = \frac{1}{10}$
- Percentages match decimals: $24\% = 0.24$, $70\% = 0.7$, $6\% = 0.06$.
- To find a percentage of something …
  1 multiply by the number of percent
  2 divide by 100.

18 Formulae

In this chapter you will learn about ...

1 giving instructions

2 using letters for numbers

3 substituting numbers for letters

---

1 Giving Instructions

Learn About It

Ian has a collection of CDs. If he buys three more how many does he have altogether?

Ian has added three CDs to his collection. You can write this as ...

The new number of CDs equals the old number of CDs plus 3

what is worked out   how is it worked out

An **instruction** describes how to work something out.

You start your instruction with what you want to work out.

Try It Out

 Write instructions for these.

Example	Peter is four times as old as his brother. Complete the sentence 'Peter's age equals ...'
Answer	Peter's age equals his brother's age 4 times.

Complete the sentence 'Ben's age equals ...' if Ben is

1 two years older than Jane

2 five years older than Claire

3 twice as old as Mira

4 one third of his dad's age.

Practice

B Write instructions for these.

> **Example**   Kamal's age if he is 5 years older than Claire.
> **Answer**   Kamal's age equals Claire's age plus 5.

1 Ken's age if he is 4 years older than Jill.
2 Sharon's age if she is 3 years older than Stan.
3 Sue's age if she is 5 years older than Brian.
4 Jade's age if she is 2 years younger than Opal.
5 Raji's age if she is 7 years younger than Parul.
6 Peter's age if he is 5 years younger than Sian.
7 Phil's age if he is twice as old as his brother Sean.
8 Marion's age if she is four times as old as Tony.
9 Robert's age if he is three times as old as Shirley.
10 Stella's age if she is half her mother's age.

C In each question there is one rule. This rule tells you how to find the bottom number from the top one. Write the rule in words.

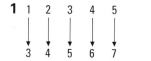      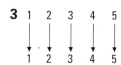

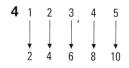   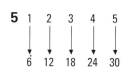

Further Practice

D Write instructions for these.

> **Example**   The total number of legs on all the tables in a house.
> **Answer**   The total number of legs equals the number of tables times 4.

1 The total number of legs on all the chairs in a classroom.
2 The number of eggs in a crate if there are 36 eggs in each layer.
3 The number of cans on a supermarket shelf if the cans are stored in packs of 6.
4 Bill's age if he is 3 years older than Ali.

5 Andrew's age if he is 8 years older than his brother.

6 Marcia's age if she is 8 years younger than Steven.

7 Mira's age if she is 2 years younger than Mukta.

8 Donna is 25 years younger than her mother.

    (a) What is Donna's age if you know her mother's age?

    (b) What is her mother's age if you know Donna's?

9 The new length when 7 m is cut from a roll of carpet.

10 Each lorry delivers 5 tonnes of rock to a building site. How much will be delivered in one day?

11 A newspaper costs 30p. How much will a shop get for the papers sold in one day?

12 If you save the same amount every week how much do you save in 7 weeks?

> **Finished Early?**
> Go to page 365

Go to page 365

T 2 Using Letters for Numbers

Learn About It

Roya has a collection of cassette tapes which fill four boxes.

The total number of tapes equals four times the number in a box.

Writing sentences to give instructions can take a long time.

Replacing the words with letters is shorter.

The total number of *t*apes is *t*.

The number in a *b*ox is *b*.

Now you write a **formula** using letters.

$$t = 4 \times b$$

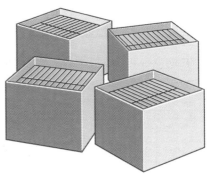

Try It Out

E Write each of these as formula using the red letters and numbers.

1 Tony's age equals Fred's age plus 4.

2 Claire's age equals Sue's age minus 3.

3 Peter's age equals Jack's age times 4.

4 Kim's age equals her dad's age divided by 3.

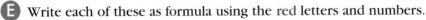

Learn More About It

The formula $t = 4 \times b$ can be shortened by leaving out the multiplication sign.
You write $t = 4b$.

Addition, subtraction, multiplication and division can all be used in a formula.

Example   The *n*umber of 5 m pieces that can be cut
from a *l*ength of carpet

Answer $n = \dfrac{l}{5}$

Key Fact

Miss out the multiplication
sign ($\times$) when using letters.

Word Check

formula a rule for working
   something out

formulae more than one formula

Try It Out

F Write each of these as a formula. Use the red letters and numbers.

1 The *m*oney raised in a sponsored swim at 20p for each *l*ength.

2 The *t*otal raised on a sponsored walk at 50p for each *m*ile.

3 The *d*istance left on a 100 km journey after travelling a number of
*k*ilometres.

4 The *n*umber of 3 m pieces that can be cut from a *l*ength of string.

Practice

G Write these as formulae. Use the red letters and numbers.

1 The total *c*ost of a magazine at £2 each week for some *w*eeks.

2 The *t*otal cost of some metres of carpet at £18 per square *m*etre.

3 The recording *t*ime on some *c*assettes of 90 minutes each.

4 The *l*ength remaining on a 10 m roll of carpet when a *p*iece has been cut off.

5 The *n*umber of chocolates left in a box of 30 when some have been *e*aten.

6 The *c*harge for special delivery of a parcel if it costs £2 for each *k*ilogram
the parcel weighs.

H Write each of these as a formula. Make it clear what the letters mean.

Example	The total *c*ost of a number of *b*ooks if they are £4 each
Working	*c* is the total cost of the books
	b is the number of books
Answer	$c = 4b$

1 The sale *p*rice of a mobile phone with £20 off the *u*sual price.

2 The weekly *w*ages earned by someone who earns £5 for each *h*our.

3 The number of *e*mpty seats in a hall with room for 500 when some seats are *t*aken.

4 The total number of seats in a *c*inema with 16 seats in each *r*ow.

5 The amount of *w*eight a person has lost if they are 4 kg below their *o*ld weight.

Further Practice

I Write each of these as a formula. Use the red letters and numbers.

1 The *n*umber of tins of *c*at food needed by cats who each eat 4 tins a week.

2 The *t*otal weight of *c*ars weighing 800 kg each.

3 The amount each *c*hild gets when a *p*rize is shared equally between 4 pupils.

4 The *w*eight of each cake when some *m*ixture is split into 5 parts.

5 The cost of a *b*ox of crisps, when you know the *n*umber of packets in each box and the price of a packet is 30p.

J Write each of these as a formula.

1 The total *p*rize money when 12 people get an equal *s*hare.

2 The sale *p*rice of a CD player with £15 off the *u*sual price.

3 The *a*nswer you get when you find ...

    (a) the sum of a *n*umber and 3   **(b)** three times a *n*umber

    (c) half a *n*umber   **(d)** three less than a *n*umber

    (e) four more than a *n*umber.

4 The total *c*ost of a meal for *f*ood and *d*rink.

Finished Early?
➡ Go to page 365

❸ Substituting Numbers for Letters

Learn About It

The formula for the total length of a car and a trailer is $l = c + t$

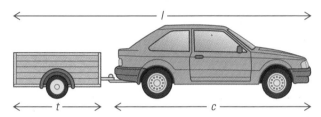

where c is the length of the car and t is the length of the trailer.

Replacing letters in a formula with numbers is called **substitution**.

If the car is 4 m long and its trailer is 3 m long then $c = 4$ and $t = 3$ so

$l = 4 + 3$
$\quad = 7\text{ m}$

> **Word Check**
> **substitute** replace with letters

Try It Out

K Find the value of …

1 $a + 3$ when a is 4.
2 $a + b$ when a is 3 and b is 5.
3 $3q$ when q is 4.
4 xy when x is 5 and y is 4.
5 $12 - u$ when u is 4.

Example	Find $\dfrac{l}{n}$ when $l = 10$ and $n = 2$.
Working	$\dfrac{10}{2}$
Answer	5

6 Find $\dfrac{a}{b}$ when $a = 12$ and $b = 3$.

Practice

L

Example	The formula for the cost of crisps bought for a party is
	$\quad C = np$
	where C is the total cost, n is the number of packets and p is the price of one packet.
	Find C when n is 20 and p is 30.
Working	$C = 20 \times 30$
Answer	$C = 600$

1 The distance (d) around the sides of a square with sides s is given by

$$d = 4s$$

Find d when …

(a) s is 5 cm   (b) s is 3.5 cm   (c) s is 2.4 m   (d) s is 1.8 km.

2 The total prize money when a prize is shared is given by the formula

$$t = pw$$

Where t is the total prize money, p is the number of prizewinners and w is the amount each wins.

Find the total prize money when …

(a) 10 winners each get £100   (b) 15 winners each get £30
(c) 25 winners each get £80   (d) 12 winners each get £20.

3 The amount of money a theatre takes is given by the formula

$$t = s + c$$

where t is the total amount of money, s is the amount of money taken for seats in the stalls and c is the amount of money taken for seats in the circle.

Find t when …

(a) s is £300 and c is £200   (b) s is £150 and c is £450
(c) s is £240 and c is £120   (d) s is £360 and c is £480.

4 The distance (d) around a rectangle with sides l and w is given by

$$d = 2l + 2w$$

Find d when …

(a) $l = 10$ cm, $w = 8$ cm   (b) $l = 16$ cm, $w = 11$ cm
(c) $l = 21$ m, $w = 12.5$ m   (d) $l = 2$ km, $w = 1.6$ km.

(M) You are given these formulae.
Copy the tables and fill in the y values.

Example $y = 3x - 1$
Answer

x	1	2	3	4
y	2	5	8	11

when x is 4
$y = 3 \times 4 - 1$
$= 12 - 1$
$= 11$

1 $y = 2x$

x	1	2	3	4
y				

2 $y = x - 1$

x	1	2	3	4
y				

3 $y = 2x + 1$

x	1	2	3	4
y				

4 $y = 2x - 3$

x	1	2	3	4
y				

5 $y = 5 - x$

x	1	2	3	4
y				

Further Practice

 **1** Find the value of …

(a) $p = q + 3$ when q is 9

(b) $l = m + n$ when m is 12 and n is 13

(c) $r = 5s$ when s is 10

(d) $u = 9e$ when $e = 3$.

2 The total charge for delivering cement is given by

$t = 12 + 9c$

Where t is the total charge in pounds and c is the weight in tonnes.

Find the total charge when …

(a) $c = 3$ tonnes (b) $c = 5$ tonnes

(c) $c = 2.5$ tonnes (d) $c = 9.5$ tonnes.

3 The cost of a special delivery parcel is given by the formula

$c = 2w + 4$

where c is the cost in pounds and w is the weight in kilograms.

Find c when …

(a) $w = 3$ kg (b) $w = 4$ kg (c) $w = 6.5$ kg (d) $w = 2.8$ kg.

You are given these formulae.

Copy the tables and fill in the y values.

1 $y = 3x$

x	1	2	3	4
y	3	6		

2 $y = x + 3$

x	1	2	3	4
y				

3 $y = 6 - x$

x	1	2	3	4
y				

4 $y = 2x + 3$

x	1	2	3	4
y				

Finished Early?
Go to page 365

19 Equations

In this chapter you will learn about …
1. writing equations
2. working backwards
3. solving equations

1 Writing Equations

Learn About It

Ray says 'When I add five to my age I get seventeen'. This means 'My age plus 5 equals 17'.

Using *a* for age Ray can write $a + 5 = 17$.

This is an **equation**. You write unknown numbers as letters.

Examples

I think of a number, subtract 4 and the answer is 16.

With *n* for the number, the equation is $n - 4 = 16$.

I think of a number, multiply by 5 and the answer is 20.

With *n* for the number, the equation is $5n = 15$.

> **Word Check**
>
> **equation** letters and numbers connected by an equals sign (=)

Try It Out

A Write these as equations using n for the number.

1 I think of a *number*, add 3 and the answer is 10.
2 I think of à *number* and add 5. The answer is 17.
3 I think of a *number*, subtract 4 and the answer is 11.
4 I think of a *number*, multiply by 5 and the answer is 15.
5 I think of a *number* and multiply it by 6. The answer is 12.

Example	I think of a *number*, divide it by 3 and the answer is 4.
Working	Use *n* for number.
Answer	The equation is $\dfrac{n}{3} = 4$

6 I think of a *number*, divide by 5 and the answer is 6.

Practice

B Write these as equations using n for the number.

1 When 3 is added to a *number* the answer is 14.
2 When 5 is added to a *number* you get 17.
3 I think of a *number* and add 7. The answer is 13.
4 I think of a *number*, add 4 and get 23.
5 I think of a *number*, add 8 and the answer is 13.
6 If 7 is added to a *number* the answer is 15.
7 19 added to an unknown *number* gives 28.
8 When you add 35 to a *number* you get 57.
9 I think of a *number* and subtract 7. The answer is 32.
10 I think of a *number*, subtract 9 and get 7.
11 I think of a *number*, take away 11 and the answer is 13.
12 If 12 is subtracted from a *number* the answer is 23.

C Write these as equations.

1 I think of a *number*, multiply by 4 and the answer is 12.
2 If a *number* is multiplied by 5 the answer is 20.
3 4 multiplied by a *number* gives 28.
4 When you multiply 6 by a *number* you get 30.
5 5 times a *number* gives 35.
6 When 8 is multiplied by a *number* you get 56.
7 I think of a *number* and multiply it by 10. The answer is 230.
8 I think of a *number*, multiply by 9 and get 63.
9 When a *number* is divided by 3 the answer is 5.
10 When a *number* is divided by 4 you get 5.
11 6 divided into an unknown *number* gives 6.
12 When you divide 5 into a *number* you get 8.

> **Finished Early?**
> 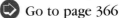 Go to page 366

Further Practice

D Write these as equations.

1 I think of a *number* and add 4. The answer is 17.
2 I think of a *number*, add 3 and get 9.
3 I think of a *number*, add 5 and the answer is 16.
4 If 6 is added to a *number* the answer is 16.
5 When 9 is added to a *number* the answer is 18.
6 When 7 is added to a *number* you get 15.
7 9 added to a *number* gives 25.
8 When you add 25 to a *number* you get 40.
9 I think of a *number* and subtract 6. The answer is 13.

10 I think of a *number*, subtract 8 and get 7.

11 I think of a *number*, take away 6 and the answer is 14.

12 If 15 is subtracted from a *number* the answer is 20.

E Write these as equations.

1 I think of a *number*, multiply by 3 and the answer is 9.

2 If a *number* is multiplied by 4 the answer is 20.

3 5 multiplied by a *number* gives 25.

4 When you multiply 6 by a *number* you get 24.

5 3 times a *number* gives 36.

6 When 6 is multiplied by a *number* you get 48.

7 I think of a *number* and multiply it by 7. The answer is 49.

8 I think of a *number*, multiply by 10 and get 120.

9 When a *number* is divided by 4 the answer is 6.

10 When a *number* is divided by 3 you get 5.

11 5 divided into a *number* gives 4.

12 When you divide 3 into a *number* you get 9.

T2 Working Backwards

Learn About It

A number machine shows a rule.

When you feed in one number, another number comes out.

3 ▮ ×6 ▷ 18

The number fed into the number machine is the **input**. The number that comes out of the number machine is the **output**.

You can check your calculations by working backwards.

The opposite of × **6** is ÷ **6** so

3 ◁ ÷6 ▮ 18

An **inverse** is the opposite of an operation. Multiplication and division are inverses. Addition and subtraction are inverses.

Try It Out

F Check these by using number machines to work backwards.

Example	36 ÷ 9 ▷ 4
Working	36 ◀── ◀×9 ── ◀─ 4
	4 × 9 = 36
Answer	So the answer is correct.

1 12 + 34 ▷ 46

2 37 − 19 ▷ 18

3 12 ×7 ▷ 84

4 96 ÷ 24 ▷ 4

Word Check

inverse the opposite of an operation

operation +, −, × or ÷

Practice

G Check these by using number machines to work backwards.

Write the correct answers for those that are wrong.

1 12 + 32 ▷ 44

2 24 + 48 ▷ 74

3 28 − 11 ▷ 17

4 74 − 28 ▷ 48

5 12 ×4 ▷ 48

6 24 ×5 ▷ 110

7 60 ÷5 ▷ 12

8 76 ÷8 ▷ 9

H Find the numbers fed into these number machines.

Example	? ×12 ▷ 36
Working	3 ◀ ÷12 36
Answer	So the missing number is 3.

1 ? + 33 ▷ 54

2 ? + 48 ▷ 104

3 ? − 24 ▷ 19

4 ? − 63 ▷ 15

5 ? ×3 ▷ 45

6 ? ×4 ▷ 84

7 ? ÷4 ▷ 7

8 ? ÷ 16 ▷ 8

9 ? ×3 ▷ 63

10 ? + 25 ▷ 54

11 ? + 19 ▷ 47

12 ? − 18 ▷ 23

13 ? ÷ 12 ▷ 6

14 ? ÷ 13 ▷ 7

15 ? ×7 ▷ 84

16 ? − 129 ▷ 43

I Check these by using number machines to work backwards.

Write the correct answers for those that are wrong.

Example	6 ×5 ▷ −7 ▷ 28
Working	Work backwards. Write down the output from each machine.

7 ◀— ◁ ÷5 — 35 ——— ◁ +7 — ◀ 28

Since we work back to 7 the answer is not correct.

6 ×5 ▷ −7 ▷ 23

Answer	Wrong. The correct answer is 23.

1 3 ×5 ▷ +4 ▷ 19   **2** 4 ×6 ▷ +8 ▷ 32

3 5 ×12 ▷ −6 ▷ 66   **4** 9 ×12 ▷ −18 ▷ 90

5 90 ÷15 ▷ +12 ▷ 18   **6** 72 ÷18 ▷ +12 ▷ 16

7 120 ÷24 ▷ −27 ▷ 33   **8** 240 ÷16 ▷ −3 ▷ 10

Finished Early?
➡ Go to page 366

Further Practice

J Check these by using number machines to work backwards.

Write the correct answers for those that are wrong.

1 15 +30 ▷ 45   **2** 39 +23 ▷ 63   **3** 35 −17 ▷ 19

4 72 −58 ▷ 14   **5** 12 ×3 ▷ 36   **6** 25 ×6 ▷ 160

7 84 ÷8 ▷ 12   **8** 144 ÷8 ▷ 18

K Find the numbers fed into these number machines.

1 ? +12 ▷ 36   **2** ? +15 ▷ 40   **3** ? −12 ▷ 18

4 ? −18 ▷ 26   **5** ? ×4 ▷ 40   **6** ? ×6 ▷ 120

7 ? ÷6 ▷ 4   **8** ? ÷8 ▷ 6

L Check these by using number machines to work backwards.

Write the correct answers for those that are wrong.

1 2 ×4 ▷ +3 ▷ 11   **2** 6 ×3 ▷ +4 ▷ 22

3 4 ×12 ▷ −16 ▷ 38   **4** 8 ×12 ▷ −16 ▷ 80

5 60 ÷12 ▷ +8 ▷ 13   **6** 84 ÷6 ▷ +12 ▷ 24

7 100 ÷5 ▷ −14 ▷ 6   **8** 128 ÷16 ▷ +32 ▷ 40

❸ Solving Equations

Learn About It

1 You can write $a + 7 = 19$ where a is your age.

This is an equation.

You can write the equation using a number machine.

a | **+7** ⟩ 19

Using the number machine in reverse gives

12 ⟨ **−7** | 19

So $a = 12$.

2 To **solve** the equation means finding the unknown number.

The number found is called the **solution**.

3 Find the solution which is not correct from these.

You can use number machines to work them out.

$x + 4 = 9$ Solution $x = 5$?
$a - 6 = 13$ Solution $a = 7$?

$\dfrac{r}{2} = 6$ Solution $r = 12$?

$5y = 30$ Solution $y = 6$?

Try It Out

Ⓜ Solve these equations using number machines.

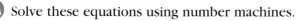

Example	Solve $s + 7 = 19$.
Working	s ⟶ **+7** ⟩ ⟶ 19
	Working backwards gives the answer.
	12 ◀ ⟨ **−7** ◀ 19
Answer	$s = 12$

1 $a + 4 = 8$ **2** $d - 5 = 3$ **3** $2x = 10$ **4** $\dfrac{n}{4} = 2$

Key Fact

To solve an equation use inverse operations.

Word Check

Solve find the unknown number
Solution the value of the number

Practice

N Solve these equations. Write them using number machines and use the reverse machines.

1 $s + 5 = 11$ 2 $d + 16 = 23$ 3 $y + 9 = 18$
4 $f + 12 = 19$ 5 $g - 3 = 14$ 6 $h - 12 = 3$
7 $v - 18 = 9$ 8 $p - 13 = 23$ 9 $4n = 20$
10 $5p = 30$ 11 $7q = 56$ 12 $12r = 60$

13 $\dfrac{a}{3} = 9$ Remember $\dfrac{a}{3}$ means $a \div 3$.   14 $\dfrac{x}{6} = 7$

◎ Write the sentences as equations and then solve them.

Use the letters highlighted for the equations.

Example	Three times a *b*oy's age is 39 years.
Working	$3b = 39$
	b ×3 ▷ 39
	13 ◁ ÷3 39
Answer	$b = 13$. The boy is 13 years old.

1 My *a*ge plus 9 equals 25.
2 My *s*avings times 4 equals £100.
3 The *n*umber of pens divided by 3 is 48.
4 The *n*umber of pupils in the class multiplied by 6 is 120.
5 The *p*rice of a stereo minus £12 equals £60.

Finished Early?
 Go to page 366

Further Practice

P Solve these equations. Write them as number machines and use the reverse machines.

1 $t + 3 = 7$ 2 $m + 4 = 9$
3 $a + 5 = 8$ 4 $b + 6 = 12$
5 $p - 4 = 12$ 6 $q - 11 = 4$
7 $r - 10 = 5$ 8 $s - 10 = 12$
9 $2x = 6$ 10 $3y = 15$
11 $8z = 24$ 12 $5w = 30$

13 $\dfrac{l}{2} = 3$ 14 $\dfrac{m}{4} = 5$

15 $\dfrac{n}{6} = 4$ 16 $\dfrac{s}{7} = 5$

17 $9a = 27$ 18 $w + 12 = 19$
19 $p - 4 = 37$ 20 $7q = 56$

Unit 9 *Algebra*

Review of Chapters 18 and 19

- An instruction describes how to work something out.
- A formula is a rule for working something out.
- A formula uses letters.
- The letters in a formula are used instead of numbers.
- Miss out the × sign when using letters.
- An equation has letters and numbers connected by an equals (=) sign.
- Putting numbers into a formula is known as substitution.
- A number machine shows a rule.
- You can check calculations by working backwards.
- An inverse is the opposite of an operation.
- To solve an equation use inverse operations.

20 Angles

In this chapter you will learn about …
1. what different kinds of angles there are
2. measuring and estimating angles
3. drawing angles accurately

T 1 Types of Angle

Learn About It

An **angle** measures how much something has turned. You usually show this with two lines.

In the middle is part of a circle. This shows which way the arm has turned.

Angles are measured in **degrees**. 20 degrees is written 20°.

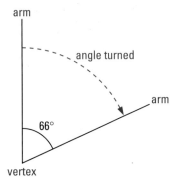

Different amounts of turning have different names.

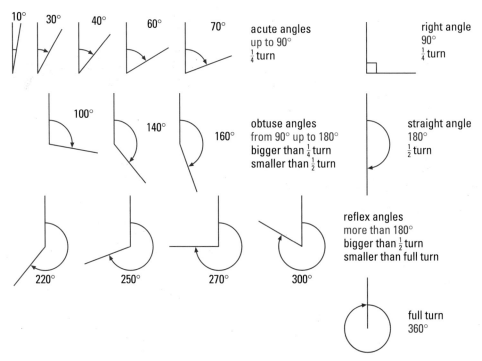

10° 30° 40° 60° 70° acute angles
up to 90°
$\frac{1}{4}$ turn

right angle
90°
$\frac{1}{4}$ turn

100° 140° 160° obtuse angles
from 90° up to 180°
bigger than $\frac{1}{4}$ turn
smaller than $\frac{1}{2}$ turn

straight angle
180°
$\frac{1}{2}$ turn

220° 250° 270° 300° reflex angles
more than 180°
bigger than $\frac{1}{2}$ turn
smaller than full turn

full turn
360°

> ## Word Check
> angle an amount of turning
> degree angles are measured in degrees
> vertex a corner of a shape

Try It Out

A Write down the type of angle each of these is.

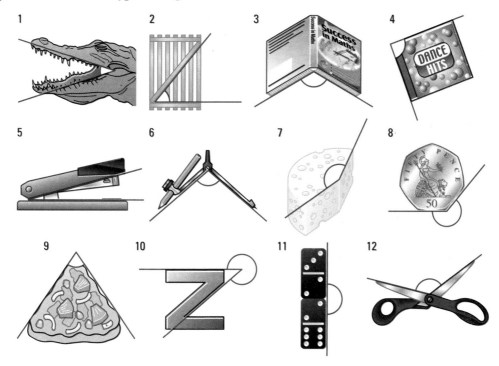

1   2   3   4

5   6   7   8

9   10   11   12

Practice

B These are the points of the compass.
These are the ways you can turn.

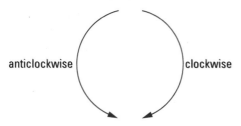

anticlockwise   clockwise

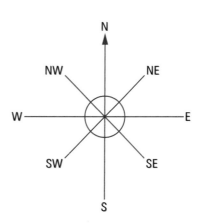

N
NW   NE
W —————— E
SW   SE
S

Look at the instructions. Work out the type of angle you turn through.

Example:	Face *North* (N), then turn *anticlockwise*
	until you are facing *North-West* (NW).
Answer	An *acute* angle.

Copy and complete the table.

Question	Face	... then turn ...	until facing	Type of angle
1	North	clockwise	East	
2	North	clockwise	North-East	
3	North	anticlockwise	South-West	
4	East	clockwise	South-East	
5	South	anticlockwise	West	
6	East	anticlockwise	North-West	
7	West	clockwise	South-West	
8	North-East	anticlockwise	North-West	
9	North-West	clockwise	South-East	
10	South	anticlockwise	North-East	

Word Check

clockwise the hands of a clock go in this direction

anticlockwise the opposite of clockwise

Ⓒ These angles are given in degrees. Work out what type of angle each one is.

Example	102°
Working	102° is between 90° and 180°.
Answer	102° is obtuse.

1 55°	**2** 12°	**3** 185°	**4** 36°	**5** 78°
6 261°	**7** 90°	**8** 15°	**9** 98°	**10** 166°
11 195°	**12** 51°	**13** 320°	**14** 180°	**15** 135°

Finished Early?
Go to page 367

Further Practice

D Here are some shapes. Copy each one and label the angles **inside** them.
Use **A** for acute, **O** for obtuse and **R** for reflex. Use ■ for right angles.

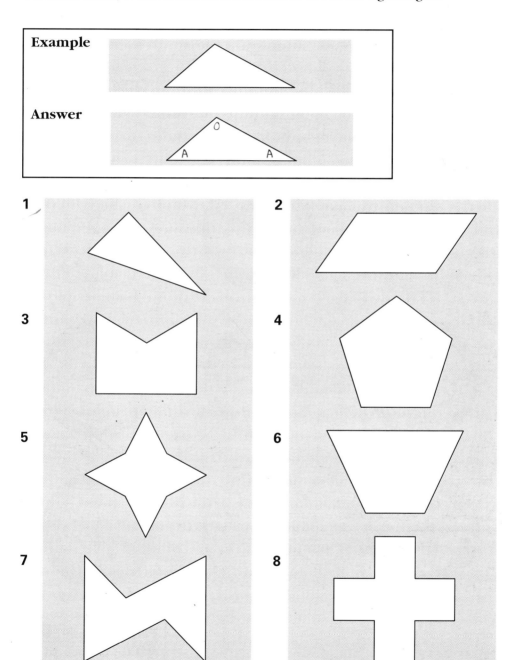

Example

Answer

1

2

3

4

5

6

7

8

E Start at the minute hand and go clockwise until you reach the hour hand.
Write down what type of angle you have to turn through.

Example **Working**

Answer obtuse

1 2 3

4 5 6

7 8 9

Finished Early?
Go to page 367

❷ Measuring and Estimating Angles

Learn About It

Protractor

This is a **protractor**.

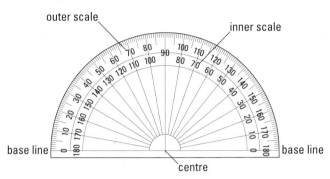

You use it to measure angles.

Sometimes you see
protractors like this.

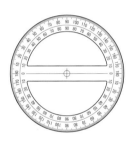

This picture shows a protractor being used to measure 130°.
It is important to have the protractor in the right place.

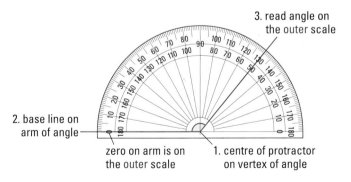

3. read angle on
the outer scale

2. base line on
arm of angle

zero on arm is on
the outer scale

1. centre of protractor
on vertex of angle

You have to use the **outer** scale. The inner scale would read 50°.
This is **wrong** because the angle is obtuse.

If the protractor is put here you can use the **inner** scale.

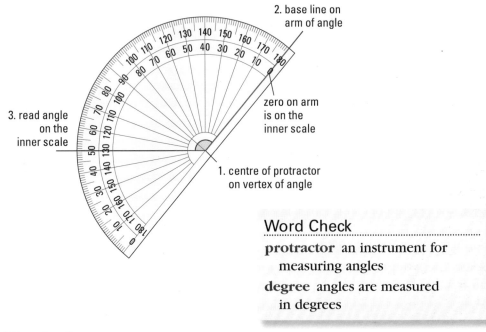

2. base line on
   arm of angle

3. read angle
   on the
   inner scale

zero on arm
is on the
inner scale

1. centre of protractor
   on vertex of angle

Word Check

protractor an instrument for
  measuring angles

degree angles are measured
  in degrees

Try It Out

F Measure these angles. Measure twice, with your outer and inner scales.
This will help you check that you are right. Turn the book round if it helps.

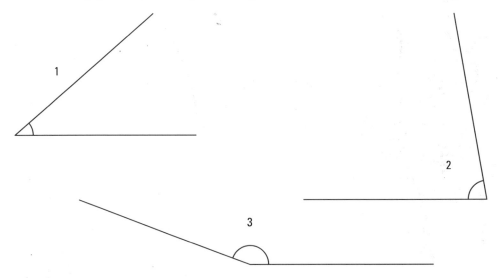

1

2

3

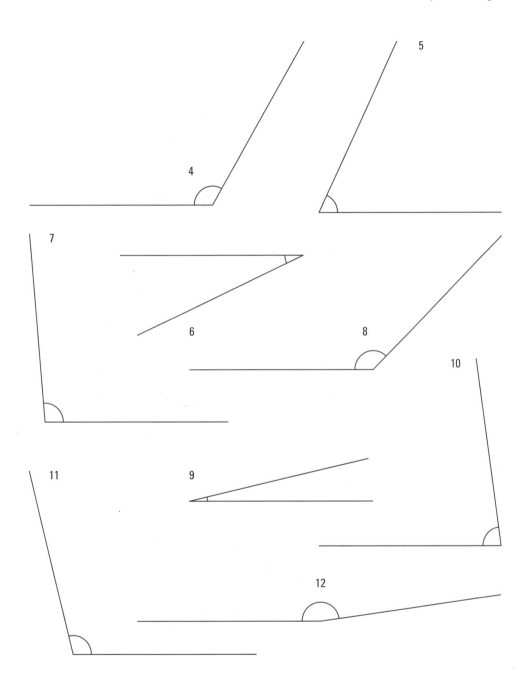

Learn More About It

You need to be able to **estimate** angles. This means to make a good guess.

Suppose you had to estimate this angle.

Imagine this red star.

Imagine it on top of the angle.

Halfway between 90° and 180° is 90° + 45° = 135°.

The angle is just more than halfway.

So a good estimate is 140°.

Always use right angles and 45° angles to make your estimates.

Try It Out

Plain paper

1 On a piece of plain paper, draw 10 different acute and obtuse angles. Number them from 1 to 10.

2 Measure them carefully with your protractor. Write them down on a **different** piece of paper.

3 Swap the angle sheet with your neighbour.

4 You now have 10 angles to estimate. Make a table in your book for the answers.

Angle number	Estimate	Actual	Error	Rating
1				
2				

Fill in the first column with numbers 1 to 10.

5 Estimate the angles. Write your estimates in the **Estimate** column.

6 Now swap tables with your neighbour. Fill in the **Actual** column for them. Use the measurements you made earlier. Then swap back.

7 Now fill in your own **Error** column.

Example	Estimate = 40°, actual = 32°.
Working	Error = 40° − 32°
Answer	Error = 8°.

8 Use this table to fill in your **Rating** for each angle.

Error	Rating
more than 20°	poor
11° to 20°	fair
6° to 10°	good
2° to 5°	very good
0° or 1°	brilliant!

9 Compare your ratings with your neighbour. Add up all the numbers in your **Error** columns. Who was better at estimating?

10 Keep the angle sheet that your neighbour gave you.

Practice

(H) **1** Estimate the angles inside these shapes.

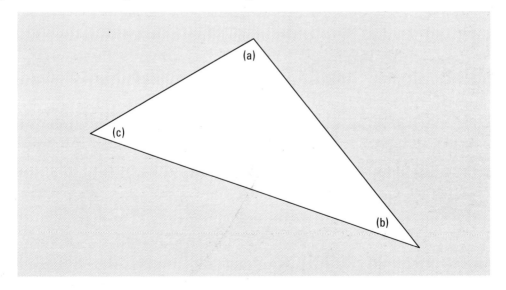

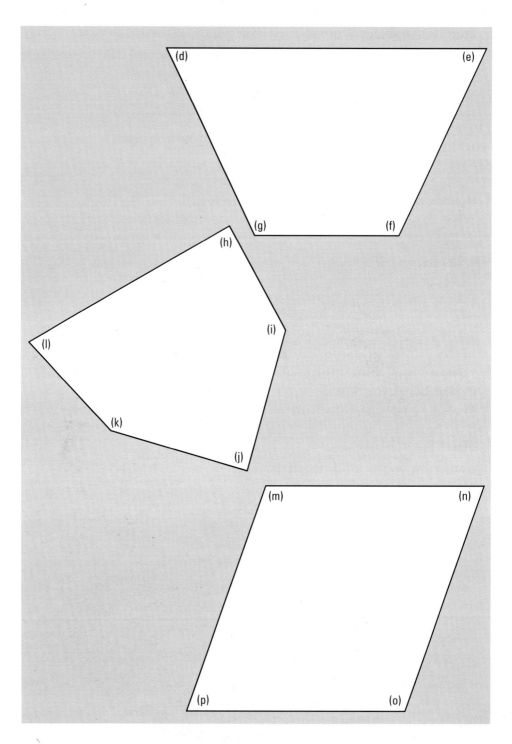

2 Measure the angles with your protractor.

1 Estimate the angles cut into the pies and cake.

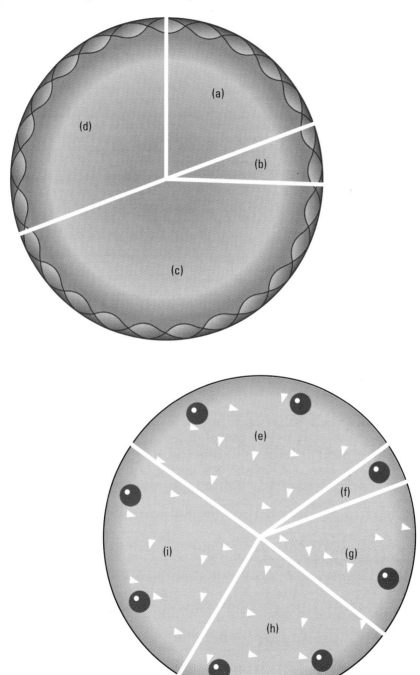

2 Measure the angles with your protractor.

Finished Early?
➡ Go to page 368

Further Practice

J Estimate these angles, then measure them. Measure each angle twice, with your outer and inner scales. This will help you check that you are right. Turn the book round if it helps.

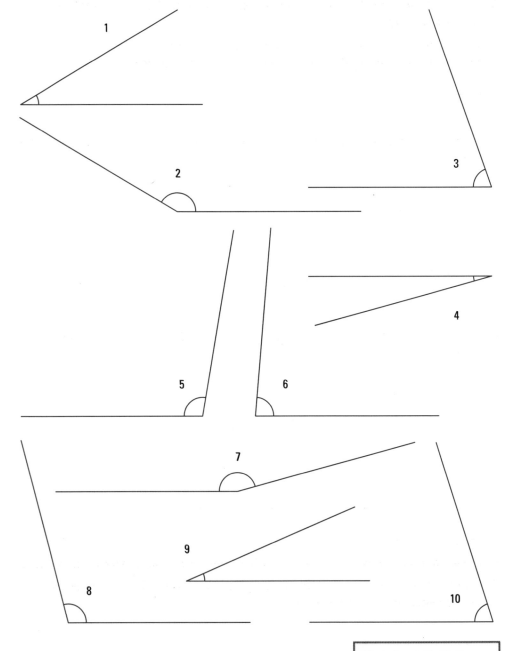

Finished Early?
Go to page 368

❸ Drawing Angles

Protractor, ruler

Learn About It

1 Follow these steps to draw an angle. Read through the steps carefully, then do it yourself.

2 Leave about half a page empty. Start with a base line for the angle. Put a mark in the middle. This mark is blue on the diagram.

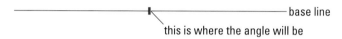

base line

this is where the angle will be

3 Place your protractor as shown. Mark 65° at the edge of the protractor. This mark is red on the diagram.

mark at 65°

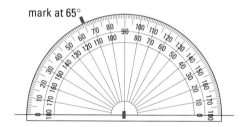

4 Take the protractor away. Join the blue mark to the red mark. Carry the line on a bit further.

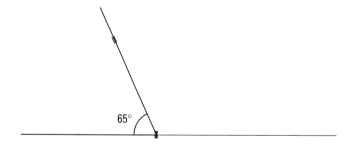

65°

5 Label the angle.

6 Leave another half page. Draw a new base line. Put a mark near in the middle.

7 Draw another 65° angle as shown on page 220. You will need to use the **other scale** on your protractor.

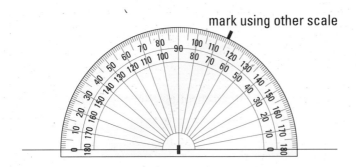

mark using other scale

8 Repeat all of these steps with 115°. They should look like this.

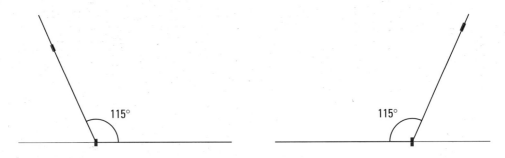

115°   115°

 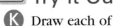 ## Try It Out

K Draw each of these angles twice, using both scales on your protractor.

1 30°   **2** 100°   **3** 85°   **4** 165°   **5** 43°   **6** 132°

Now swap with a neighbour. Measure their angles with your protractor.
Mark their work.

Practice

L Each question has two angles. Draw a base line and make two marks 6 cm
apart. Draw the first angle at the left mark and the second one at the right.
Carry the lines on far enough to cross. This makes a triangle. Measure the
length of these two lines, from the base line to where they cross.

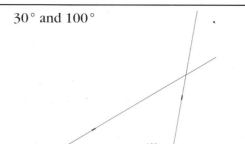

Example 30° and 100°
Working

Answer 7.7 cm and 3.9 cm

1 30° and 60°   **2** 50° and 50°   **3** 25° and 35°   **4** 140° and 20°
5 60° and 60°   **6** 90° and 45°   **7** 22° and 110°   **8** 77° and 41°

M Draw these diagrams accurately.

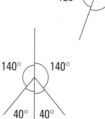

1   2   3
4   5   6

Finished Early?
➡ Go to page 368

Further Practice

N Draw each of these angles twice, using both scales on your protractor.

1 30°   **2** 100°   **3** 80°   **4** 65°   **5** 45°
6 135°   **7** 37°   **8** 82°   **9** 113°   **10** 13°

O Using a base line of 7 cm, use these angles to draw triangles. Measure the two new sides of each triangle, from the base line to where they cross.
For an example, see Practice **L** above.

1 30°, 50°   **2** 40°, 40°   **3** 15°, 55°   **4** 110°, 20°
5 65°, 65°   **6** 38°, 92°   **7** 14°, 152°   **8** 64°, 46°

Finished Early?
➡ Go to page 368

21 Angle Relationships

In this chapter you will learn about ...
- **1** angles together on a straight line
- **2** angles in a triangle
- **3** angles around a point

P **1** Angles on a Straight Line

 Ruler, protractor

Learn About It

1 A 180° angle is called a **straight angle** because its arms make a straight line.

Draw a horizontal line about 10 cm long. Leave about 5 cm space clear above it. Make a mark in the middle, like this.

2 Now add a line like this. It 'cuts' the straight angle into two parts.

These are called **adjacent** angles.

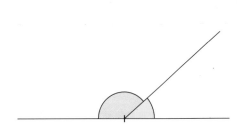

3 With your protractor, measure the angle on the left of the cut (our blue angle). Now measure the angle on the right (our yellow angle). They should add up to 180°.

4 Draw another two similar diagrams. Put the 'cut' in a different place each time.
Record all your measurements in a table.

Angle on left	Angle on right	Total, left + right

5 Whenever you cut a straight angle into pieces, the pieces still make 180°.

Key Fact

Angles together on a straight line add up to 180°.
Adjacent angles add up to 180°.

Word Check

angle an amount of turning
straight angle half a complete turn, 180°
adjacent angles angles together on a straight line

Try It Out

Example Find the missing angle in this diagram.

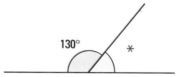

Working $130° + {}^* = 180°$
$130° + 50° = 180°$

Answer ${}^* = 50°$

1

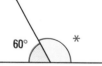

2

3

4

5

6

7

8

B What angle goes with the given angle to make 180°?

Example:	45°
Working:	180° – 45° = 135°
Answer:	135°

1 30° **2** 50° **3** 15° **4** 45° **5** 130°

6 120° **7** 105° **8** 155° **9** 57° **10** 71°

11 99° **12** 104° **13** 162° **14** 116° **15** 147°

Practice

C Aidan's homework was about angles on a straight line. He was supposed to make the angles in each diagram add up to 180°. He got some right and some wrong. In each question, work out the total of the angles and write it down. Then give it a ✓ or a ✗.

1

60° 120°

2

25° 155°

3

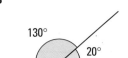

130° 20°

4

110° 40°

5

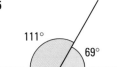

111° 69°

6

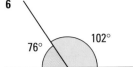

76° 102°

7

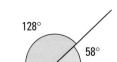

128° 58°

8

54° 166°

How many did Aidan get right?

D You can have more than two angles on a straight line. All the angles together still add up to 180°.

Some of the diagrams have been turned round to make them look different. You still find the answers in the same way.

Some questions have more than one *. In each question every * is the same size angle.

Example

Working   50° + 30° = 80°
                180° – 80° = 100° (find what is left)

Answer   * = 100°

1

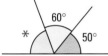

60°   50°   *

2

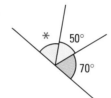

*   50°   70°

3

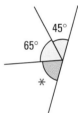

45°   65°   *

4

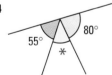

80°   55°   *

5

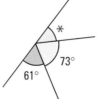

*   73°   61°

6

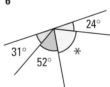

24°   31°   52°   *

7

82°   *   *

8

*   65°   *

Finished Early?
 Go to page 369

Further Practice

E Find the missing angle in each diagram.

1
60° *

2
80° *

3
* 130°

4
* 155°

5
* 67°

6
126° *

7
60° * 70°

8
62° 50° *

Finished Early?
➡ Go to page 369

T 2 Angles in a Triangle

Learn About It

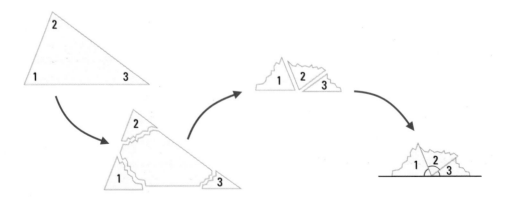

You can put the angles at the vertices (corners) of a triangle together to make a straight angle. This means that the angles in a triangle always add up to 180°.

Key Fact

Angles in a triangle add up to 180°.

Word Check

vertex a corner of a shape

vertices more than one vertex

triangle a flat shape with 3 straight sides

You can use this fact to help you work out an angle you don't know.

Try It Out

F Sally-Anne was supposed to make the angles in each triangle add up to 180°. She has got some of them right and some wrong. For each question, write down the total of Sally-Anne's angles, then give it a ✓ or a ✗.

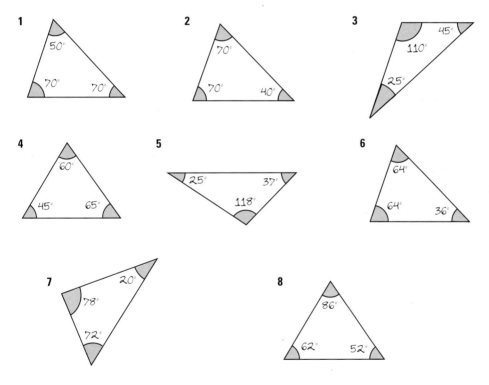

How many did Sally-Anne get right?

Learn More About It

Special Triangles

In an **isosceles** triangle, two angles are the same.

In an **equilateral** triangle, all three angles are the same (60°).

In a **right-angled** triangle, one angle is 90°.

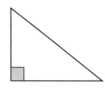

A **scalene** triangle has three different angles.

Word Check

isosceles a triangle with two angles the same

equilateral a triangle with all three angles the same

scalene a triangle with three different angles

Try It Out

G Here are the angles in some triangles. For each triangle, write down what type it is and why.

1 60°, 30°, 90°

2 120°, 30°, 30°

3 70°, 75°, 35°

4 80°, 50°, 50°

5 80°, 80°, 20°

6 46°, 123°, 11°

7 54°, 111°, 54°

8 90°, 45°, 45°

9 60°, 60°, 60°

10 32°, 116°, 32°

Practice

 Work out the missing angles in these triangles.

Example

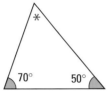

Working $70° + 50° + * = 180°$
  so $120° + * = 180°$
  $120° + 60° = 180°$

Answer $* = 60°$

1

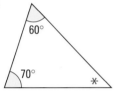

2

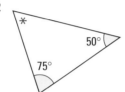

3

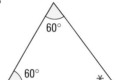

4

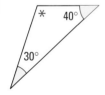

5

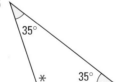

6

7

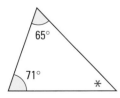

8

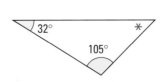

I These triangles are all special types.

Make a sketch of each one. Work out the missing angles, then write down what type it is.

> **Example**
>
>
>
> **Working**   180° – 40° = 140° (*2 × angle* *)
>   140° ÷ 2 = 70°
>
> **Answer**   * = 70°
> **Check**   40° + 70° + 70° = 180°

1

45°

2

60°

3

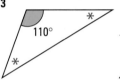

110°

4

76°

5

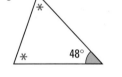

48°

6

28°

7

8

22°

9

10

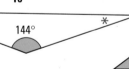

144°

11

36°

> **Finished Early?**
> ➡ Go to page 370

Further Practice

J Draw five different triangles. Make them quite big (about two on a page). Label the corners of each one A, B and C, like this.

A ——————— B

C

Measure the angles in each triangle. Record them in a table like this.

Angle A	Angle B	Angle C	Total, A + B + C

To fill in the last column, add up the angles you've measured. You should get answers very close to 180°.

K In each question, you are given two angles from a triangle. Find the other one. If it helps, draw a sketch of each triangle.

1 30°, 80°	**2** 80°, 90°	**3** 20°, 20°	**4** 40°, 60°
5 130°, 20°	**6** 140°, 30°	**7** 105°, 45°	**8** 32°, 42°
9 162°, 12°	**10** 74°, 45°	**11** 16°, 18°	**12** 147°, 3°

> **Finished Early?**
> ➡ Go to page 370

❸ Angles Round a Point

Learn About It

1 Sheena faces North, then makes a full turn. She has turned through 360°.

She faces North and turns until she is facing South-East.
She has turned through 135°.

N

(a)
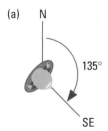

(b)
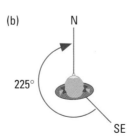

To face North again she turns through 225°.

The angles she turned through, together, make a full turn.

$135° + 225° = 360°$.

2 Measure the angles in this diagram.

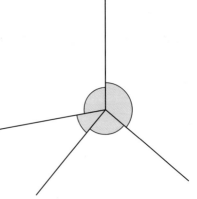

Write them down and add them
together. Do you get 360°?

3 Draw two diagrams like this.
You can have as many lines as you like.
Make sure they all meet at a single point.
Measure and label the angles.
Do you get 360°?

> # Key Fact
> Angles round a point add up
> to 360°.

4 You can use this to work out an angle you don't know.

> **Example**
>
>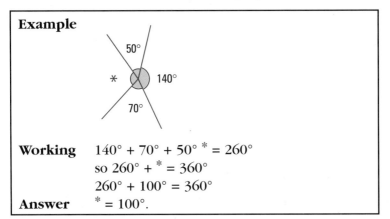
>
> **Working** $140° + 70° + 50°$ * $= 260°$
> so $260° +$ * $= 360°$
> $260° + 100° = 360°$
> **Answer**   * $= 100°$.

5 This means that you can measure
reflex angles easily.
These lines make an obtuse angle
and a reflex one.
Measure the obtuse angle with
your protractor.
Now subtract your measurement
from 360°. This is the reflex angle.

Try It Out

L Work out whether each pie chart is possible or impossible.

1
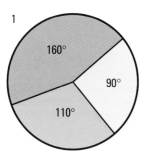

2
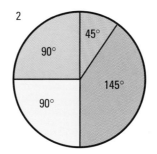

3
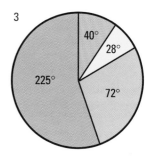

4
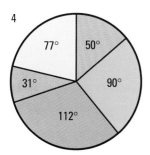

5
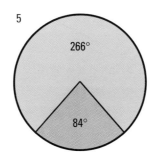

6
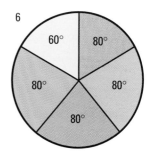

Learn More About It

1 You can now measure **reflex** angles.

These lines make an obtuse angle and a reflex one.

Measure the obtuse angle with your protractor.

Now subtract your measurement from 360°. This is the reflex angle.

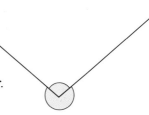

2 Draw a reflex angle of 310°.

Try It Out

180° Protractor

 Measure these reflex angles.

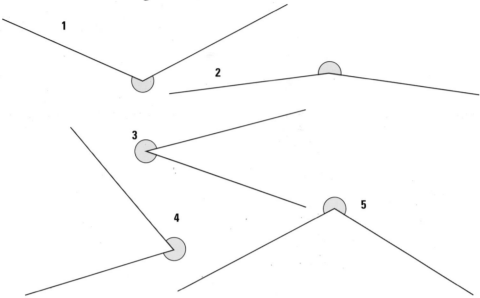

N Practice

Copy the diagrams, work out the missing angles and mark them on your diagrams.

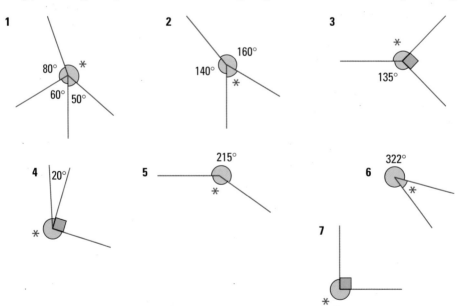

Draw these reflex angles.

1 190° **2** 270° **3** 330° **4** 205° **5** 305° **6** 197° **7** 234° **8** 298°

> **Finished Early?**
> ⇨ Go to page 371

Further Practice

Copy the diagrams, work out the missing angles and mark them on your diagrams.

1
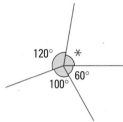

2
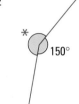

3
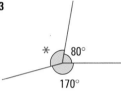

4
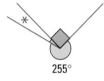

5
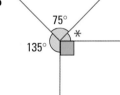

6
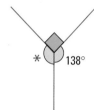

7

Q Measure these reflex angles.

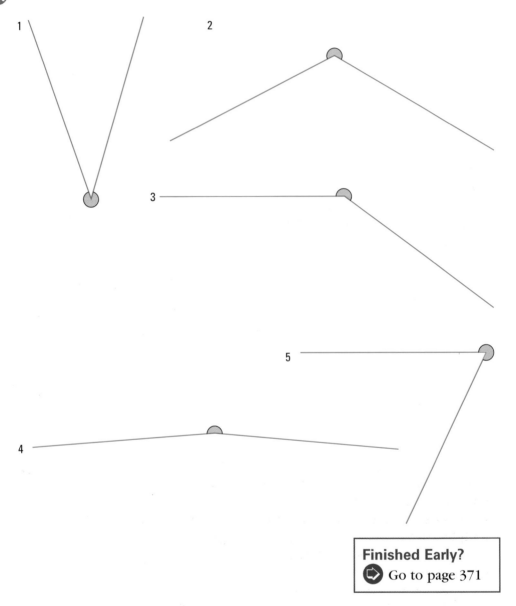

1

2

3

5

4

Finished Early?
➡ Go to page 371

Unit 10 *Angles*

Summary of Chapters 20 and 21

- There are different types of angles.

Type of angle	Size
acute	up to 90°
right	exactly 90°
obtuse	more than 90°, up to 180°
straight	exactly 180°
reflex	more than 180°, up to 360°
whole turn	exactly 360°

- To estimate angles, use right angles and 45° angles. Imagine an 8-pointed star, like the one above.
- Always check that you are using the correct scale on your protractor. Look at the type of angle. Is the answer sensible?
- Angles on a straight line add up to 180°.

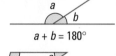

$a + b = 180°$

- Angles in a triangle add up to 180°. $c + d + e = 180°$
- **Scalene** triangles have all three angles different.
- **Isosceles** triangles have two angles the same.
- **Equilateral** triangles have all three angles the same (60°).
- **Right-angled** triangles have one right angle.
- Angles around a point add up to 360°.
- To measure a reflex angle:
  1. Measure the acute or obtuse angle.
  2. Subtract it from 360°.
- To draw a reflex angle:
  1. Subtract it from 360°.
  2. Draw the acute or obtuse angle.

$f + g + h + i = 360°$

22 Multiples and Factors

In this chapter you will learn …
1. when one number is a multiple of another number
2. when one number is a factor of another number
3. about special kinds of numbers called prime numbers and square numbers

P 1 Multiples

 A *Hundred Grids* sheet

Learn About It

1. The numbers 2, 4, 6, 8, 10, … are from the 2× table. They are called **multiples** of 2. **Multiples** comes from **multiply**.

2. This is a *hundred grid*. Some multiples of 2 have been coloured yellow. On a copy of this grid, colour in all the multiples of 2 you can find. Use light colours.

1	2	3	4	5	6	7	8	9	10
11	12	13	14	15	16	17	18	19	20
21	22	23	24	25	26	27	28	29	30
31	32	33	34	35	36	37	38	39	40
41	42	43	44	45	46	47	48	49	50
51	52	53	54	55	56	57	58	59	60
61	62	63	64	65	66	67	68	69	70
71	72	73	74	75	76	77	78	79	80
81	82	83	84	85	86	87	88	89	90
91	92	93	94	95	96	97	98	99	100

3. The numbers 3, 6, 9, … are numbers from the 3× table. They are the multiples of 3. On this grid, they have been coloured green. Copy and finish this colouring on another grid.

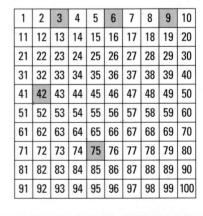

1	2	3	4	5	6	7	8	9	10
11	12	13	14	15	16	17	18	19	20
21	22	23	24	25	26	27	28	29	30
31	32	33	34	35	36	37	38	39	40
41	42	43	44	45	46	47	48	49	50
51	52	53	54	55	56	57	58	59	60
61	62	63	64	65	66	67	68	69	70
71	72	73	74	75	76	77	78	79	80
81	82	83	84	85	86	87	88	89	90
91	92	93	94	95	96	97	98	99	100

Try It Out

A Use more grids to colour in multiples of
4, then 5, then 6, ... up to 12.

B Look for patterns in the grids you have coloured. Write a sentence to describe
each pattern you find. Try to find at least one for each multiple.

Word Check

multiples of a number are
the numbers in its
multiplication table, e.g.
multiples of 4 are 4, 8, 12, 16.

Learn More About It

1 Multiples of 2 Look at your grid of multiples of 2. Look at the units of
each one. They have something in common. Write down what it is.

2 Multiples of 10 To check if a number is a multiple of 10, look at the units
digit. Multiples of 10 have something in common. Write down what it is.

3 Multiples of 5 To check if a number is a multiple of 5, look at the units
digit. Multiples of 5 have something in common. Write down what it is.

4 Multiples of 3 To check if a number is a multiple of 3, you need to work
out its digit sum. Every number has a **digit sum**. Add all the digits in the
number together. Do this again and again until you have just a single digit.
This is the digit sum.

Example	Find the digit sum of 174.
Working	1 + 7 + 4 = 12 (This has two digits, so do it again.)
	1 + 2 = 3 (This has one digit, so you've finished.)
Answer	The digit sum of 174 is 3.

Look at your grid of multiples of 3. Work out five of the digit sums.
They should all have something in common. Write down what it is.

5 Multiples of 9 To check if a number is a multiple of 9, you need digit sums
again. Investigate the multiples of 9.

Try It Out

C Test all the numbers in each cloud to see if they are multiples of the middle number.

Write down the ones that **are** multiples.

Show any working you do.

Cloud 1 (middle **2**): 266, 85, 723, 6310, 15 346, 3767, 2202, 53, 65 536, 534, 54, 225 377, 1024, 12 345, 5600, 80

Cloud 2 (middle **3**): 132, 59, 357, 777, 502, 63, 1086, 735, 4522, 155 620, 613, 252, 3345, 561, 66 027, 19 542, 881

Cloud 3 (middle **5**): 6125, 55, 1202, 234, 6510, 300, 256, 77 634, 4505, 1000, 532, 15 437, 2555, 446 000, 3564

Cloud 4 (middle **9**): 81, 561, 1521, 2800, 2134, 279, 105 508, 42, 1053, 600, 216, 92, 900, 8181, 120 550, 531, 31 113, 441

Cloud 5 (middle **10**): 5262, 155, 130, 6000, 700, 5780, 5479, 520, 124, 5783, 120, 28 080, 25 501, 3200, 377, 455

Practice

D In this cloud, there are multiples of different numbers.

Find as many numbers as you can that are …

1 multiples of 2   **2** multiples of 10   **3** multiples of 5
4 multiples of 3   **5** multiples of 9   **6** multiples of 20.

Note: some numbers can be used for more than one question.

3045   5715   165
18 015   246   521 685   69 558   1 043 370
2286   173 895   347 790   1320   11 430
1845   1230   208 674   3690   1905   21 618
762   3810   990   15 240   144 120   869 475
36 030   7206
615   1 391 160   108 090
9525   495
738   330   66   90 075   198
54 045   4920   825

Finished Early?
➡ Go to page 372

Further Practice

E Test all the numbers on each block to see if they are multiples of the middle number.

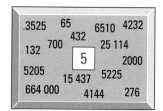

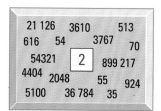

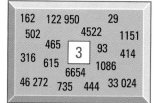

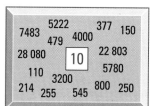

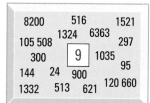

Write down the ones that **are** multiples.

Finished Early?
➡ Go to page 372

② Factors

Learn About It

Look at this arrangement of 12 flowers.

They are set out in 3 rows of 4.

The 12 flowers can be arranged differently.

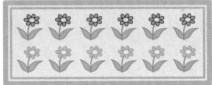

Now they are in 2 rows of 6.

Factors come in pairs, like 3 and 4, or 2 and 6.

3 and 4 are both **factors** of 12, because:
- 12 can be divided exactly by 3 **and** by 4
- 12 is a multiple of 3 **and also** a multiple of 4.

2 and 6 are also **factors** of 12, because …
- 12 can be divided exactly by 2 **and** by 6
- 12 is a multiple of 2 **and also** a multiple of 6.

1 and 12 are also a pair of factors.

> ### Word Check
> **factor of a number**
> any whole number that divides into it exactly, without leaving a remainder

You can show all of the factors in a **factor diagram**.

The diagram also shows how the factors link up together.

the numbers in the circles are factors of 12

this shows that 2 and 6 make a pair

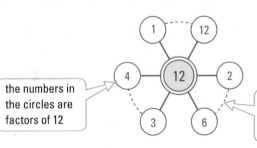

Try It Out

F You have a number of square tiles. Find all the different rectangles that you can make.

Use a factor diagram to help, then put the factors in order.
The number in brackets tells you how many rectangles to find.

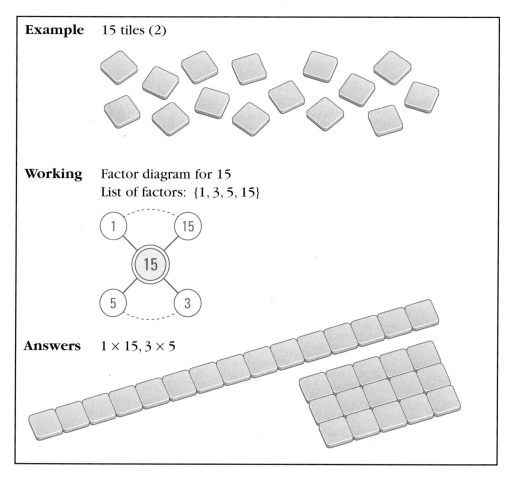

Example   15 tiles (2)

Working   Factor diagram for 15
List of factors: {1, 3, 5, 15}

Answers   1 × 15, 3 × 5

1 6 tiles (2)	**2** 8 tiles (2)	**3** 10 tiles (2)	**4** 12 tiles (3)
5 14 tiles (2)	**6** 18 tiles (3)	**7** 20 tiles (3)	**8** 22 tiles (2)
9 24 tiles (4)	**10** 27 tiles (2)	**11** 30 tiles (4)	**12** 50 tiles (3)

Practice

G Answer *yes* or *no* to these questions.

If the answer is *yes*, find the other factor that pairs up with the one in the question.

Example	Is 4 a factor of 28?
Working	See if 4 will divide exactly into 28.
	$28 \div 4 = 7$ (exactly).
Answer	*yes*, 4 is a factor of 28. The other factor in the pair is 7.

1 Is 2 a factor of 36?   **2** Is 3 a factor of 36?   **3** Is 5 a factor of 21?

4 Is 10 a factor of 230?   **5** Is 6 a factor of 15?   **6** Is 9 a factor of 45?

7 Is 4 a factor of 222?   **8** Is 7 a factor of 56?   **9** Is 8 a factor of 56?

10 Is 12 a factor of 132?   **11** Is 11 a factor of 132?   **12** Is 15 a factor of 235?

13 Is 20 a factor of 150?   **14** Is 100 a factor of 400?   **15** Is 25 a factor of 375?

16 Is 30 a factor of 370?   **17** Is 50 a factor of 600?   **18** Is 60 a factor of 600?

H Find the missing factors from these lists. The factors have been written in order of size. They are inside curly brackets. You could draw factor diagrams to help.

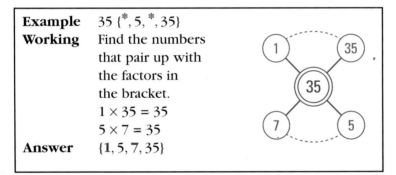

Example	35 {*, 5, *, 35}
Working	Find the numbers that pair up with the factors in the bracket.
	$1 \times 35 = 35$
	$5 \times 7 = 35$
Answer	{1, 5, 7, 35}

1 86 {1, *, 43, *}

2 75 {1, *, 5, *, 25, 75}

3 96 {1, 2, *, 4, *, *, 12, 16, *, 32, *, 96}

4 78 {1, *, *, 6, *, *, 39, 78}

5 102 {1, 2, *, 6, *, 34, *, *}

6 124 {1, 2, *, 31, *, *}

Finished Early?
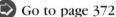 Go to page 372

Further Practice

Jim has to plant bulbs in straight rows. He must have the same number of bulbs in each row. Find all the different ways that he can do it.

Use a factor diagram to help, then put the factors in order.

The number in brackets tells you how many ways to find.

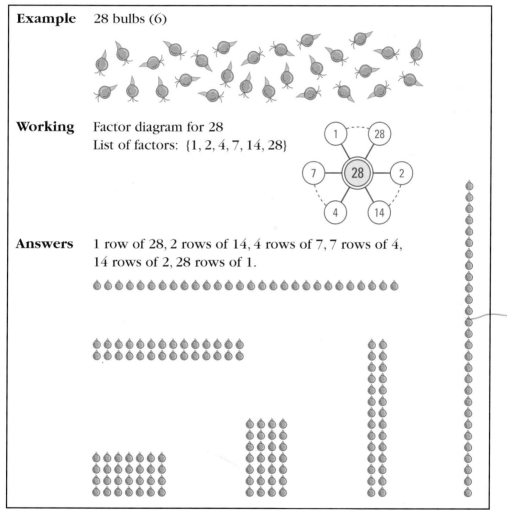

Example   28 bulbs (6)

Working   Factor diagram for 28

List of factors: {1, 2, 4, 7, 14, 28}

Answers   1 row of 28, 2 rows of 14, 4 rows of 7, 7 rows of 4, 14 rows of 2, 28 rows of 1.

1 45 bulbs (6)   **2** 60 bulbs (12)   **3** 70 bulbs (8)   **4** 72 bulbs (12)

5 80 bulbs (10)   **6** 88 bulbs (8)   **7** 140 bulbs (12)   **8** 250 bulbs (8)

9 360 bulbs (24)   **10** 432 bulbs (20)

Finished Early?
Go to page 372

P ③ Squares and Primes

Learn About It

1 You can make a pattern of dots from a number.
It helps to know what the factors are.
Look at 15. You can make rectangles.

3 rows of 5 dots:    5 rows of 3 dots:

You can make them because 3 and 5 are factors of 15.
You can also make a long line: 1 row of 15 dots:

The factor diagram for 15 looks like this:

2 Here is a rectangle with 16 dots:
There are 2 rows of 8 dots.

You can also make a long line: 1 row of 16 dots:

Here is another way of arranging 16 dots:
It is a square. There are 4 rows of 4 dots.
There are only a few numbers that do this.
They are called **square numbers**.

Look at the factor diagram for 16:

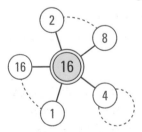

4 is a '**solo factor**'. It has to be joined
to itself.

> **Key Fact**
> Square numbers make square patterns.

> **Key Fact**
> Square numbers have one solo factor.

3 4 is being multiplied by itself. Remember that you can use a power to write this.

$4 \times 4 = 4^2$. You say 'four **squared**'.

4 Draw a dot pattern and a factor diagram for 9.

Word Check

square number made by multiplying numbers by themselves

squared (^{2}) multiplied by itself

solo factor a factor that doesn't belong in a pair

Try It Out

Squared paper

1 Write down a list of all the square numbers up to 100. (Don't panic - there are only 10!)

Start like this: $1^2 = 1 \times 1 = 1$

$2^2 = 2 \times 2 = 4$, etc.

2 Draw a dot pattern for each one.

3 Draw a factor diagram for each one.

Learn More About It

1 Some numbers can **only** be drawn in a line, like 7:

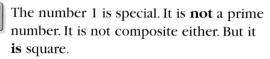

These numbers are called **prime** numbers.

The factor diagram for 7 looks like this:

There are only two factors.

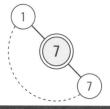

2 Draw a dot pattern and a factor diagram for 5.

3 Numbers that make rectangles or squares of dots are called **composite** numbers.

The number 1 is special. It is **not** a prime number. It is not composite either. But it **is** square.

Key Fact

Prime numbers only have two factors: 1 and the number itself.

Key Fact

Composite numbers have more than two factors.

Word Check

prime number can only be divided by 1 or itself: makes lines of dots only

composite number has more than 2 factors: makes rectangular or square dot patterns

Try It Out

1 To make a list of prime numbers, you need to test each number in turn. There are two kinds of numbers you **don't** need to test. What are they?

2 Work through the numbers from 1 to 50. Draw dot patterns if you need to. Each time you find a prime number, add it to your list.

3 **(a)** What is the biggest prime number below 50?
   (b) What is the first prime number after 50?

4 **(a)** What is the biggest prime number below 100?
   (b) What is the first prime number after 100?

Practice

Test each of these numbers to see what kind it is. Draw dot patterns if you wish.
If it is prime, write *prime*.
If it is composite, write *composite*. List its factors.
A composite number might also be square. Check this. If it is, write *square* as well.

Example	39
Working	$39 = 3 \times 13$
Answer	39 is composite. Its factors are 1, 3, 13, 39.

1 53	**2** 63	**3** 73	**4** 101	**5** 111	**6** 121
7 134	**8** 144	**9** 154	**10** 149	**11** 159	**12** 169
13 215	**14** 225	**15** 235	**16** 301	**17** 311	**18** 321

Further Practice

Hundred grid

1 On a blank *hundred grid*, colour in all the square numbers you can find.
2 Now work out the square numbers between 101 and 200 (there are only 4!)
3 On another grid, colour all the prime numbers up to 50. You could use your list from Try It Out **K**.
4 Now work out which of the numbers between 50 and 100 are prime. Colour these squares on your grid.

Test each of these numbers to see what kind it is. Draw dot patterns if you wish.

If it is prime, write *prime*.
If it is composite, write *composite*. List its factors.
A composite number might also be square. Check this. If it is, write *square* as well.

1 21	**2** 31	**3** 41	**4** 33	**5** 43	**6** 53
7 120	**8** 123	**9** 125	**10** 147	**11** 150	**12** 196

Finished Early?
➡ Go to page 373

23 Patterns and Sequences

In this chapter you will learn about ...
1. number patterns
2. rules for patterns
3. writing rules using formulas

① Number Patterns

Learn About It

1 These telephone numbers are easy to remember. Each has some kind of pattern. Fill in the missing numbers so that they have a pattern. There may be more than one possible answer.

Now make up your own special telephone number.

Telephone Numbers

Gas	123321
Water	456456
Electricity	987654
Doctor	1122
Taxi	5252
Builders	7777
Council	024
Garage	1999
Hospital	1357

2 Here are the number patterns you already know. Copy and complete the list. Use a whole page of your exercise book.

You can add new number patterns later.

3 Write down the next two numbers for each pattern in your list.

Number Patterns

Counting numbers	1,2,3,4,5
Even numbers	2,4,6,8,10
Odd numbers	1,3,5,7,9
Multiples of 3	3,6,9,12,15
Multiples of 5	
Multiples of 10	
Square numbers	1,4,9,16

4 Copy these dot triangles.
The numbers of dots are called **triangular numbers**.
Draw the next two dot triangles. Write the triangular numbers underneath.

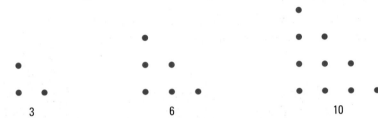

1   3   6   10

 A4 sheet of paper

5 Fold a sheet of paper in half. Fold it in half
again, as many times as you can. Open out the
sheet and count the number of rectangles. It
should be one of these numbers.

2   4   8   16   32   ...

Let's call these **doubling numbers**.
With each fold you double the number of rectangles.
What are the next two numbers?

6 Most number patterns do not have special names.
Each new section of fence needs 3 more pieces of wood.

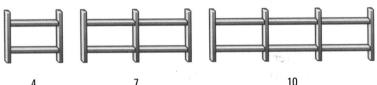

4   7   10

These numbers increase by 3 at a time.
Draw the next two fence patterns.
Write their numbers underneath.

Try It Out

 1 Write down the name of each of these number patterns. You may need
to look at your list.

(a) 1   4   9   16   25   (b) 4   8   12   16   20
(c) 1   3   5   7   9   (d) 1   3   6   10   15

These number patterns do not start at the beginning. Write down their names.

(e) 6   8   10   12   14   (f) 6   9   12   15   18
(g) 4   9   16   25   36   (h) 15   20   25   30   35

2 Sui Fung is given £10 for his birthday. He adds £3 each week.
    Savings   £10   £13   ...
Write down his savings for the next four weeks.

Practice

B **1** Each row of dominoes pushes over the next. The numbers show the toppled dominoes.

(a) Write down the first five numbers in the pattern.

(b) What is the name of this number pattern?

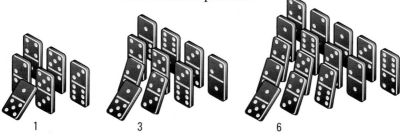

1   3   6

2 (a) Copy and complete these calculations.

$1 = 1$

$1 + 2 + 1 = 4$

$1 + 2 + 3 + 2 + 1 =$

$1 + 2 + 3 + 4 + 3 + 2 + 1 =$

$1 + 2 + 3 + 4 + 5 + 4 + 3 + 2 + 1 =$

(b) What pattern do the answers make?

(c) Find the next two numbers.

3 Here are some matchstick patterns.

(a) Copy the patterns.

(b) Draw the next two patterns.

(c) Write the numbers underneath.

(d) What is the number pattern called?

(i)
3   5

(ii)
3   1

(iii)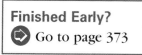
3

(iv)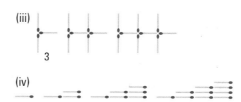

Finished Early?

➡ Go to page 373

Further Practice

1 Write down the names of these number patterns. Look at your list if you need to. Copy the patterns and fill in the missing numbers.

(a) $8, \ldots, 10, 11, 12$

(b) $2, 4, 6, \ldots, 10$

(c) $1, \ldots, 6, 10, 15$

(d) $1, 4, \ldots, 16, 25$

(e) $5, 10, 15, \ldots, 25$

(f) $1, \ldots, 2, 3, 5, \ldots$

(g) $6, 9, 12, \ldots, 18$

(h) $10, 9, \ldots, 7, 6$

2 These brick walls are being built. For each one write down …

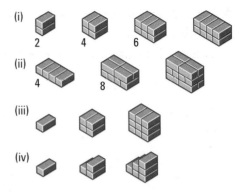

(a) the numbers of bricks

(b) the name of the number pattern

(c) the next two numbers in the pattern.

3 Rafiq works 10 hours for a gardener in the summer holidays. The gardener offers Rafiq three ways of being paid.

A 50p each hour

B 1p the first hour, 2p the second hour, 4p the third hour, doubling each time

C 10p the first hour, 15p the next, 20p the next, 25p the next, and so on

(a) What are the names of the number patterns in B and C?

(b) Calculate the total amount Rafiq would be paid each way.

> **Finished Early?**
> ➡ Go to page 373

P ② Rules for Patterns

Learn About It

1 What is the next number in this pattern?

    2   5   8   11   14   ....

You need to know the **rule** to find it. The rule for this pattern is 'add 3'.

```
   +3      +3      +3      +3
  ⌢       ⌢       ⌢       ⌢
 2       5       8       11
```

2 You can write this rule as a number machine ⬛ +3 ⟫ .

This pattern starts with 2, so you can write it like this 2 ⬛ +3 ⟫ for short.

3 The number pattern 3 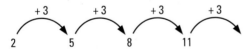 starts with 3 and has the rule 'add 2'.

Write down the next five numbers. Describe the number pattern.

4 Write down the first six numbers of the pattern 2  . Describe the number pattern.

5 This machine has printed a number pattern. What is the rule?

3   8   13   18   23   ?

You can often find the rule by looking at the **differences** between the numbers:

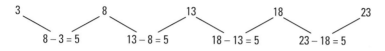

3   8   13   18   23

8 − 3 = 5   13 − 8 = 5   18 − 13 = 5   23 − 18 = 5

The rule is **+5** .

6 Calculate the differences. Write down the rule for this number pattern.

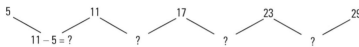

5   11   17   23   29

11 − 5 = ?   ?   ?   ?

7 Here are the first few triangular numbers.

1   3   6   10   15

+ 2   + 3   + 4   + 5   + 6

The differences also make a pattern. Work out the next three triangular numbers.

Word Check

rule tells you how to find the next number in a pattern.

difference the result of subtracting one number from another

Try It Out

1 Write down the first six numbers in these patterns. If the pattern has a name, write it down.

(a) 1 +2   (b) 11 +3   (c) 3 +4

(d) 6 +2   (e) 12 +4   (f) 20 −1

2 Find the rule for these patterns. If the pattern has a name, write it down.

(a) 4, 8, 12, 16 ?   (b) 0, 1, 2, 3, 4 ?

(c) 18, 24, 30, 36 ?   (d) 10, 12, 14, 16 ?

(e) 100, 90, 80, 70 ?   (f) 33, 30, 27, 24, 21 ?

Practice

E **1** Write down the first five numbers in these patterns. If you know the name of the pattern, write it down.

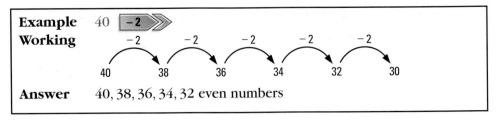

Example 40 | **– 2** ⟫
Working
$$-2 \qquad -2 \qquad -2 \qquad -2 \qquad -2$$
40   38   36   34   32   30

Answer 40, 38, 36, 34, 32 even numbers

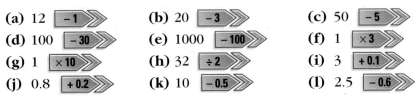

(a) 12 | **– 1** ⟫   (b) 20 | **– 3** ⟫   (c) 50 | **– 5** ⟫

(d) 100 | **– 30** ⟫   (e) 1000 | **– 100** ⟫   (f) 1 | **× 3** ⟫

(g) 1 | **× 10** ⟫   (h) 32 | **÷ 2** ⟫   (i) 3 | **+ 0.1** ⟫

(j) 0.8 | **+ 0.2** ⟫   (k) 10 | **– 0.5** ⟫   (l) 2.5 | **– 0.6** ⟫

2 There are five number patterns beginning with 30.

    (a) Write down the five number patterns, from beginning to end.
    (b) Write each number pattern using a number machine.

3 **(a)** Calculate the differences between the numbers of this pattern.

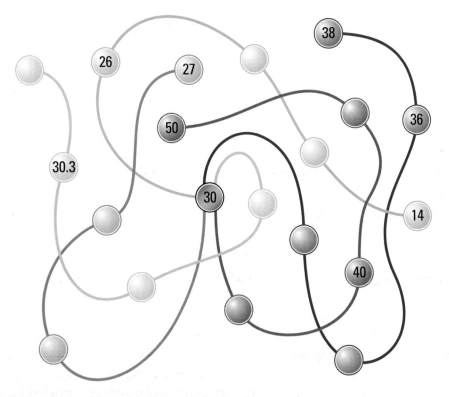

(b) Now find the next two numbers in the pattern.

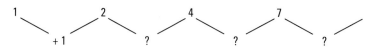

(c) Use differences to find the next two numbers in this pattern.

1 6 12 19 27 …

> **Finished Early?**
> ➡ Go to page 374

Further Practice

F

1 Each of these number patterns is in your list. Write down the first five numbers. If you know the name of the pattern, write it down.

(a) 1 [+2 »] (Start with 1. The rule is 'add 2'.)

(b) 2 [+2 »]   **(c)** 5 [+5 »]   **(d)** 2 [+0.5 »]   **(e)** 3 [×2 »]

(f) 500 [−50 »]   **(g)** 1 000 000 [÷10 »]   **(h)** 5 [−0.1 »]

2 Find the rules for these patterns.

(a) 5, 6, 7, 8, 9 [? »]

(b) 30, 40, 50, 60, 70 [? »]

(c) 4, 8, 12, 16, 20 [? »]

(d) 10, 9, 8, 7, 6 [? »]

(e) 20, 18, 16, 14 [? »]

(f) 100, 90, 80, 70 [? »]

(g) 5, 5.1, 5.2, 5.3 [? »]

(h) 1000, 900, 800, 700 [? »]

> **Finished Early?**
> ➡ Go to page 374

❸ Writing Rules Using Formulae

Learn About It

A **sequence** is a list of numbers in order. For example:

2 4 6 8 10 12 ….

Each number has a *position* in the sequence.

Position	1st	2nd	3rd	4th	5th	6th	…
Term	2	4	6	8	10	12	…

The numbers in a sequence are called **terms**. So, the 4th term is 8. And the 6th term is 12.

The numbers in this sequence are the even numbers. So, the 7th term is 14. And the 8th term is 16.

Word Check

sequence list of numbers in order

term one of the numbers in a sequence

Try It Out

G **1** Find the 3rd, 5th and 6th terms of 5, 7, 9, 11, 13 …

2 Find the 2nd, 4th and 6th terms of 20, 19, 18, 17, 16 …

3 Find the 1st, 6th and 7th terms of 5, 10, 15, 20, 25 …

4 Find the 5th and 6th terms of 1, 10, 100, 1000 …

Learn More About It

Ivor is investigating patterns made with matches.

   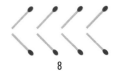

2   4   6   8

He counts the number of matches in each pattern.

The first pattern has 2 matches. The second pattern has 4 matches. And so on.

Ivor makes a table.

Pattern number	1st	2nd	3rd	4th
Number of matches	2	4	6	8

He notices that the number of matches is always twice the pattern number. For example, the 4th pattern has $2 \times 4 = 8$ matches.

So, Ivor knows that the 5th pattern will have $2 \times 5 = 10$ matches. And the 10th pattern will have $2 \times 10 = 20$ matches.

Ivor writes down a formula for finding the number of matches. The numbers go up in 2s, like the 2 times table. So the rule is $2 \times$.

Number of *M*atches = $2 \times$ pattern *n*umber

Then he writes the formula using letters.

$M = 2n$

Try It Out

H **1** Copy these matchstick patterns.

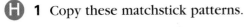

2 Write the number of matches underneath each pattern.

3 Copy and complete this table.

Pattern number, *n*	1st	2nd	3rd	4th
Number of matches, *M*				

What is the rule for the numbers of matches?

4 Write down a formula for finding the number of matches.

5 Write the formula using letters.

6 Use your formula to find the number of matches in the ...

   (a) 5th pattern   **(b)** 10th pattern   **(c)** 100th pattern.

Practice

1 Describe these patterns and find the terms. You may need to look at your list of number patterns.

   (a) Find the 3rd and 6th terms of $1, 3, 5, 7, \ldots$

   (b) Find the 5th and 6th terms of $9, 12, 15, 18 \ldots$

   (c) Find the 3rd and 5th terms of $1, 4, 9, 16 \ldots$

   (d) Find the 3rd, 7th and 20th terms of $1, 2, 3, 4, 5, 6 \ldots$

   (e) Find the 2nd and 5th terms of $1, 3, 6, 10 \ldots$

2 (a) Complete a table like this for each matchstick pattern.

Pattern number, *n*	1st	2nd	3rd	4th
Number of matches, *M*				

   (b) Find a formula for the number of matches. Write the formula using letters.

   (c) Use your formula to find the number of matches in the 20th pattern.

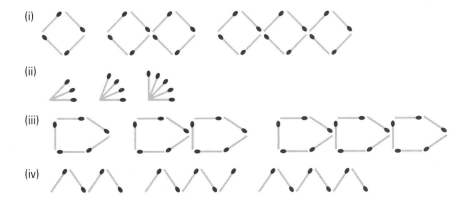

(i)

(ii)

(iii)

(iv)

3 Write down a formula that gives the terms of these sequences.
Use your formula to find the 20th term.

Example	4 8 12 16
Working	Write down the positions of the terms.

Position, n	1st	2nd	3rd	4th
Term, T	4	8	12	16

Answer	Term = $4 \times$ position or $T = 4n$
	20th term = $4 \times 20 = 80$

(a) 10   20   30   40   **(b)** 11   12   13   14

(c) 50   100   150   200   250   **(d)** 0.1   0.2   0.3   0.4

Finished Early?
➡ Go to page 374

Further Practice

J A shop sells four types of cassette tape. The tables show the cost of each type.
Find a formula for the cost of each type of tape. Write your formula using letters.

Example	Gold tapes

Number of tapes, n	1	2	3	4	5
Cost, £C	3	6	9	12	15

Working	The formula is: Cost = $3 \times$ number of tapes.
Answer	$C = 3n$

(a) Chromium Tapes

Number of tapes, n	1	2	3	4	5
Cost, £C	2	4	6	8	10

(b) Hi Band Tapes

Number of tapes, n	1	2	3	4	5
Cost, £C	4	5	6	7	8

(c) Pro Tapes

Number of tapes, n	1	2	3	4	5
Cost, £C	4	8	12	16	20

Finished Early?
➡ Go to page 374

Unit 11 *Number Relationships*

Summary of Chapters 22 and 23

- **Multiples**
  Multiples of 2: 2, 4, 6, 8, 10, 12, 14, ... units digit is 2, 4, 6, 8 or 0.
  Multiples of 3: 3, 6, 9, 12, 15, 18, 21, ... digit sum is 3, 6 or 9.
  Multiples of 5: 5, 10, 15, 20, 25, 30, ... units digit is 5 or 0.
  Multiples of 9: 9, 18, 27, 36, 45, 54, 63, ... digit sum is 9.
  Multiples of 10: 10, 20, 30, 40, 50, 60, 70, ... units digit is 0.
- **Factors** of a number are numbers that divide it exactly.
  The factors of 12 are {1, 2, 3, 4, 6, 12}.
- Factors come in **pairs**. The factor pairs for 12 are 1 and 12, 2 and 6, 3 and 4.
- Sometimes a factor pairs up with itself.
  The factors of 25 are {1, 5, 25}; 1 pairs with 25 and 5 pairs with 5.
  Numbers like this are the **square** numbers.
- **Prime** numbers have no factors except 1 and themselves.
  Prime numbers: 2, 3, 5, 7, 11, 13, 17, ...
  Numbers that are not prime are called **composite**.
- **Number Patterns**
  Counting numbers: 1, 2, 3, 4, 5, 6, 7, ...
  Even numbers: 2, 4, 6, 8, 10, 12, 14, ...
  Odd numbers: 1, 3, 5, 7, 9, 11, 13, ...
  Triangular numbers: 1, 3, 6, 10, 15, 21, 28, ...
  Square numbers: 1, 4, 9, 16, 25, 36, 49, ...
  Doubling numbers: 2, 4, 8, 16, 32, 64, 128, ...
- A **rule** tells you how to find the next number in a pattern.

Pattern number, *n*

Number of matches, *M*   3   6   9

The **formula** for this pattern is...
number of *M*atches = 3 × pattern *n*umber
or $M = 3n$

24 Length and Weight

In this chapter you will learn about …
1. length and distance
2. weight
3. converting units

P 1 Length

Learn About It

1 This ruler is marked in **centimetres (cm)**. A 1p coin is about 2 cm across.

(a) Copy this table.

Object	Length
Match	
Washing machine	

(b) Write these objects in your table, from shortest to longest. Two have been done for you.

(c) Match each object with a length. Write the answers in your table. Remember to write cm at the end of each length. The arrows show the lengths.

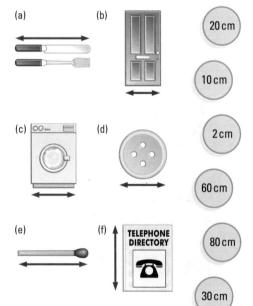

Ruler

2 There are 10 **millimetres (mm)** in a centimetre. A credit card is about 1 mm thick.

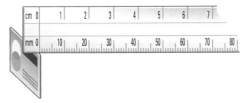

Use your ruler to measure these objects in millimetres. Write the answers in this table. Remember to write mm at the end of each length.

Object	Size
Thickness of a £1 coin	
Width of a paper clip	
Thickness of a piece of chalk	
Diameter of a 5p coin	
Width of a 1st class stamp	
Height of a first class stamp	

3 There are 100 centimetres in a **metre (m)**. A giant footstep is about 1 metre long.

Look at the descriptions on the next page.

Match each description with a length. Write them in a table, from smallest to largest. Remember to write m at the end of each length.

Word Check

diameter width of a circle

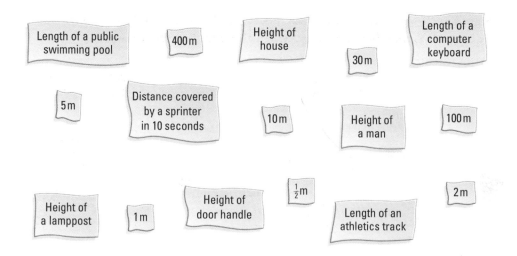

Length of a public swimming pool

400 m

Height of house

30 m

Length of a computer keyboard

5 m

Distance covered by a sprinter in 10 seconds

10 m

Height of a man

100 m

Height of a lamppost

1 m

Height of door handle

$\frac{1}{2}$ m

Length of an athletics track

2 m

4 There are 1000 metres in a **kilometre (km)**. You can walk a kilometre in about 10 minutes. **Estimate** how many kilometres the railway station is from your school. Write down your estimate. Compare it with your neighbour's estimate.

In many countries, long distances are measured in kilometres.

(a) Copy the table.

(b) Calculate the lengths of the train journeys. Write the answers in your table. Remember to write km at the end of each length.

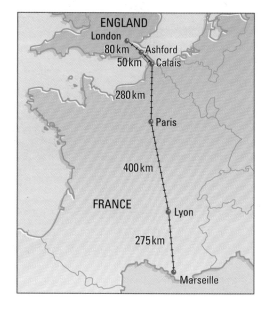

ENGLAND
London
80 km — Ashford
50 km — Calais
280 km
Paris
400 km
FRANCE
Lyon
275 km
Marseille

Journey	Distance
Marseille to Lyon	
Marseille to Paris	
Paris to London	
London to Marseille	

5 In the UK, long distances are still measured in **miles**. A mile is about $1\frac{1}{2}$ km. It takes about 15 minutes to walk a mile.

Match each description with a length. Write them in a table, from shortest to longest. Remember to write miles at the end of each distance.

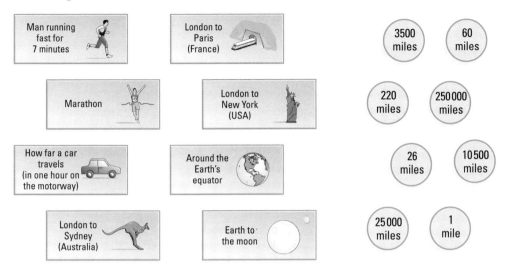

6 Millimetre (mm), centimetre (cm), metre (m), kilometre (km) and mile are called **units of length**.

Word Check

....

estimate your best guess

units of length millimetre (mm), centimetre (cm), metre (m), kilometre (km), mile

Try It Out

A Dana rushed her homework. She put all the lengths in the wrong places. Copy her table and put the lengths in the correct places. Remember to write the correct unit (mm, cm, m, km or miles) at the end of each length.

Description	Length or distance
Thickness of an exercise book	675 km
Thickness of this book	10 m
Length of a pencil	2 cm
Height of a front door	7 mm
Height of a lamppost	875 miles
Width of a public swimming pool	4 miles
Walk in England for 1 hour	2 m
Marseille to Paris	15 cm
North of Scotland to south of England	5 m

Practice

B **1** **(a)** Use a ruler to draw three lines between 1 cm and 15 cm long. Make sure they are an exact number of centimetres. Secretly write down their lengths.

  (b) Show the lines to your partner. They have to guess their lengths. Write down the guesses next to the exact lengths.

  (c) Swap around several times. Are your estimates improving?

  (d) Make more estimates using lines between 1 mm and 30 mm long.

2 Hold your hands apart. Guess the distance between them, in centimetres. Your partner can then measure the distance. Write down your guess and the exact length. Swap around several times.

> **Finished Early?**
> ⇨ Go to page 375

Further Practice

C **1** Choose the correct length or distance. Not all the circled lengths are used.

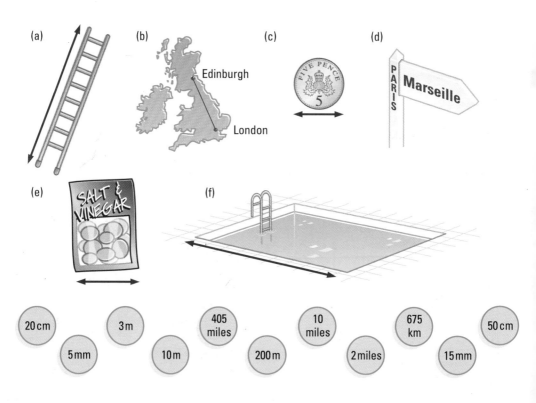

2 The distances on this map are in miles.

(a) Copy this table.

Journey	Length
Leeds to Liverpool	
London to Birmingham **via** Bristol	
London to Liverpool (shortest route)	
Bristol to London to Leicester to Leeds	
Round trip from London to all other places (shortest route)	

Leeds

Liverpool 70

95

100

Birmingham 40 Leicester

90 110 100

Bristol 115 London

(b) Calculate the lengths of the journeys. Write the answers in your table. Remember to write miles at the end of each length.

(c) Write down all the ways to get from Bristol to Leeds. You must not visit a place more than once.

(d) Work out the distance for each journey.

(e) Which is the shortest journey?

> **Word Check**
>
> **via** visiting

> **Finished Early?**
> ➡ Go to page 375

❷ Weight

Learn About It

1 Small objects are weighed in **grams (g)**.

2 Match each object with a weight. Write them in a table, from smallest to largest. Remember to write g at the end of each weight.

150 g   10 g

1 g   400 g

740 g   30 g

5 g   75 g

3 Heavier objects are measured using **kilograms (kg)**.

There are 1000 grams in a kilogram.

Match each object with a weight. Write them in a table, from smallest to largest. Remember to write kg at the end of each weight.

4 There are 1000 kilograms in a **tonne (t)**. A group of 15 adults weighs about a tonne.

Copy this table.

Use your table to help answer these questions. Remember to write t at the end of each weight.

Object	Weight
Small car	1 t
Range Rover	2.5 t
Minibus	5 t
Coach	15 t
Fire engine	25 t
Container lorry	50 t
Boeing 747	150 t

(a) A pick-up truck carries a small car and a Range Rover. What weight does it carry?

(b) Which weighs the most, 10 small cars or a coach?

(c) A coach contains 60 people. What is the total weight?

(d) A ferry carries 10 small cars, 2 Range Rovers, a minibus, 2 coaches and a container lorry. What weight does it carry?

5 Another word for weight is **mass**. Gram, kilogram and tonne are called **units of mass**.

Write down the missing units for these objects.

Word Check
....
mass another word for weight
units of mass gram (g),
    kilogram (kg) and tonne (t)

Try It Out

D Match each object with a weight. Write them in a table, from smallest to largest. Remember to write the correct unit (g, kg or t) at the end of each weight.

Practice

E

1 Choose an object from one of the tables in your exercise book. Secretly write it down with its weight. Ask your partner to guess its weight. Write down the guess next to the actual weight. Swap around several times.

2 One of you thinks of a familiar object, e.g. a cat. Both of you guess its weight. Write down your guesses. Decide whose estimate is best. Use the tables in your exercise book to help you. Take turns at choosing objects.

> **Finished Early?**
> ➡ Go to page 375

Further Practice

F

1 (a) List these objects in order, from lightest to heaviest.

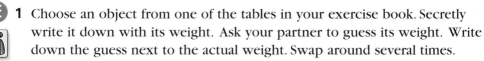

Child's racing bicycle	£1 coin
Minibus	1 litre bottle of water
Apple	Pencil
Heaviest weight lifted above head	Bag of shopping
Medium can of tomatoes	

(b) Find the weight of each object from the tables in your exercise book. Add the weights to your list.

2 Match each object with a weight. Write them in a table, from smallest to largest. Remember to write the correct unit (g, kg or t) at the end of each weight.

Finished Early?
➡ Go to page 375

⊤ ③ Converting Units

Learn About It

This ruler shows both centimetres (cm) and millimetres (mm).

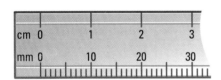

Centimetres (cm) are bigger units than millimetres (mm).
Each cm contains 10 mm.

So, 1 cm = 10 mm
2 cm = 2 lots of 10 mm = 2 × 10 mm = 20 mm
3 cm = 3 lots of 10 mm = 3 × 10 mm = 30 mm

To **convert** cm (bigger units) to mm (smaller units), *multiply* by 10.

Example	Convert 2.5 cm to mm
Working	2.5 × 10 = 25
Answer	2.5 cm = 25 mm

Example	Convert 0.7 cm to mm
Working	0.7 × 10 = 7
Answer	0.7 cm = 7 mm

To convert mm (smaller units) to cm (bigger units), *divide* by 10.

Example	Convert 30 mm to cm
Working	30 ÷ 10 = 3
	This shows there are 3 lots of 10 mm in 30 mm
Answer	30 mm = 3 cm

Example	Convert 23 mm to cm
Working	23 ÷ 10 = 2.3
Answer	23 mm = 2.3 cm

Key Fact

To convert bigger units to smaller units *divide*. mυιτιρυ

To convert smaller units to bigger units *multiply*. ∪ιΛιτↄ

Word Check

convert change

conversion table shows how many smaller units are contained in a bigger unit

The **conversion table** below helps you convert other units. It shows you the numbers to multiply and divide by.

Units of length
1 centimetre (cm) = 10 millimetres (mm)
1 metre (m) = 100 centimetres (cm)
1 kilometre (km) = 1000 metres (m)

Units of mass
1 kilogram (kg) = 1000 grams (g)
1 tonne (t) = 1000 kilograms (kg)

Try It Out

1 Convert the following units. Use the conversion table to help you.

(a) 3 km to m   (b) 2 kg to g   (c) 5 cm to mm

(d) 3 t to kg   (e) 2.4 cm to mm   (f) 20 m to cm

(g) 1.74 t to kg   (h) 5.83 km to m   (i) 4.125 kg to g

Example	Convert 2.3 kg to g
Working	To convert bigger units (kg) to smaller units (g), *multiply*. The conversion table shows: 1 kg = 1000 g. So, multiply by 1000. 2.3 × 1000 = 2300
Answer	2.3 kg = 2300 g

2 Convert the following units. Use the conversion table to help you.

(a) 700 cm to m   (b) 2000 g to kg   (c) 120 mm to cm

(d) 5000 kg to t   (e) 154 cm to m   (f) 5430 g to kg

(g) 17 mm to cm   (h) 2 mm to cm

Example	Convert 543 cm to m
Working	To convert smaller units (cm) to bigger units (m), *divide*. The conversion table shows: 1 m = 100 cm. So, divide by 100. $543 \div 100 = 5.43$
Answer	543 cm = 5.43 m

3 Convert the following units. First decide if you have to multiply or divide. Use the conversion table to find the number to multiply or divide by.

(a) 4 m to cm   (b) 2000 g to kg   (c) 40 mm to cm

(d) 2 t to kg   (e) 400 cm to m   (f) 4 t to kg

(g) 1500 kg to t   (h) 8700 m to km   (i) 480 cm to m

Learn More About It

Dagna has bought 2 m of material to make a skirt.

The skirt pattern uses centimetres. So, she **converts** 2 m to cm.

2 m = 2 × 100 cm = 200 cm.

Dagna cuts off 60 cm for her skirt. This leaves her with 200 − 60 = 140 cm of material.

She converts 140 cm back to m.

140 ÷ 100 = 1.40

So 140 cm = 1.4 m.

She has 1.4 m of material left.

Pierre and Yvonne are travelling to Leicester, 100 miles away. In France they use kilometres. Pierre knows that 1 mile is about $1\frac{1}{2}$ km. He converts 100 miles to km like this: $100 \times 1\frac{1}{2}$ km = 100 km + 50 km = 150 km.

Pierre writes his answer like this: 100 miles ≈ 150 km. The ≈ sign means 'approximately equal to'.

Yvonne likes to be more accurate. She knows that 1 mile ≈ 1.6 km, so she calculates: 100 × 1.6 km = 160 km. Yvonne's answer is: 100 miles ≈ 160 km.

Key Fact

1 mile ≈ $1\frac{1}{2}$ km (more accurate is 1.6 km).

The ≈ sign means 'approximately equal to'.

Leicester
100 miles

Try It Out

H 1 Morley has opened a 1.5 kg bag of flour. His recipe for cakes uses grams.

(a) Convert 1.5 kg to g.

Morley uses 300 g for the cakes.

(b) How much flour does he have left over, in grams?

(c) Convert your answer to kg.

2 Convert these distances to kilometres, without using a calculator.

Example	4 miles
Working	1 mile is about $1\frac{1}{2}$ km. Multiply by $1\frac{1}{2}$
	$4 \times 1\frac{1}{2} = 4 + 2 = 6$
Answer	4 miles ≈ 6 km

(a) 8 miles   (b) 12 miles   (c) 60 miles

(d) 16 miles   (e) 120 miles   (f) 80 miles

(g) 240 miles   (h) 2000 miles   (i) 100 000 miles

3 Convert these distances to kilometres (1 mile = 1.6 km). Use a calculator if you need to.

(a) 10 miles   (b) 2 miles   (c) 5 miles

(d) 50 miles   (e) 100 miles   (f) 1000 miles

(g) 200 miles   (h) 45 miles

Practice

1 Convert these units.

(a) 2.65 kg to g   (b) 0.7 cm to mm   (c) 72 cm to m

(d) $\frac{1}{4}$ t to kg   (e) 2.45 m to cm   (f) $\frac{3}{4}$ m to cm

(g) 0.055 kg to g   (h) 12.5 mm to cm   (i) 50 m to km

2 Hunter drives 104 miles in England and 249 km in France. How far does he drive altogether, in km?

3 (a) Elsa has 3.75 t of sand delivered. Convert this to kg.

(b) She uses 1450 kg. How much does she have left, in kg.

(c) Another 1.5 t of sand is delivered. How much sand does she have, in tonnes?

> **Finished Early?**
> ➡ Go to page 375

Further Practice

1 Convert these units.

(a) 4 kg to g   × 1000   **(b)** 300 cm to m   ÷ 100

(c) 45 cm to mm   × 10   **(d)** 15 km to m   × 1000

(e) 1700 kg to t   ÷ 1000   **(f)** 2 kg to g   ×

(g) 70 mm to cm   ÷   **(h)** 5 t to kg   ×

(i) 1400 g to kg   ÷   **(j)** 157 cm to m   ÷

2 Write down these snakes in order, from smallest to largest.

> *Hint: convert the lengths to centimetres first.*

Cobra	1.4 m	Thread	0.6 m
Boa	240 cm	Viper	130 cm
Python	3.4 m	Adder	400 mm
Shieldtail	210 mm	Mamba	160 cm

3 The distances on this map are in miles.

Convert them to kilometres.

(a) Birmingham to Leicester

(b) Leeds to Liverpool

(c) Bristol to Birmingham

(d) London to Liverpool via Birmingham

(e) Leicester to Bristol via Birmingham

(f) Birmingham to Leicester to Leeds to Liverpool to Birmingham

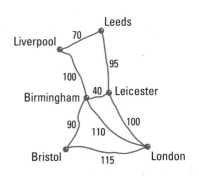

> **Finished Early?**
> ➡ Go to page 375

25 Measuring

In this chapter you will learn about ...
- **1** reading scales
- **2** measuring length
- **3** weighing

1 Reading Scales

Learn About It

 Tracing paper

1 The numbers on this scale go up in tens. Trace the scale.

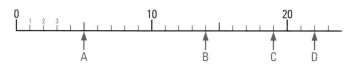

2 There are 10 spaces between 0 and 10. So each space is worth 1 unit. The small numbers go up in ones.

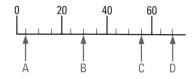

(a) Fill in the small numbers on your scale.
(b) Which numbers do the arrows point to?

3 There are 5 spaces between 0 and 10 on this scale.

So each space is worth 10 ÷ 5 = 2 units. The small numbers on this scale go up in twos.
(a) Trace the scale.
(b) Fill in the small numbers.
(c) Which numbers do the arrows point to?

4 Trace this scale.

   (a) How much is each small space worth?

   (b) Which numbers do the arrows point to?

   Only fill in the small numbers if you need to.

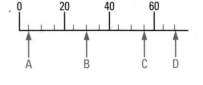

5 Some scales don't start at 0.
There are 5 spaces between 200 and 300.
So each space is worth 100 ÷ 10 = 10 units.
The small numbers go up in 20s.
Which numbers do the arrows point to?
Only trace the scale if you need to.

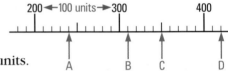

6 This is a decimal scale.

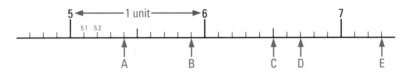

There are 10 spaces between 5 and 6. So each space is worth $\frac{1}{10}$ or 0.1 unit.
Which numbers do the arrows point to?

7 Sometimes you need to **estimate** when reading a scale.

Imagine the scale divided into equal parts.

Arrow (i) points to about 4.

The other arrows point to numbers too. Estimate them.

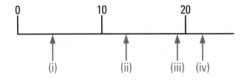
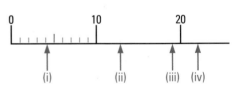

Word Check
....
estimate make your best guess

8 Scales are used to measure real amounts like weight, length and time.

This knob controls the temperature (°C) on a washing machine. What temperature has been set?

Temperature

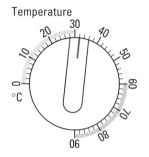

Try It Out

A **1** **(a)** How many units is each small space worth?

(b) Which numbers do the arrows point to? Estimate arrow C and D.

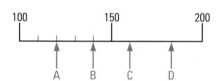

Practice

B **2** Which numbers do the arrows point to?

1
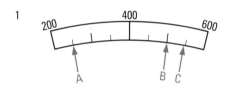

2
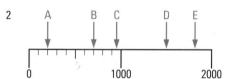

3
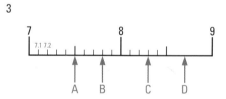

4
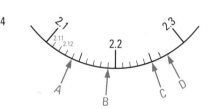

5
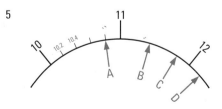

6
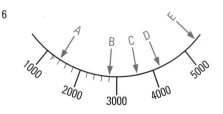

C **3** Which measurements do the arrows point to? Don't forget to write the units (cm, mm, °C, etc.) after the numbers.

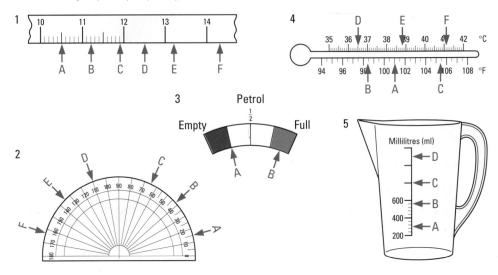

4 Read the arrows in both miles and kilometres.

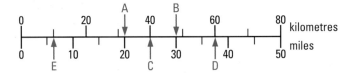

Further Practice

D **5** Which numbers do the arrows point to?

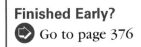

1

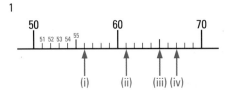

3

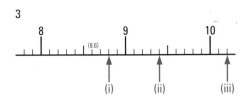

2

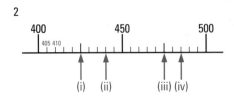

4

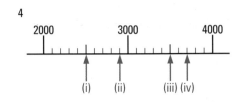

Finished Early?
➡ Go to page 376

Finished Early?
➡ Go to page 376

NUMBER SKILLS Count in steps of 0.1, 0.5, 5, 100, add HTU, know multiples of $\frac{1}{8}$

② Measuring Length

Learn About It

Ruler

1 The red line is exactly 4.6 cm long.

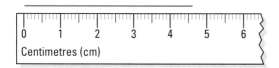

To change the answer to millimetres (mm), multiply by 10.

4.6 cm = 4.6 × 10 mm = 46 mm

2 Measure the lengths of these lines. Be as accurate as you can. Write your answers in both centimetres and millimetres.

(a) ——————————————————————

(b) ——————————————————

(c) ——————————

(d) ————————————————

(e) ———

> ### Word Check
> **accurate** close to the exact number

3 The blue line is closer to 7 cm than 6 cm.

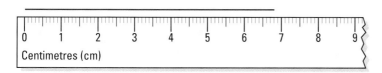

Its length is 7 cm, to the nearest cm.

4 This line is 3.5 cm long.

3.5 is halfway between 3 and 4 cm. When this happens we round it up. This line is 4 cm long, to the nearest cm.

5 Measure these lines. Write your answers to the nearest cm.

(a) ————————————————

(b) ——————————

(c) ——————————————————

(d) ———————————

(e) —————————

(f) ———————————————————

Try It Out

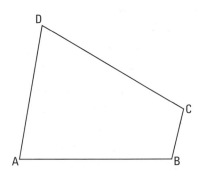

E Measure the sides of this shape. Write each answer three ways: centimetres, millimetres and to the nearest cm.

Learn More About It

1 The car in this picture is 1 cm long. In real life, the car is 2 m long.

So, 1 cm in the picture stands for 2 m in real life. This is called the **scale** of the picture.

Write it like this for short. | 1 cm to 2 m.

Or like this. | 1 cm : 2 m

2 The red shop is 4 cm wide in the picture. In real life, the red shop is $4 \times 2\,m = 8\,m$ wide.

Measure these lengths in centimetres.

(a) length of lorry   **(b)** height of bus stop
(c) length of row of shops

The yellow shop is 4.3 cm high in the picture. In real life, the yellow shop is $4.3 \times 2\,m = 8.6\,m$ high.

Measure these lengths in centimetres.

(d) height of lorry   **(e)** height of man
(f) height of lamppost

Now convert your answers to real-life lengths in metres.

Try It Out

1 The scale for this map of Roman roads is 1 cm to 30 miles.

On the map, the distance from Corinium to Ratae is 2.3 cm. So, the real distance is 2.3 × 30 = 69 miles.

Measure these distances in centimetres. Some of your answers will be decimals.

(a) Aquae Sulis to Corinium   **(b)** Lindum to Londinium

(c) Ratae to Lindum   **(d)** Aquae Sulis to Londinium

2 Convert your answers to real-life lengths in miles.

Word Check

scale what 1 cm stands for

Practice

A piece of string about 20 cm long

1 This line is divided into parts. The first part is AB.

A   B   C   D

Measure the length of each part. Write your answers in:

(a) millimetres

(b) centimetres

(c) to the nearest cm

2 Use a piece of string to find the lengths of the dotted country walks, in centimetres. Some of your answers will be decimals.

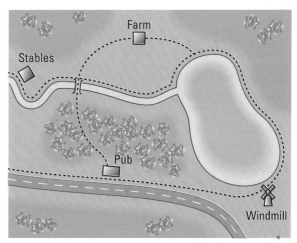

(a) pub to windmill

(b) farm to pub

(c) stables to lake

(d) farm to windmill around lake

(e) round trip: pub to farm to windmill to pub

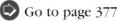
Scale: 1 cm to 400 m

3 Convert your answers in question 2 to real distances in metres.

4 Convert your answers in question 3 to kilometres.

Finished Early?

➥ Go to page 377

Further Practice

1 Measure, in centimetres, the lengths shown by the arrows. Some of your answers will be decimals.

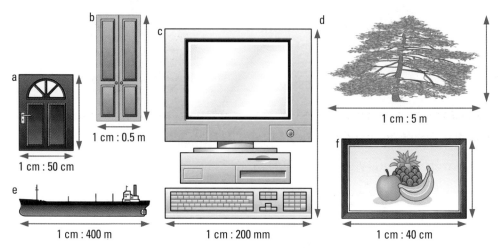

2 Convert your answers in question 1 to real-life lengths. The scale is given beneath each object.

3 Convert your answers in question 1 to millimetres.

4 Write your answers to question 1 to the nearest cm.

> **Finished Early?**
> ➡ Go to page 377

❸ Weighing

Learn About It

These are the weights usually sold with weighing scales.

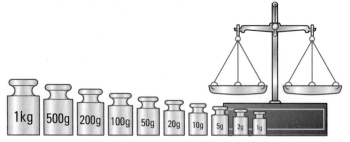

It's easy to weigh 75 g of flour.

Put these weights in one pan: 50 g, 20 g, 5 g. Pour flour into the other pan until the scales balance.

This floppy disk weighs somewhere between 20 g and 25 g.

You can be more accurate by weighing several floppy disks at a time.
This pack of 10 floppy disks weighs about 230 g.

So each floppy disk weighs about
230 g ÷ 10 = 23 g.

The more floppy disks you weigh,
the more accurate your answer.
40 floppy disks weigh about 930 g.

So each floppy disk weighs about
930 g ÷ 40 = 23.25 g.

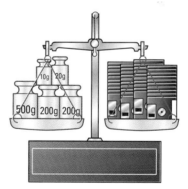

This box contains 200 floppy disks.

You can work out its weight by multiplying.
1 floppy disk weighs about 23.25 g
So 200 disks weigh about 200 × 23.25 g = 4650 g

Convert large weights to kilograms by dividing:
4650 g ÷ 1000 = 4.65 kg

Try It Out

Example	20 pencils weigh 120 g. How much does one weigh?
Working	120 g ÷ 20 = 6 g
Answer	One pencil weighs 6 g

1 **(a)** 75 nails weigh 600 g. How much does one weigh?
   (b) 80 tea bags weigh 200 g. How much does one weigh?
   (c) 24 paving stones weigh 720 kg. How much does one weigh?
   (d) 6 apples weigh 960 g. How much does one weigh?
   (e) 25 crisps weigh 30 g. How much does one weigh?
   (f) 500 bricks weigh 1200 kg. How much does one weigh?

2 Use your answers to question 1 to answer these questions.

Example	How much does a box of 200 pencils weigh, in kilograms?
Working	One pencil weighs 6 g.
	So 200 pencils weigh 200 × 6 g = 1200 g.
	Convert to kilograms: 1200 ÷ 1000 = 1.2
Answer	A box weighs 1.2 kg

   (a) How much does a bag of 300 nails weigh, in kilograms?
   (b) How much does a box of 250 tea bags weigh, in grams?
   (c) A path needs 60 paving stones. How much *Hint: 1 t = 1000 kg*
       do 60 paving stones weigh, in tonnes?
   (d) How much does a box of 50 apples weigh, in kilograms?
   (e) How much does a packet containing 60 crisps weigh, in grams?
   (f) A wall needs 750 bricks. How much do 750 bricks weigh, in tonnes?

 # Practice

 Answer these questions by multiplying or dividing.

1 100 paper clips weigh 50 g.
   (a) How much does one paper clip weigh?
   (b) How much do 5000 paper clips weigh, in kg?
   (c) How many paper clips are contained in a 300 g pack?

2 A portion of chips weighs 220 g.
   (a) A canteen serves 45 portions. How much do these weigh altogether, in kg?
   (b) A portion contains about 25 chips. How much does one chip weigh?

3 A bar of chocolate has 20 squares. Oi Tai finds that it weighs between 250 g and 260 g.
   (a) Divide 250 g and 260 g by 20.
   (b) What do your answers tell you?

4 Barney finds that 40 spoons of sugar weigh between 190 g and 210 g.

  (a) Find the two weights that a spoon of sugar weighs between.

  (b) How much do 100 spoons of sugar weigh?

Merlin the Magician mixes these ingredients into a magic potion.

Dew Drop	250g
Elf Wing	150g
Spider	200g
Tail of Rat	300g

  The mixture fills 200 bottles.

1 How much mixture does he make?

2 How much mixture does each bottle contain?

3 How much Elf Wing does each bottle contain?

4 How much Spider does each bottle contain?

5 How much Tail of Rat does each bottle contain?

Finished Early?
➡ Go to page 377

Further Practice

1 15 biro pens weigh 90 g.

  (a) How much does each biro weigh?

  (b) How much does a box of 50 biros weigh?

2 20 hazelnuts weigh 70 g.

  (a) How much does one hazelnut weigh?

  (b) How much does a bag of 60 hazelnuts weigh?

3 6 boxes of tissues weigh 1.5 kg.

  (a) Convert 1.5 kg to g.

  (b) How much does one box of tissues weigh?
  Each box contains 200 tissues.

  (c) How much does one tissue weigh?

4 12 people get into a lift. Each person weighs 75 kg.

  (a) What is their total weight?

  (b) The safe limit for the lift is 1 tonne. Do these people weigh over the limit?

5

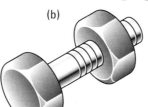

(a) 50 of these bolts weigh 600g. How much does one bolt weigh?

(b) 30 of these nuts and bolts weigh 480g. How much does one nut and bolt weigh?

(c) How much does one nut weigh?

Finished Early?
➡ Go to page 377

26 Time, Timetables and Calendars

In this chapter you will learn about ...

1. calculating time
2. timetables
3. calendars

1 Calculating Time

Learn About It

There are 24 hours in a day.

A 12-hour clock shows the hours 1 to 12.

The hour hand starts at 12 midnight.

It makes a whole 12-hour turn through the morning to 12 noon (midday).

Then it makes another 12-hour turn through the afternoon to 12 midnight.

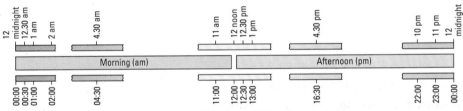

A 24-hour clock shows hours and minutes.

24-hour clock times have four digits.

The digital clock starts at 00:00 (midnight).

It runs through the morning to 12:00 (noon).

Then through the afternoon and evening up to 23:59 and finishes at 00:00 (midnight again).

Key Fact

1 minute = 60 seconds	1 week = 7 days
1 hour = 60 minutes	1 year = 365 days
1 day = 24 hours	1 year = 12 months

Try It Out

1 Convert to 24-hour clock times.

Example	4.30am
Answer	04:30 (Put an extra 0 to make 4 digits)

Example	4.30pm
Working	Add 12 hours to pm times
Answer	16:30

(a) 5pm **(b)** 9.00am **(c)** 11.00pm **(d)** 1am
(e) 4.15am **(f)** 1.25pm **(g)** 12 noon **(h)** 12.30pm
(i) 12.05am **(j)** 10.20pm **(k)** 12 midnight **(l)** Midday

2 Convert to 12-hour clock times.

Example	04.00
Working	Times before 12:00 are am. Remove the first 0.
Answer	4.00am (or 4am)

Example	23:55
Working	Times after 12:00 are pm. Subtract 12 hours.
Answer	11.55pm

(a) 04:00 **(b)** 19:00 **(c)** 01:00 **(d)** 11:00
(e) 10:30 **(f)** 13:15 **(g)** 12:00 **(h)** 00:25
(i) 23:59 **(j)** 00:00 **(k)** 20:05 **(l)** 03:20

Learn More About It

Rashida has a 4-hour video tape.
She knows that 1 hour = 60 minutes.
So 4 hours = 4 × 60 minutes = 240 minutes.
This is written on the side of her tape.

Rashida recorded *Star Trek*, which lasts 2 hours 5 minutes. She wants to know how many minutes recording time are left on her tape.

First, she converts hours to minutes.
2 hours = 2 × 60 minutes = 120 minutes.
So *Star Trek* lasts 120 + 5 = 125 minutes.
This leaves 240 – 125 = 115 minutes recording time on her tape.
Rashida converts 115 minutes back to hours and minutes like this.
60 minutes is 1 hour. This leaves 115 – 60 = 55 minutes.
So 115 minutes = 1 hour 55 minutes.

Try It Out

B **1** **(a)** Hal has a 3-hour video tape. How many minutes recording time is there?

(b) He records *The Black Knight*, which lasts 1 hour 40 minutes. How many minutes is this?

(c) How many minutes of recording time are left?

(d) Change your answer to hours and minutes.

2 Each programme is recorded on a separate 4-hour tape. How much time is left on each?

(a) *One Foot In The Grave* which lasts 40 minutes

(b) *The Gypsy Moths* which lasts 1 hour 42 minutes

(c) *The Man Who Would Be King* which lasts 129 minutes

Learn More About It

Rashida wants to record *Citizen Smith*. She needs to know how long it is.

It starts at 5.30pm and finishes at 6.10pm. She works out the length like this.

5.30pm to 6.00pm is 30 minutes.
6.00pm to 6.10pm is a further 10 minutes.

So *Citizen Smith* lasts 30 + 10 = 40 minutes.

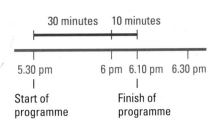

Try It Out

C **1** Hal wants to record *The Young Ones*.

(a) When does it start?

(b) When does it finish?

(c) How long does the programme last?

(d) Change the start and finish times to 24-hour clock times.

Repeat question 1 for these programmes.

2 *Blackadder the Third*

3 *Bottom*

4 *The Sullivans*

TV Guide	
7.00am	The Sullivans
9.05	Doctor Who
12.05pm	Eastenders
3.00	The Bill
5.30	Citizen Smith
6.10	FILM: Biggles
8.00	The Brittas Empire
8.40	Blackadder the Third
9.20	One Foot in the Grave
10.00	Bottom
10.40	The Young Ones
11.25	The Comic Strip Presents

Practice

D **1** Convert these times to seconds.

Example	4 minutes
Working	1 minute = 60 seconds
	4 × 60 = 240
Answer	4 minutes = 240 seconds

(a) 3 minutes   **(b)** 20 minutes   **(c)** 2 minutes 30 seconds

(d) 7 minutes 20 seconds   **(e)** $5\frac{1}{2}$ minutes   **(f)** $\frac{1}{4}$ minute

(g) 1.5 minutes   **(h)** 3.25 minutes

2 Convert these times to minutes and seconds.

Example	200 seconds
Working	1 minute = 60 seconds
	$3 \times 60 = 180$ seconds
	$200 - 180 = 20$ seconds
Answer	200 seconds = 3 minutes 20 seconds

(a) 80 seconds   **(b)** 120 seconds   **(c)** 94 seconds

(d) 150 seconds   **(e)** 600 seconds   **(f)** 254 seconds

Write these as fractions of a minute.

(g) 30 seconds   **(h)** 45 seconds

3 Find when these programmes finish.

Example	*National Lottery on Tour.* Starts 7.50pm. Lasts 20 minutes.
Working	7.50pm to 8.00pm is 10 minutes
	8.00pm to 8.10pm is another 10 minutes, making
	20 minutes altogether.
Answer	Programme finishes at 8.10pm.

(a) *A Little Piece of Home.* Starts 8.00pm. Lasts 10 minutes.

(b) *Blankety Blank.* Starts 5.50pm. Lasts 30 minutes.

(c) *Windrush Gala.* Starts 9.30pm. Lasts 1 hour 50 minutes
   (add the hours first).

(d) *Pioneers.* Starts 6.25pm. Lasts 35 minutes.

(e) *Fun Song Factory.* Starts 6.50am. Lasts 20 minutes.

(f) *GMTV.* Starts 6.00am. Lasts 3 hours 25 minutes.

(g) *The New Adventures of Superman.* Starts 10.15am. Lasts 2 hours
   10 minutes.

(h) *High Plains Drifter.* Starts 11.40pm. Lasts 1 hour 40 minutes.

4 Write down all the start times in question 3 as 24-hour clock times.

Finished Early?
🡆 Go to page 378

Further Practice

E 1 Convert to 24-hour clock times.

(**a**) 6.00am   (**b**) 5pm   (**c**) 2am

(**d**) 11.45pm   (**e**) 3.20am   (**f**) 12.15am

2 Convert these times to seconds.

(**a**) 6 minutes   (**b**) 2 minutes   (**c**) 1 minute 30 seconds

(**d**) 5 minutes 18 seconds   (**e**) $1\frac{1}{2}$ minutes   (**f**) 2.5 minutes

3 Convert these times to minutes and seconds.

(**a**) 70 seconds   (**b**) 130 seconds   (**c**) 92 seconds

(**d**) 170 seconds   (**e**) 240 seconds   (**f**) 262 seconds

Write these using fractions.

(**g**) 15 seconds (as a fraction of a minute)   (**h**) 90 seconds

4 Rashida has set her video for these programmes.

(**a**) Calculate the lengths of the programmes. Write your answers in hours and minutes.

(**b**) Write the start and finish times as 12-hour clock times.

Programme	Start	Finish
1	17.30	18.05
2	21.00	22.35
3	23.10	00.30
4	02.15	04.15
5	10.45	12.15

P 2 Timetables

Learn About It

1 This train leaves Brighton at 10:26. So it's called the 10:26 from Brighton.

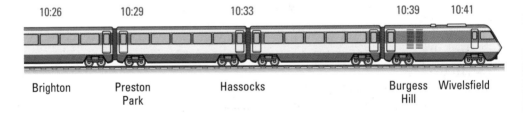

10:26   10:29   10:33   10:39   10:41

Brighton   Preston Park   Hassocks   Burgess Hill   Wivelsfield

(**a**) When does it arrive at Preston Park?

(**b**) How long does it take?

(**c**) How long does the train take to travel between Hassocks and Wivelsfield?

2 The 10:26 goes all the way to Kings Cross. The times are written in a column in a timetable.

The dots … show that this train doesn't stop at Balcombe.

(a) When does the train arrive at Kings Cross?

(b) How long does it take to travel from Burgess Hill to East Croydon?

Railway timetable

Brighton	10 26
Preston Park	10 29
Hassocks	10 33
Burgess Hill	10 39
Wivelsfield	10 41
Haywards Heath	10 46
Balcombe	…. ….
Three Bridges	10 55
Gatwick Airport	11 00
East Croydon	11 17
London Bridge	11 31
London Blackfriars	11 37
City	11 39
Farringdon	11 41
Kings Cross	11 45

3 The timetable below shows the times of different trains from Brighton to Kings Cross. Each column is for a different train. The first column is for the 10:26 from Brighton.

Railway timetable — Brighton to Kings Cross

Brighton	10 26	10 39	10 57	11 26	11 39	11 57	12 20	12 26	12 39	12 57	13 20
Preston Park	10 29	10 42	… …	11 29	11 42	… …	… …	12 29	12 42	… …	… …
Hassocks	10 33	10 49	… …	11 33	11 49	… …	… …	12 33	12 49	… …	… …
Burgess Hill	10 39	… …	11 07	11 39	… …	12 07	… …	12 39	… …	13 07	… …
Wivelsfield	10 41	… …	11 09	11 41	… …	12 09	… …	12 41	… …	13 09	… …
Haywards Heath	10 46	10 57	11 14	11 46	11 57	12 14	12 33	12 46	12 57	13 14	13 33
Balcombe	… …	… …	11 19	… …	… …	12 19	… …	… …	… …	13 19	… …
Three Bridges	10 55	11 10	11 26	11 55	12 10	12 26	… …	12 55	13 10	13 26	… …
Gatwick Airport	11 00	11 15	11 30	12 00	12 15	12 30	12 45	13 00	13 15	13 30	13 45
East Croydon	11 17	11 32	11 47	12 17	12 32	12 47	13 02	13 17	13 32	13 47	14 02
London Bridge	11 31	11 46	12 01	12 31	12 46	13 01	13 16	13 31	13 46	14 01	14 16
London Blackfriars	11 37	11 52	12 07	12 37	12 52	13 07	13 22	13 37	13 52	14 07	14 22
City	11 39	11 54	12 09	12 39	12 54	13 09	13 24	13 39	13 54	14 09	14 24
Farringdon	11 41	11 56	12 11	12 41	12 56	13 11	13 26	13 41	13 56	14 11	14 26
Kings Cross	11 45	12 00	12 15	12 45	13 00	13 15	13 30	13 45	14 00	14 15	14 30

Source: based on data from Railtrack plc.

(a) Look at the second column. When does this train leave Brighton?

(b) How many trains leave Brighton before 12:00?

4 The red times show when the trains stop at Gatwick Airport. The first train stops at 11:00.

(a) When does the next train stop at Gatwick?

(b) When does the last train stop at Gatwick?

(c) Sanjit missed the 12:00 from Gatwick. When is the next train he can catch?

5 Find the train that stops at Gatwick at 13:00. Look along the column of times.

(a) When does it leave Hassocks?

(b) When does it arrive at Farringdon?

6 Rodger lives in Brighton. On Tuesday he has to be at Gatwick Airport by 12:20. Look at the row of Gatwick Airport times. 12:30 is too late. 12:15 is alright. This train leaves Brighton at 11:39 (look at the top of the column). Rodger must catch this to be on time.

On Wednesday he has to be at Gatwick Airport by 13:10. What is the latest train he can catch from Brighton?

(F) Try It Out

Look at the Brighton to Kings Cross timetable on page 289 to answer these questions.

1 How many trains does the timetable show?

2 **(a)** When does the 10:57 from Brighton arrive at Kings Cross?
(b) How long does it take?

3 Gerald missed the 10:57 from Brighton. When does the next train leave?

4 One of the trains arrives at Kings Cross at 14:00. When does it leave Brighton?

5 **(a)** When does the first train stop at Balcombe?
(b) How often does a train stop there?

6 **(a)** When does the 10:41 from Wivelsfield arrive at Kings Cross?
(b) How long does the journey take?

7 You are meeting a friend at Kings Cross at 12:50.

(a) What is the latest train you can catch from Wivelsfield?
(b) If you miss this train, when is the next?
(c) How long will your friend have waited?

Practice

(G) Copy and complete this table. (Use the railway timetable on page 289.)

Journey	Depart	Arrive	Journey time (minutes)
Brighton to East Croydon	12 20	13 02	
Burgess Hill to City	11 07		
Balcombe to Farringdon		13 11	
Haywards Heath to Kings Cross	12 14		
London Bridge to	12 31		10
.... to London Bridge	12 39		52
Gatwick Airport to		13 56	
Brighton to Gatwick Airport	12 39		

Buses run every half hour from Portsmouth to Brighton.

Bus timetable Portsmouth to Brighton
Mon to Sat

Portsmouth	.....	.....	.....	.....	.....	.....	0645		1645 1715 1745
Havant	.....	.....	.....	.....	.....	.....	0717		1717 1747 1817
Emsworth Square	.....	.....	.....	.....	.....	.....	0725		1725 1755 1825
Chichester	.....	.....	0600	0630	0655	0720	0750		1750 1820 1850
Bognor Regis	.....	.....	0620	0650	0715	0742	0812	every	1812 1842 1907
Littlehampton Anchor	.....	.....	0646	0716	0741	0811	0841	30 min	1841 1911 1932
Ferring War Memorial	.....	.....	0703	0733	0803	0833	0909		1903 1933 1951
Worthing South Street	0635	0700	0723	0753	0823	0853	0923		1923 1953 2008
Shoreham High Street	0645	0712	0740	0810	0840	0910	0940		1940 2020
Hove King Alfred	0658	0727	0757	0827	0857	0927	0957		1957 2033
Brighton	0710	0740	0810	0840	0910	0940	1010		2010 2045

Source: based on data from Pindar.

1 Dynand lives in Chichester.

   (a) What is the earliest bus he can catch to Brighton?

   (b) How long is the journey?

2 On Wednesday, Dynand gets to the bus stop at 7.30am.

   (a) How long must he wait for a bus?

   (b) When does this bus arrive in Brighton?

3 On Thursday, Dynand gets to the bus stop at 11.00am.

   (a) How long must he wait for a bus?

   (b) When does this bus arrive in Brighton?

4 On Friday, Dynand has to be in Brighton by 2.15pm.

   (a) Write 2.15pm as a 24-hour clock time.

   (b) What is the latest time he can arrive in Brighton?

   (c) What is the latest bus he can catch from Chichester?

> **Finished Early?**
> ➡ Go to page 379

Further Practice

1 (a) How many trains does the timetable show?

   (b) When does the first train leave Carlisle?

   (c) When does this train arrive in Glasgow?

   (d) One of the trains arrives in Glasgow at 15:30. When does it leave Carlisle?

Carlisle to Glasgow

Carlisle	0612	0645	0812	0948	1110	1307	1423
Gretna Green	0623	0656	0823	0959	1121	1321	1434
Annan	0632	0705	0831	1008	1129	1330	1442
Dumfries	0650	0722	0848	1024	1146	1346	1459
Sanquhar	0716	.....	0914	.....	1212	1412	1525
Kirkconnel	0721	.....	0919	.....	1217	1417	1530
New Cumnock	0730	.....	0927	.....	1226	1426	1539
Auchinleck	0738	.....	0936	.....	1234	1435	1548
Kilmarnock	0756	.....	0954	.....	1252	1452	1607
Glasgow	0837	.....	1041	.....	1330	1530	.....

Source: based on data from Railtrack plc.

Fulla, Oran and Andrew are meeting up in Glasgow.

2 Fulla lives in Annan.

   (a) What is the first train she can catch?

   (b) When does it arrive in Glasgow?

   (c) How long does the journey take?

3 Oran lives in New Cumnock. He arrives at the station at 9.15am.

(a) When is the next train to Glasgow?

(b) When does it arrive in Glasgow?

(c) How long does the journey take?

4 Andrew lives in Kirkconnel. He just misses the 09:19 train to Glasgow.

(a) When is the next train to Glasgow?

(b) When does it arrive in Glasgow?

(c) How long does the journey take?

> **Finished Early?**
> ➡ Go to page 379

P ③ Calendars

Learn About It

1 A year is divided into 12 **months**. Copy their names:

January	February	March	April	May	June
July	August	September	October	November	December

You can remember the number of days in each month using this rhyme:

'Thirty days have September, April, June and November. All the rest have 31, except February, which has 28 days and 29 days in a leap year'

(a) Write out the months in order: January (31), February (28), etc.

(b) The 5th month is May. What is the 10th month? How many days does it have?

2 Here is the calendar for May 2000. Kerry has circled her dental appointments. The first one is on Friday 12th May 2000. You can write this date quickly as 12/5/00.

May 2000

Mon	Tue	Wed	Thu	Fri	Sat	Sun
1	2	3	4	5	6	7
8	9	10	11	(12)	13	14
15	(16)	17	18	19	20	21
22	23	24	25	26	(27)	28
29	30	31				

(a) Write down her other appointments using both ways.

(b) Copy the calendar. Leave space for June's calendar later.

3 Look at the column for Thursday. There are four dates. So there are four Thursdays in May. The first Thursday is on the 4th. Write down the dates of the …

(a) second Thursday

(b) first Saturday

(c) third Wednesday

(d) last Friday.

4 Class 7A are given some homework on Friday 19th May. They have to hand it in 10 days later.

Bill counts 10 days on the calendar.

Galen calculates 19 + 10 = 29. So it is due on the 29th May. She sees this is a Monday on the calendar.

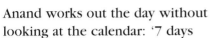

Anand works out the day without looking at the calendar: '7 days from today is also a Friday, 8 for Saturday, 9 for Sunday, 10 for Monday.'

(a) 4th May is a Thursday. What day of the week is 12 days later? Use your calendar.

(b) 9th May is a Tuesday. What day of the week is 11 days later? Use Galen's or Anand's method.

5 Look at the calendar for May again. The last day is Wednesday 31st. So the 1st day of June must be a Thursday. Copy and complete the calendar for June. Write it next to your May calendar.

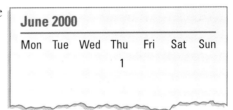

June 2000

Mon	Tue	Wed	Thu	Fri	Sat	Sun
			1			

Try It Out

1 **(a)** What is the 8th month of the year?
  (b) How many days does it have?

2 Use your calendars to write down the date of …

  (a) the third Tuesday in May   **(b)** the last Sunday in May
  (c) the first Monday in June   **(d)** the last Friday in June.

3 Write your answers to question 2 like this date: 12/5/00.

4 Chandler starts his exam revision on 3rd June.

  (a) What day of the week is this?
  (b) His first exam is in 9 days time. What day of the week is this?
  (c) His next exam is 11 days after the first exam. What day of the week is this?

Practice

1 **(a)** How many weekends are there in June 2000?
  (b) How many Tuesdays are there in May 2000 after the 4th?
  (c) How many weekdays (Monday to Friday) are there in May 2000?

2 Some people say that a week begins on Monday.

  (a) How many whole weeks are there in May 2000?
  (b) How many in June 2000?
  (c) What would your answers be if a week begins on Sunday?

L How long does each of these events last? Write your answers in weeks and days.

> **Example** Sea voyage from 20th May to 5th June
> **Working** Count the days on your fingers: 20th, 21st, 22nd up to 31st. That's 12 days. Then add the first 5 days of June, giving 12 + 5 = 17 days.
> **Answer** The voyage lasts 2 weeks 3 days.

1 Music festival from 6th May to 21st May.

2 School trip from 13th June to the end of the month.

3 Bicycle race from 30th May to 2nd June.

4 French language course from 22nd May to 9th June.

5 Art exhibition from 16th May to 15th June.

6 Funfair from 27th June to 3rd July.

> **Finished Early?**
> Go to page 379

Further Practice

M **1** These people are going on holiday Which day and date do they return to work?

> **Example** Tan Tin leaves on 29th May for 8 days.
> **Working** Count 8 days on your calendars: Mon 29th **May**, Tue 30th, Wed 31st, Thur 1st **June**, Fri 2nd, Sat 3rd, Sun 4th, Mon 5th (last day of her holiday).
> **Answer** Tan Tin returns to work on Tuesday 6th June.

1 Malik leaves on 1st May for 10 days.

2 Poppy leaves on 30th May for 7 days.

3 Gebhard leaves on 20th May for 2 weeks.

4 Son leaves on 18th May for 3 weeks.

5 Kalma leaves on 25th June for 8 days.

N **2** A **leap** year has an extra day: 29th February. A leap year can be exactly divided by 4. For example, 2000 is a leap year because 2000 ÷ 4 = 500. Which of these years are leap years?

(a) 1994   **(b)** 2010   **(c)** 1648   **(d)** 2050

(e) When is the next leap year after 2222?

> **Finished Early?**
> Go to page 379

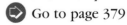

Unit 12 *Measures*
Summary of Chapters 24, 25 and 26

- **Units of length**

  1 centimetre (cm) = 10 millimetres (mm)

  1 metre (m) = 100 centimetres (cm)

  1 kilometre (km) = 1000 metres (m)

  1 mile is about 1.5 km (1.6 km is more accurate)
- You can estimate length by rounding to the nearest cm. For example, 2.7 cm can be rounded to 3 cm.
- The numbers on a scale go up in equal amounts. There are 5 divisions between 20 and 30. Each division is worth 10 ÷ 5 = 2 units.

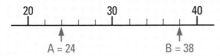

- A map scale tells you what 1 cm stands for in real life, e.g. a map scale of 1 cm to 30 miles means 1 cm on the map represents 30 miles on the ground.
- **Units of mass**

  1 kilogram (kg) = 1000 grams (g)

  1 tonne (t) = 1000 kilograms (kg)
- **Units of time**

  1 minute = 60 seconds

  1 hour = 60 minutes

  1 day = 24 hours

  1 week = 7 days

  1 year = 52 weeks and 1 day = 365 days

  1 year = 12 months
- To change 12-hour clock times to 24-hour clock times …
- put a 0 before am times e.g. 7.25 am is the same as 07.25
- add 12 to pm times e.g. 4.30 pm is the same as 16.30
- Thirty days have September, April, June and November. All the rest have 31, except February which has 28 and 29 in a leap year.
- A leap year can be divided by 4, e.g. 1984

27 Perimeters and Areas

In this chapter you will learn about …
1. the perimeter of a shape
2. counting areas
3. calculating areas

T1 The Perimeter of a Shape

Learn About It

If you run around the edge of this pitch how far have you run?

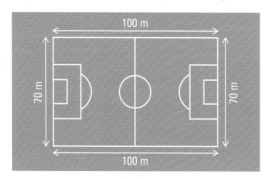

The total distance around the pitch is 100 + 70 + 100 + 70 = 340 m.
So you have run 340 m.

The **perimeter** of the football pitch is 340 m.

The perimeter of any shape is the total distance around its edges.

Look at this shape drawn on 1 cm squared paper.

Each square has sides length 1 cm so you can count the squares to find the perimeter.

Perimeter = 16 cm

Rectangles

Here the missing lengths are 10 − 5 = 5 cm
and 8 − 3.5 = 4.5 cm.

So perimeter = 3.5 + 10 + 8 + 5 + 4.5 + 5 = 36 cm.

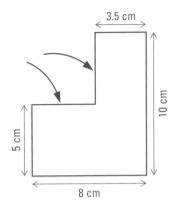

Word Check

perimeter the distance around
the edges of a shape

rectangle a four-sided shape with
right-angled corners

Try It Out

A Find the perimeters of these shapes.

The squares of the grid are 1 cm. Draw them on squared paper if you wish.

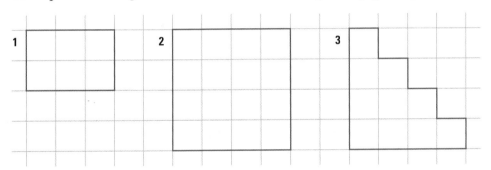

B Find the perimeters of these shapes.

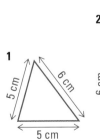

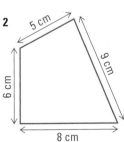

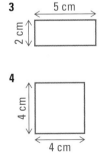

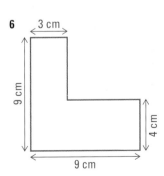

Practice

C Find the perimeters of these shapes. The squares of the grid are 1 cm squares.

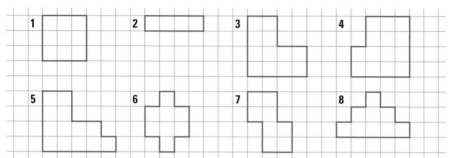

D Find the perimeters of these.

1 Della's diary
3 the pond in Phil's garden
5 the side of Ria's house
7 superstore car park
9 Green Acres Farm

2 Phil's garden
4 the paving in Phil's garden
6 superstore
8 Crawley Woods

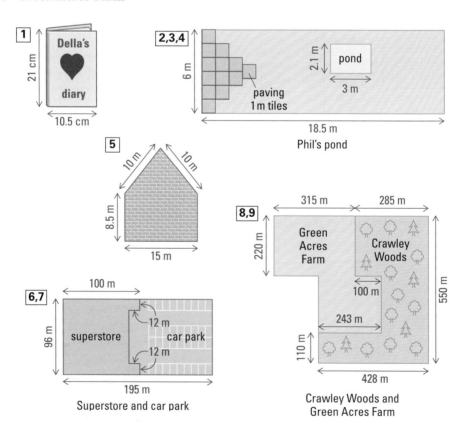

1 Della's
♥ diary
21 cm
10.5 cm

2,3,4
6 m
2.1 m
pond
3 m
paving
1 m tiles
18.5 m
Phil's pond

5
10 m   10 m
8.5 m
15 m

6,7
100 m
96 m
superstore
12 m
car park
12 m
195 m
Superstore and car park

8,9
315 m   285 m
220 m
Green Acres Farm
Crawley Woods
100 m
243 m
110 m
428 m
550 m
Crawley Woods and Green Acres Farm

Further Practice

E Find the perimeters of these shapes by counting. The squares of the grid are 1 cm.

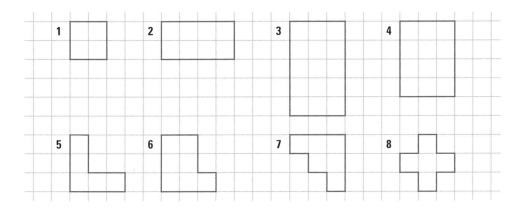

F Find the perimeters of these.

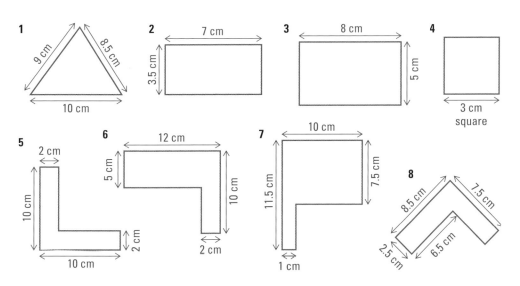

Finished Early?
Go to page 380

T 2 Counting Areas

Learn About It

Area is the amount of space that a flat shape takes up.

You measure it in squares.

A square with 1 cm sides is 1 cm². You say this as 'one square centimetre'.

Use this for small areas, ➤

e.g. a piece of paper, your hand, a picture.

A square with 1 m sides is 1 m² 'one square metre'.

Use this for larger areas, ➤

e.g. the floor of your classroom, a football pitch.

This triangle is drawn on centimetre squares; you have three whole squares and three half squares.

$1 \text{ m}^2 = 100 \times 100 = 10000 \text{ cm}^2$

Area = $3 + \frac{1}{2} + \frac{1}{2} + \frac{1}{2}$

$= 4\frac{1}{2} \text{ cm}^2$

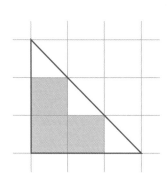

Jason spilt blue paint on the paving slabs in his garden.

8 squares are all covered with paint. 3 squares are more than half covered.

You can estimate the area covered in paint by adding these.

Estimated area = $8 + 3 = 11 \text{ m}^2$.

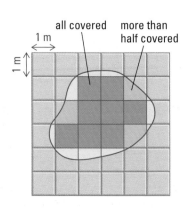

Try It Out

Find the areas of these shapes.

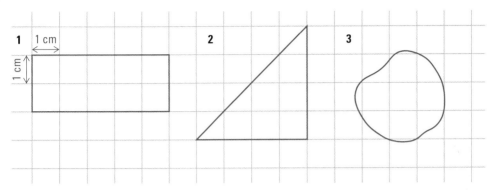

1 1 cm

1 cm

2

3

Practice

1 Mira is helping her dad plan a pond in the garden. They mark out the area with string to form a grid of 1 m squares. Then they use a hose pipe to try out shapes for the pond. For each of them Mira estimates the area.
What are the areas of these ponds?

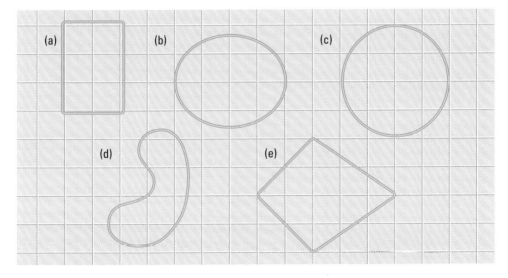

(a) (b) (c)

(d) (e)

2 Mira's dad buys a plastic sheet to line the pond and hold the water.
They need twice the pond area to allow for the depth.
The plastic costs £12.50 per m².
Work out the cost of the plastic for each pond in question 1.

3 Mira's dad plans to spend £250 on the garden.
How much would he have left to spend on plants with each of the ponds?

1cm squared paper

4 Design a rectangular garden with an area of $120m^2$. Use 1 cm squared paper. You can put in …

a lawn   a shed   a paved area   flower beds   a pond   bushes

Mark clearly the different parts of your garden and find their areas.

5 On squared paper draw around …

(a) your left hand   **(b)** your right hand.

Work out the area in each case.

Are your answers to **(a)** and **(b)** the same?

Further Practice

I Find the areas of these shapes by counting the squares.

The gridlines are 1 cm apart. Copy them onto squared paper if you need to.

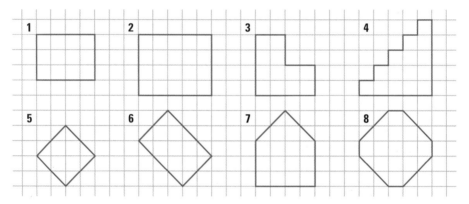

J Estimate the areas of these shapes.

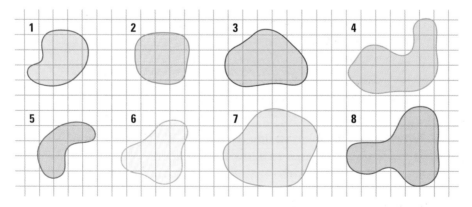

Finished Early?

➡ Go to page 380

Calculating Areas

Learn About It

Squared paper

1 Draw ten different rectangles on squared paper. Make them different sizes and shapes. Find the area of each rectangle by counting the squares. Write the area inside the rectangles.

2 Record the length, width and area of each rectangle in a table.

What do you notice about the length, width and area of your rectangles?

3 Multiplying the length and the width gives the number of squares in the rectangle. This equals the area.

Area = length × width

Area of this football pitch
$$= 100 \times 70$$
$$= 7000 \text{ m}^2$$

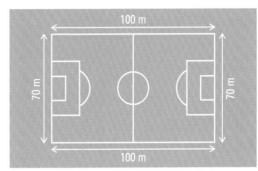

4 You can often split a shape into rectangles to help you find its area.

This is Kidmore school and playground.

To find the area of the playground divide it into two rectangles and add the areas:

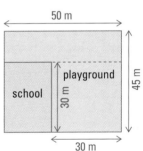

area of the top rectangle   = 50 × 15   = 750 m²
area of the other rectangle = 30 × 30   = 900 m²
area of playground   = 750 + 900 = 1650 m²

5 You can use length × width to find areas even when the lengths of the sides are not whole numbers.

Area of Della's diary = 21 × 10.5
                  = 220.5 cm²

Key Fact

Area of a rectangle = length × width

Try It Out

K Find the areas of these shapes.

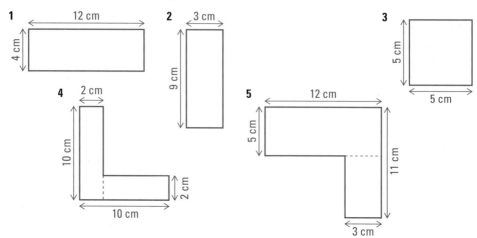

Practice

L Calculate the area of each of these.

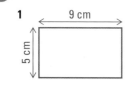

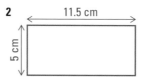

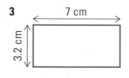

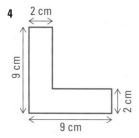

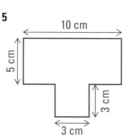

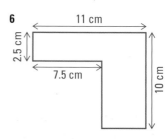

M This is a plan of Phil's garden.

Find the area of …

1 the whole garden

2 the pond

3 the paving.

Apart from the pond and the paving the garden is to be sown with grass seed.

4 Find the area to be grassed.

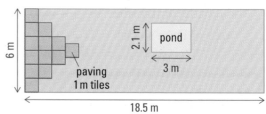

N This is a plan of the flat where Katy lives.

1 Find the area of …

(a) bedroom 1
(b) Katy's room
(c) the living room
(d) the bathroom
(e) the kitchen.

2 Katy's mum buys her a rug for her bedroom.

If the rug is 2 m by 3.1 m find …

(a) the area of the rug
(b) the area of the floor not covered by the rug.

[Plan of flat showing: top measurements 3.6 m and 2.8 m; bedroom 1 (4 m), kitchen (2.5 m), hall, Katy's room (3.4 m), bathroom (3 m), 1.8 m, living room (4.8 m), bottom 6.4 m]

Further Practice

O Find the areas of these shapes.

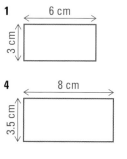

1 6 cm × 3 cm

4 8 cm × 3.5 cm

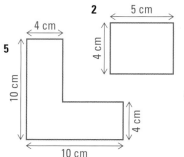

2 5 cm × 4 cm

5 L-shape: 4 cm, 10 cm, 4 cm, 10 cm

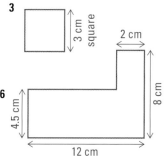

3 3 cm square

6 Shape: 4.5 cm, 2 cm, 8 cm, 12 cm

P This is the plan of part of Kidmore School.

1 Find the areas of …

(a) Miss Clarke's room
(b) Mrs Hunjan's room
(c) Mr Hassan's room
(d) Mr James's room
(e) The Hall.

2 (a) What is the area of the corridor if it is 2 m wide?

(b) If carpet costs £20 per m² how much would it cost to carpet the corridor?

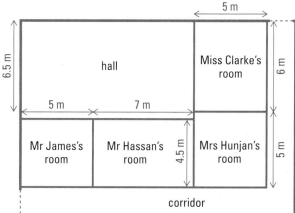

[Plan of Kidmore School showing: hall (6.5 m, 5 m, 7 m), Miss Clarke's room (5 m, 6 m), Mr James's room, Mr Hassan's room (4.5 m), Mrs Hunjan's room (5 m), corridor]

Finished Early?
➡ Go to page 380

28 Volume and Capacity

In this chapter you will learn about ...
1. filling space
2. boxes
3. liquids

1 Filling Space

Learn About It

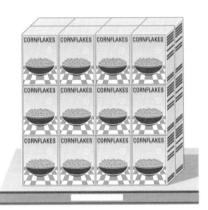

1. Claire has a job in a supermarket.
   She fills shelves.
   She fills this space with cornflake packets.

   Claire fills it like this.
   Each layer has $4 \times 2 = 8$ packets.
   There are 3 layers.
   So there are $8 \times 3 = 24$ packets.

2. Can you tell which shelf has more space from the number of packets?

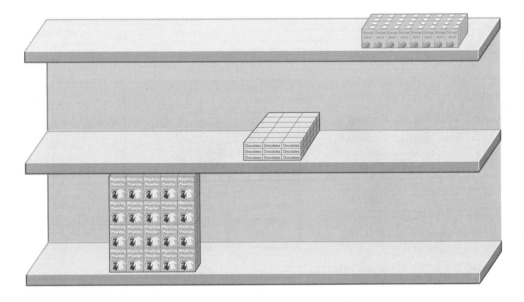

3 Suppose you fill space with cubes all of side 1cm.
The number of cubes gives the **volume**.
The volume is the amount of space taken
up. There are 24 cubes.

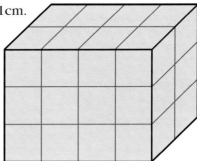

Try It Out

A Write down the number of cubes in each of these.

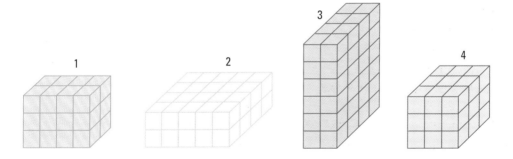

Practice

B Find the number of 1 cm cubes in each of these.

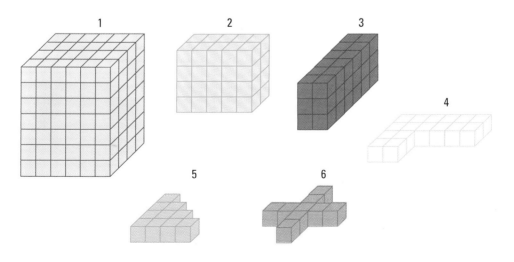

C Find the number of 1 cm cubes in each of these.

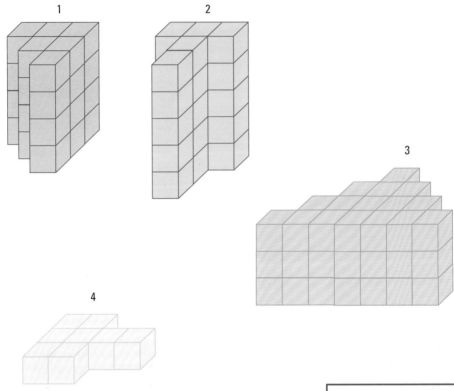

1   2   3

4

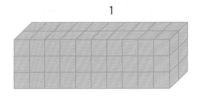

> **Finished Early?**
> Go to page 381

Further Practice

D Find the number of 1 cm cubes in these.

1   2

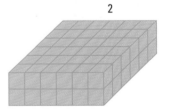

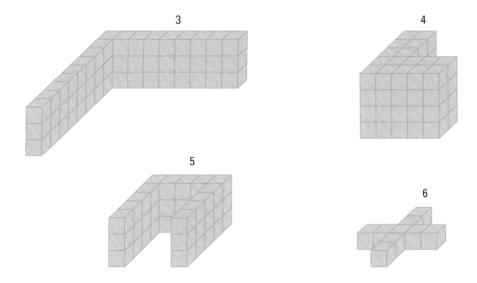

Boxes

Learn About It

The **volume** of an object is the amount of space it takes up.
Volume is measured by how many cubes fill the object.
For big objects you use m^3.

For small objects you use cm^3.

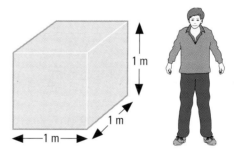

Look at this box.

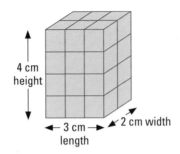

There are $3 \times 2 = 6$ cubes in each layer.
There are 4 layers. So the number of cubes $= 6 \times 4 = 24$.
The volume of the box $= 24 \, \text{cm}^3$.
Boxes are called **cuboids** in mathematics.

> Volume of a cuboid = length $\times$ width $\times$ height.

Other words can be used for the lengths, e.g. width, breadth, height.
This formula works for any sides, even when they are not whole numbers.

Example This box is 3.5 m long, 2.4 m wide
and 1.2 m high.
The volume of the box is
$3.5 \times 2.4 \times 1.2 = 10.08 \, \text{m}^3$.

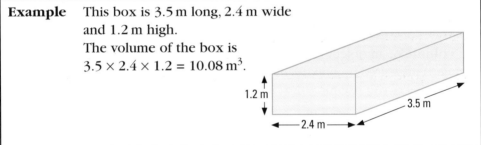

Key Fact

Volume of a cuboid = length
$\times$ width $\times$ height

Word Check

volume the amount of space in
an object
cuboid a rectangular box shape

Try It Out

List these objects in order of volume, starting with the smallest.

Calculate the volume of these cuboids.

1 4 cm by 3 cm by 2 cm

2 7 cm by 4 cm by 3 cm

3 a cube with sides 3 cm

4 2.5 cm by 3.5 cm by 4 cm

Practice

Calculate the volumes of these cuboids.

Remember to put all the lengths in the same units.

Example	A cupboard 40 cm long, 90 cm deep and 1 m high
Working	Put all lengths in metres.
	Volume = $0.4 \times 0.9 \times 1 = 0.36 \, \text{m}^3$
Answer	$0.36 \, \text{m}^3$

1 a block 5 cm by 7 cm by 10 cm

2 a cube of side 8 cm

3 a long metal bar 2 m by 4.5 cm by 13.5 cm

4 a piece of wood 12.5 cm by 4 cm by 1.5 cm

5 a metal sheet 17 cm by 4 cm by 0.5 cm

6 a room 2.4 m by 3.2 m by 2.5 m

1 One computer disc measures 9.3 cm by 9 cm by 0.3 cm.

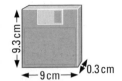

   (a) Find the volume of a disc.

   (b) Find the volume of 25 discs piled on top of each other.

2 Raj has 30 cassette tapes.

  Each tape is 7 cm high by 11 cm wide by 1.7 cm deep.

   (a) Find the volume of one tape.

   (b) Find the volume of all 30 tapes.

   (c) If the tapes are on a shelf, how long must the shelf be?

3 Shirin is stacking shelves in a supermarket.

  Large cornflakes boxes are 20 cm wide by 8 cm deep by 22 cm high.

   (a) Find the volume of one box.

      Shirin is told to make a big display 5 boxes high in the shape of a box.

      He is told to use 150 boxes.

   (b) Find the volume of Shirin's display.

   (c) Draw a sketch to show how you would stack the boxes.

   (d) Work out the lengths of the sides of your stack. Use these to calculate its volume.

4 Each block in a child's set is a 2 cm cube. There are 96 blocks in the set.

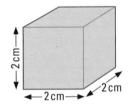

   (a) Find the volume of each block.

   (b) Find the volume of the set.

   (c) Draw a box to store the cubes and mark in its measurements.

   (d) Find the volume of your storage box.

5 Bricks are 20 cm long by 10 cm wide by 6 cm high.

  A stack of bricks has a volume of 48 000 cm^3.

  How many bricks are in the stack?

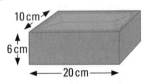

6 A washing machine measures 60 cm by 60 cm at the base and is 90 cm high.

   (a) Find its volume.

      It is to go under a counter top 3 m long, 60 cm deep and 90 cm high.

   (b) Find the amount of space under the counter top.

   (c) Find the volume left when the washing machine is fitted.

Finished Early?
➡ Go to page 381

Further Practice

Calculate the volumes of these cuboids.

1	4 cm by 6 cm by 3 cm	**2**	5 cm by 9 cm by 4 cm
3	7.5 cm by 3 cm by 5 cm	**4**	2 m by 3 m by 5.5 m
5	4 m by 5.2 m by 6 m	**6**	a cube of side 5 m

1 A CD in its case measures 12.5 cm high by 14 cm wide by 1 cm deep.

   (a) Find the volume of one CD.

      Sarah has 20 CDs on a shelf.

   (b) Find the volume of all 20.

   (c) What length of shelf is taken up by 20 CDs?

2 Steve is working in a supermarket. He is told to make a big stack of these boxes of lightbulbs.

   (a) Find the volume of one box.

   Steve is told to make 60 boxes into a block as a display.

   (b) Draw one way that he could stack them.

   (c) Mark in the length of the sides of the stack.

   (d) Find the volume of the stack and check that this is the same as the volume of the 60 boxes.

3 This book measures 17 cm wide by 2 cm thick by 24 cm high.

   (a) Find the volume of one book.

   (b) Thirty books are stored on a shelf. Find their volume.

   (c) A shelf is 80 cm long. What volume of books can it hold?

Hint: first find the number of books.

4 A factory stacks boxes of video recorders.
Each box is 40 cm long by 30 cm wide by
10 cm high.

(a) Find the volume of one box.
(b) Find the volume of 80 boxes.

Finished Early?
➡ Go to page 381

T ③ Liquids

Learn About It

The volume of a carton of juice is about $8 \times 3 \times 10 = 240 \text{ cm}^3$.

The amount of juice in a carton is measured in millilitres.
Amount of juice = 240 millilitres, or 240 ml for short.
The amount of liquid that fills an object is called its **capacity**.
Capacity is measured in millilitres or litres. 1 litre = 1000 ml.
Capacity in millilitres is equal to volume in cm^3.
It helps to get a rough idea of sizes.
A small spoon is about 5 ml.

> ## Key Fact
> $1 \text{ cm}^3 = 1 \text{ ml}$
> $1 \text{ litre} = 1000 \text{ ml}$

A medium size carton of milk
contains 1 litre.

A small pool in a garden would contain about 1000 litres.
To convert from one unit to another you multiply
or divide by 1000.

Examples

1 250 ml in litres = 250 ÷ 1000
          = 0.25 litre.

2 3 litres in ml = 3 × 1000
          = 3000 ml.

Pints are old British units of capacity. They have been used in Britain for a
very long time. 1 pint is approximately 500 ml ($\frac{1}{2}$ litre).

Key Fact

Capacity is measured in litres or millilitres.

Word Check

capacity the amount of liquid that fills an object.

Try It Out

List these items in order of capacity, smallest first.

| Tin of paint 500 ml | Soy sauce 150 ml | Bucket 10 litres | Shampoo 250 ml | Vinegar 568 mls | Milk carton 250 ml | Can of drink 250 ml |

1 Change these into millilitres (ml).

  (a) 2 litres   **(b)** 5 litres   **(c)** 0.5 litres   **(d)** 1.5 litres

2 Change these into litres.

  (a) 4000 ml   **(b)** 800 ml   **(c)** 2500 ml

3 A petrol can is 30 cm long, 25 cm wide and 20 cm high.

  (a) Find its volume in cm^3.

  (b) Change the volume to litres.

  (c) If petrol costs 60p per litre how much will it cost to fill the can?

Practice

1 Change these into millilitres.

Example	0.7 litres
Working	0.7 litres = 0.7 × 1000 litres
Answer	700 litres

  (a) 0.8 litres   **(b)** 0.6 litres   **(c)** 0.3 litres   **(d)** 2.7 litres

2 Change these to litres.

  (a) 300 ml   **(b)** 480 ml   **(c)** 2400 ml   **(d)** 3650 ml

1 Julie is trying to decide which blackcurrant drink to buy.
The bottle has a capacity of 700 ml and the carton is 8 cm by 6 cm by 14 cm.
If both are full, which has most drink?

2 A carton containing 1 litre of milk is 7 cm by 7 cm by 21 cm high.
How much empty space is there in the carton?

3 Cough Cure medicine is made in the factory in tanks 2 m by 1 m by 0.5 m high.

   (a) What is the volume of the tank in m^3?
   (b) How many litres are there in the tank?
   (c) A full tank is used to fill 4000 bottles of Cough Cure. How many ml are
   there in each bottle?
   (d) Cough Cure is taken in 5 ml spoonfuls. How many spoonfuls are there
   in a bottle?

4 A petrol tank measures 60 cm by 50 cm by 30 cm.

   (a) Find its volume in cm^3.
   (b) Find its capacity in litres.

Further Practice

1 Change these to millilitres.

   (a) 0.4 litre   **(b)** 0.6 litre   **(c)** 0.9 litre   **(d)** 1.2 litre

2 Change these to litres.

   (a) 150 ml   **(b)** 250 ml   **(c)** 3000 ml   **(d)** 2500 ml

1 A fish tank is 60 cm long, 40 cm wide and the
water is 30 cm deep.
Find the amount of water in the tank ...

   (a) in millilitres
   (b) in litres.

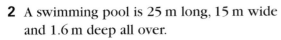
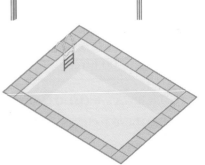

2 A swimming pool is 25 m long, 15 m wide
and 1.6 m deep all over.

   (a) Change all the lengths to cm.
   (b) Find the volume of the pool in cm^3.
   (c) How many litres is this?
   (d) How long does it take to fill the
   pool if water can be poured in at
   750 litres per minute?

> **Finished Early?**
> Go to page 382

Unit 13 *Mensuration*

Summary of Chapters 27 and 28

- Perimeter is the distance around the edges of a shape.
- Area is the amount of space in a shape.
- You can find the area of a composite shape by adding the areas of the parts.
- Area of a rectangle = length $\times$ width.
- Area is measured in cm^2 or m^2.
- Volume is the amount of space in an object.
- Volume is measured in cm^3 or m^3.
- Volume of a cuboid = length $\times$ width $\times$ height.
- Capacity is the amount of liquid that fills a container.
- Capacity is measured in millilitres (ml) or litres (l).
- 1 ml will fill a container of volume $1\,cm^3$.
- 1000 ml = 1 litre.

29 Averages

In this chapter you will learn ...
1. how to calculate the mean
2. how to calculate the mode and the median
3. how to compare two sets of data using averages and the range

An **average** tells you roughly what is happening in a single number.
There are three kinds of average: **mean**, **median** and **mode**.

1 The Mean

Learn About It

Last summer 5 children collected a total of £30 for charity.
You can get a rough idea of how much each person collected by dividing the total £30 by 5. This gives the **mean**.
Mean amount collected = £30 ÷ 5 = £6.
In other words, each person collected £6 on average.
These are the actual amounts they collected.

Bill £3   Carl £5   Sarah £6   Monica £7   Lewis £8

Bill and Carl collected below average amounts.
Monica and Lewis collected above average amounts.
This summer the children collected more money for charity.

Bill £2   Carl £5   Sarah £6   Monica £10   Lewis £12

Monica worked out the total first: £2 + £5 + £6 + £10 + £12 = £35.
Then she divided the total by 5 to get the mean: £35 ÷ 5 = £7.
Monica noticed that none of them actually collected £7.
The mean does not have to be one of the **values** used to calculate it.

Key Fact

To calculate the mean ...
- add up all of the values
- divide the total by the number of values.

Word Check

average mean, median or mode

mean one way to find the average of a set of data.

data information

value number (a single piece of data)

Try It Out

A A school football team played 10 matches this term. These are the goals they scored.

> 4   3   5   1   2   3   6   4   1   1

1 Calculate the total goals they scored.
2 Calculate the mean number of goals.
3 In how many matches did the team score more than the mean?

Learn More About It

Jack runs the school shop.

He records the number of apples sold each day.

> Monday 6   Tuesday 8   Wednesday 12   Thursday 9   Friday 7

At the end of the week he counts up the total number of apples sold:

> 6 + 8 + 12 + 9 + 7 = 42

Then he calculates the mean.

> Mean = 42 ÷ 5 = 8.4 apples **per** day.

Jack said, 'That's impossible. You can't sell 8.4 apples.'
The mean is sometimes an impossible value.
Although it looks strange, it is not wrong.

> **Word Check**
>
> **per** each

Try It Out

B **1** Calculate the mean of these numbers.

(a) 2 2 5	**(b)** 5 7 9
(c) 4 8	**(d)** 1 7 8 2
(e) 2 2 3 5 2 1 9 4	**(f)** 10 8 5 3 9 4 7 2 1 5

2 Mary is learning to type. She counted the number of mistakes she made on 8 pages of typing:

> 5   6   3   3   4   0   5   2

(a) Calculate the total number of mistakes she made.

(b) Calculate the mean number of mistakes she made.

(c) On how many pages did she make below the mean number of mistakes?

Practice

C **1** Here are the sizes, in cm, of some birds in a zoo.

Calculate the mean size for each type of bird. Do not use your calculator.

Example	Sunbird 9 11 13
Working	Total = 9 + 11 + 13 = 33.
	There are 3 numbers, so divide the total by 3.
	33 ÷ 3 = 11
Answer	The mean size is 11 cm.

(a) hummingbird   6   7   8   9   10
(b) flycatcher   9   15
(c) crow   22 ˙ 32   38   52
(d) sparrow   10   10   11   11   13

2 Here are the sizes, in cm, of some animals.
Calculate their means.

(a) deer   58   64   122   66
(b) beaver   34   36   40   41
(c) cheetah   200   205   215   220   220   230   236
(d) bat   3.5   3.7   3.9   4.0   4.3
(e) rat   5.2   6.1   6.3   7.2   7.4   8

3 Siobhan counted the matches in 10 boxes.

28   27   31   32   31   32   29   30   30   32

(a) Calculate the mean number of matches in a box.
(b) The box says 'Average contents: 30 matches'. Is this reasonable?
(c) Siobhan missed a few matches when she was counting. How does this affect the mean that she calculated?

Finished Early?
 Go to page 382

Further Practice

D **1** Here are the sizes, in cm, of some animals in a zoo.
Calculate the mean for each animal.

(a) sand lizard   5   5   6   8   9
(b) python   100   400   700
(c) turtle   10   12   15   19
(d) gecko   2.6   3.9   4.9
(e) anteater   16   16   17   18   18   20   20   21   21   22

2 Joshua plays table tennis. He scored these points in 5 games.

   3 5 8 13 21.

(a) Calculate his mean score.

(b) Which scores are below the mean?

(c) Which scores are above the mean?

Here are Joshua's scores in the next 4 games.

   8 9 17 24

(d) Find the mean of all Joshua's scores.

(e) Has Joshua improved?

3 FuelCo say that a litre of their unleaded petrol is 1p lower than the average price. A motorist found these prices at 7 petrol stations.

(a) Calculate the mean price of a litre of petrol.

(b) Do you agree with FuelCo?

Petrol Station	Price of 1 litre (pence)
FuelCo	70.3
LibOil	72.9
Americo	69.1
AfricOil	70.9
PPP	73.1
Gold10	72.1
Mogul	69.3

Finished Early?

➡ Go to page 382

The Mode and Median

Learn About It

'How many PE lessons would you like each week?', the teacher asked her class. She wrote down their answers on the board.

0 0 0 0 1 1 1 1 1 2 2 2 2 2 2 2 2 2 2 3 3 3 3 4 4

Brian quickly calculated the mean to be 1.8.

'We should have 1.8 PE lessons each week, Miss,' he said.

Mary said, 'That doesn't make sense. We should have 2 lessons a week because that's the most popular choice.'

Mary is right. There are more 2s than any other number. So 2 is the most common number. It is called the **mode** or **modal value**.

Sometimes the mode is a more useful average than the mean.

Word Check

mode (**modal value**) the most common number

Try It Out

E In a sponsored swim 10 children swam these lengths:

1 1 3 4 4 5 5 5 5 8

What is the modal number of lengths?

Learn More About It

Moira took 5 maths tests during the year. These are her marks out of 20.

16 20 19 2 18

Moira didn't do well on one of her tests because she was ill.
Her maths teacher, Miss Jones, added up her marks: $16 + 20 + 19 + 2 + 18 = 75$.
Then she calculated Moira's mean mark: $75 ÷ 5 = 15$.
This seems unfair because Moira got more than 15 on four of her tests.
Miss Jones solves the problem.
She will use Moira's middle mark as her average.
First, she needs to arrange Moira's marks
from smallest to largest.

2 16 18 19 20

The middle mark is 18. This is called
the **median**. Moira got 18 marks per
test, on average.

> **Word Check**
> **median** the middle of a list of
> numbers arranged from
> smallest to largest

Try It Out

F Harry makes paper aeroplanes. He is flying *Condor* in a competition.
The longer it stays in the air, the better.

These are his flying times, in seconds:

33 42 31 30 7

1 Rearrange the times from shortest to longest.

2 Find the median time.

3 Harry was allowed to repeat his last flight, because *Condor* hit the wall.
This flight lasted 28 seconds. Replace 7 by 28 and calculate his median
again. What do you notice?

Learn More About It

Six children collected the following amounts for charity.

£6   £12   £9   £2   £5   £8

Mary rearranged them from smallest to largest but could not find a middle number.

?

£2   £5   £6   £8   £9   £12

Her teacher said, 'When there is an *even* number of values, find the middle two. The median is halfway between them.'
The middle two values are £6 and £8.
Halfway between £6 and £8 is £7. (You can calculate this by: 6 + 8 = 14 and then 14 ÷ 2 = 7.)
The median amount collected is £7 per person.

Key Fact

To find the median …
- arrange the values from smallest to largest
- the median is the middle value
- if there are two middle values, the median is halfway between.

Try It Out

La Belle is a French restaurant. These are the numbers of customers served this week.

Tuesday 4   Wednesday 6   Thursday 5   Friday 12   Saturday 14   Sunday 7

Find the median number of customers served.

Practice

1 These children rolled a die until it turned up 6.

(a) Rearrange the numbers from smallest to largest for each person.
(b) Find the median for each person.

Example	Elvina 4 1 2 5 2 6
Working	(a) Write the numbers from smallest to largest: 1, 2, 2, 4, 5, 6.
	(b) There are two middle numbers, 2 and 4. Halfway between 2 and 4 is 3.
Answer	The median is 3.

Rosheen	2	5	4	2	6		
Martin	1	3	2	3	1	3	6
June	3	5	1	3	6		
Lai Mai	4	4	4	6			
Peter	2	5	2	4	5	1	6

2 Find the mode for each person in question 1.

Example	Elvina 4 1 2 5 2 6
Answer	The mode is the most common number, 2

3 In the school quiz, a team of 5 pupils each had to complete a puzzle as quickly as possible. Here are their times, in seconds:

Gabriel 28   Philippa 31   Ceri 23   Penelope 64   Liaqat 34

(a) Calculate the median time taken.

(b) Calculate the mean time taken.

(c) Penelope dropped one of her pieces on the floor. That's why she took so long. Is the mean or the median the fairest average for the team?

Finished Early?
➡ Go to page 383

Further Practice

1 Find the mode for these sets of numbers.
Remember, the mode is the most common number.

(a) 2, 3, 3, 4, 5, 5, 5, 6, 7, 7
(b) 1, 2, 3, 4, 5, 6, 6, 7, 8
(c) 1, 1, 1, 2, 3, 3, 3, 3, 5, 5, 5, 6
(d) 50, 50, 40, 70, 30, 40, 60, 60, 40, 30

2 Find the median for these sets of numbers.

(a) 6, 5, 8, 1, 2
(b) 6, 12, 4, 8, 8, 5, 10
(c) 6, 5, 3, 8, 1, 2
(d) 4, 6, 2
(e) 6, 12, 4, 8, 8, 5, 10, 11
(f) 28, 15, 30, 52, 14, 30, 45, 26, 9, 60

3 These are the hourly rates of pay for 6 people.

Bank manager £28   Teacher £10   Plumber £7
Clerk £6   Milkman £5   Shop assistant £4

(a) Calculate the median hourly rate.

(b) Calculate the mean hourly rate.

(c) Is this newspaper report correct?

(d) Do you agree with the newspaper report?
Explain your answer.

Daily Flyer

Average wage hits
£10 per hour!

Finished Early?
➡ Go to page 383

Comparing Sets of Data

Learn About It

1 Patrick plays computer football. He played 10 games against his computer. These are the goals he scored.

   0 1 1 2 2 2 3 3 4 5

Calculate the mean, median and mode.

2 Patrick bought a joystick for his computer and played 10 more games. These are the goals he scored.

   0 0 1 1 1 1 2 2 3 4

Calculate the mean, median and mode again.

3 Is Patrick better or worse playing with his joystick? Write a sentence to explain your answer.

Try It Out

A few weeks later Patrick records the goals he scored in another 10 games.

   0 1 2 2 2 3 3 4 5 6

1 Calculate the mean, median and mode.

2 Compare these averages with those you calculated in Learn About It step 2. Is Patrick getting better at using his joystick? Explain your answer.

3 Compare these new averages with those you calculated in Learn About It step 1. Is Patrick scoring more goals using his joystick?

Learn More About It

1 Mr Butler makes brooms. His machine is set to cut broom handles 120 cm long. Something has gone horribly wrong! He measures the lengths of 5 broom handles.

   95 cm   104 cm   121 cm   130 cm   145 cm

There is a big difference between the smallest handle (95 cm) and the largest handle (145 cm). This difference is called the **range**.

Range = largest value – smallest value

      = 145 – 95 = 50 cm.

Mr. Butler's machine is cutting a wide range of broom handles.

2 He gets the machine repaired and measures 5 more handles.

    117 cm   119 cm   120 cm   120 cm   122 cm

Calculate the range.

Is the machine working correctly now? Explain your answer.

Key Fact

To find the range, subtract the smallest value from the largest value.

Word Check

range the difference between the smallest and largest values

Try It Out

K Mr Butler's drilling machine is set to cut 20 mm holes in the broom heads.

If the hole is too small, the handle won't fit. If the hole is too large, the head falls off.

On Monday, Mr Butler measured 5 holes.

    21   18   20   19   19

On Friday, he measured another 5 holes.

    21   23   18   25   16

1 Find the smallest and largest holes drilled on Monday. Use your answers to calculate the range.

2 Calculate the range of holes drilled on Friday.

3 The drilling machine was not working properly on one of these days. Which day was this? Explain your answer.

Practice

Watch or clock with seconds hand

L Work in groups of five. Make sure you can all see a watch or clock with a seconds hand. When the seconds hand reaches 0, close your eyes and count 60 seconds in your head. Open your eyes and write down the number of seconds on the clock. Copy each other's times. You should now have five times written in your exercise book.

1 Calculate the mean and range.

2 Ask another group of classmates for their mean and range. How do your results compare?

Practise counting along with the clock for 60 seconds. Then repeat the experiment with your group.

3 Calculate the mean and range.

4 Has your group improved their estimation of time?

> **Finished Early?**
> ➡ Go to page 383

Further Practice

1 Calculate the range of these numbers

Example	7	22	5
Working	Range = biggest – smallest = 22 – 5 = 17		
Answer	Range is 17		

(a)	4	6	3	9	15	
(b)	150	60	95	200	100	50
(c)	5.2	4.9	4.9	5.3	4.6	4.4	5.1
(d)	3000	800	2500	1800	4000	900	3600

2 Sam is entering a frisbee competition. He has two frisbees, *Skimmer* and *Tornado*. He throws each frisbee 5 times and records the distances to the nearest 10 m.

Skimmer	50	40	90	73	51
Tornado	56	59	63	58	64

(a) Calculate the median and range for each frisbee.
(b) Which frisbee is more reliable? Explain your answer.
(c) If Sam has only one throw in the competition, which frisbee should he use?
(d) If the best of five throws wins, which frisbee should Sam use? Why?

Unit 14 *Processing Data*

Summary of Chapter 29

- There are three kinds of **average**: mean, median and mode.
- To calculate the **mean** …
  - add up all of the values
  - divide the total by the number of values.

Example: Find the mean of 5, 6, 6, 9, 10

Working: Total = 5 + 6 + 6 + 9 + 10 = 36
There are 5 values (numbers), so divide by 5
$36 \div 5 = 7.2$

Answer: The mean is 7.2 (the mean does not have to be one of the values used to calculate it.)

- To find the **median** …
  - arrange the values from smallest to largest
  - the median is the middle value
  - if there are two middle values, the median is halfway between.

Example: Find the median of 8, 4, 3, 7

Working: Arrange values from smallest to largest: 3, 4, 7, 8
The middle values are 4 and 7
Halfway between 4 and 7 is 5.5
(Add up the values: 4 + 7 = 11
Divide by 2: $11 \div 2 = 5.5$)

Answer: The median is 5.5

- The **mode** or **modal value** is the most common value. The mode of the values 2, 2, 2, 3, 4, 4, 5 is 2.
- The **modal class** contains the most data.
- The **range** is the difference between the smallest and largest values. The range of the values 9, 5, 2, 8 is 9 − 2 = 7.
- You can compare means, medians, modes and ranges.

30 Chance

In this chapter you will learn about ...
1. probability words and numbers
2. calculating probability
3. probability experiments

Probability

Learn About It

Some things are more likely to happen than others.

It is **impossible** to jump over the moon.

It is **unlikely** you will get a six with a roll of the die.

You are **unlikely** to see a rainbow tomorrow.

There is an **even chance** of flipping heads with a coin.

You are **likely** to learn to drive.

The sun is **certain** to rise tomorrow.

Probability tells you how likely something is. You can show probabilities using a probability scale.

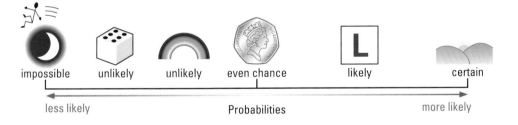

| impossible | unlikely | unlikely | even chance | likely | certain |

less likely ← Probabilities → more likely

Try It Out

A **1** Copy this probability scale.

| impossible | unlikely | even chance | likely | certain |

2 Decide how likely these things are.
>   A If you drop a playing card it will land face up.
>   B An aeroplane will crash.
>   C If you jump in the air you will come back down.
>   D Something will fall off your desk next lesson.
>   E You can stand on the ceiling.
>   F You will learn to drive.
>   G You will miss the bull's-eye with a single dart.

3 Write the letters A to G on your probability scale.

Learn More About It

Probability is measured using numbers from 0 to 1.

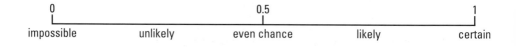

| 0 | | 0.5 | | 1 |
| impossible | unlikely | even chance | likely | certain |

It is impossible to run a mile in 1 minute.
The probability is 0.

It is unlikely you will break a leg.
The probability is less than $\frac{1}{2}$.

You have an even chance of flipping tails with a coin.
The probability is $\frac{1}{2}$.

It is likely you will celebrate your 70th birthday.
The probability is more than $\frac{1}{2}$.

You are certain to close this book. The probability is 1.

| 0 | | 0.5 | | 1 |
| impossible | | even chance | | certain |

Word Check

probability a measure of how likely something is; it is a number between 0 and 1

impossible cannot happen; probability of 0

very unlikely probability close to 0

unlikely probability of less than $\frac{1}{2}$

even chance probability of $\frac{1}{2}$

likely probability of more than $\frac{1}{2}$

very likely probability close to 1

certain must happen; probability of 1

Try It Out

1 Some of these numbers are probabilities. Some are not.

$$0.7 \quad -\tfrac{1}{2} \quad \tfrac{3}{4} \quad 1.2 \quad 0 \quad 0.99 \quad \tfrac{1}{4} \quad -1 \quad 0.5 \quad 1\tfrac{1}{2} \quad 0.01 \quad 25$$

Which are the probabilities?

2 (a) Choose a probability for each description. The probabilities are written in the circles.

$$\boxed{0} \qquad \boxed{1} \qquad \boxed{\tfrac{1}{2}} \qquad \boxed{\text{less than } \tfrac{1}{2}} \qquad \boxed{\text{more than } \tfrac{1}{2}}$$

> **A** If you get bitten by a mosquito it will be on your left side.

> **B** Some trees will lose their leaves in Autumn.

> **C** One of your teachers owns a pet.

> **D** A cat will give birth to a dog.

> **E** There is a Loch Ness monster.

(b) Copy this probability scale.

$$0 \qquad\qquad\qquad \tfrac{1}{2} \;(0.5) \qquad\qquad\qquad 1$$

(c) Write the letters A, B, C, D and E on your probability scale.

Practice

1 Probabilities are often written as fractions.

Example	1 in 10 people are left handed.
Working	1 in 10 can be written as the fraction $\frac{1}{10}$.
Answer	The probability of someone being left-handed is $\frac{1}{10}$.

(a) Write these probabilities as fractions.
  A 1 in 2 households have a tumble dryer.
  B 1 in 4 bills are paid using plastic cards.
  C 7 out of 100 people have National Savings Certificates.
  D 97 out of every 100 people watch TV each week.
  E 6 out of 10 people listen to music each week.
(b) Draw a probability scale.
(c) Write the letters A, B, C, D and E on your probability scale, showing the fractions.

> **Finished Early?**
> ➡ Go to page 384

Further Practice

1 Write each probability word next to a probability number.

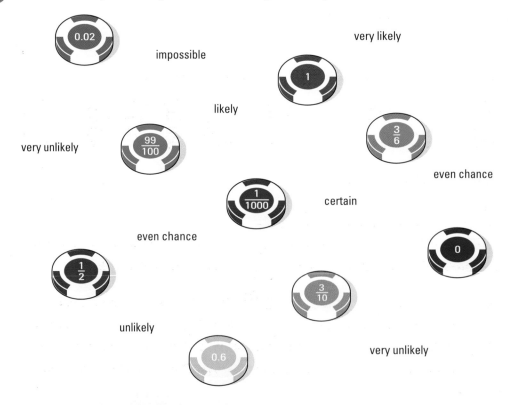

NUMBER SKILLS **Identify numbers between 0 and 1, order fractions from smallest to largest and decimals**

2 (a) Choose a probability for each description. The probabilities are written in the circles.

A   You will be asleep at midnight.

B   A matchbox falls on its end.

C   Someone's birthday is on 30th February.

D   There is an even number of hairs on your head.

E   You will stop writing at the end of this lesson.

(b) Draw a probability scale.

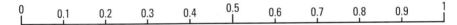

(c) Write the letters A, B, C, D and E on your probability scale.

Finished Early?
➡ Go to page 384

Calculating Probability

Learn About It

Rory buys a bag of Liquorice Allsorts. He has 10 sweets left.

His favourite sweet is

Rory shakes a sweet from the bag.
There is a 1 in 10 chance it is his favourite.
The probability 1 in 10 can be written as the fraction $\frac{1}{10}$. That's 0.1 as a decimal.

The probability that Rory will get a 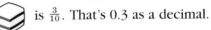 is $\frac{3}{10}$. That's 0.3 as a decimal.

The probability that Rory will get a 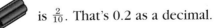 is $\frac{2}{10}$. That's 0.2 as a decimal.

The probability that Rory will get a round sweet is $\frac{7}{10}$. That's 0.7 as a decimal.

The probability that Rory will get a green sweet is 0, because it is impossible.

The probability that Rory will get a Liquorice Allsort is 1, because it is certain.

Try It Out

 1 Sui Main says, 'Pick a straw.' There are 3 long straws
out of 6. So, the probability of choosing a long straw
is $\frac{3}{6}$.

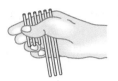

A   B   C   D   E

(a) Write down the probabilities of choosing a long straw.
(b) Copy the probability scale.

```
0        1        2        3        4        5        1
         6        6        6        6        6
|_____|_____|_____|_____|_____|_____|
```

(c) Write the letters A, B, C, D and E on your scale.

2 Look again at diagrams A to E in question 1.
  (a) Write down the probabilities of choosing a short straw.
  (b) Draw a new probability scale.
  (c) Write the letters A, B, C, D and E on your scale.

Practice

 1 This spinner is spun once.

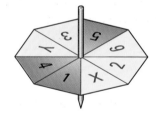

Example	What is the probability that the spinner lands on a number below 6?
Working	There are 5 numbers below 6 (these are 5, 4, 3, 2, 1). There are 8 sides to the spinner.
Answer	The probability is 5 out of 8, which is written $\frac{5}{8}$.

What is the probability the spinner lands on …
A a number   B a letter   C a red number
D the number 7   E the letter X   F a letter or a number
G an even number?

Write the letters A to G on a probability scale like this

```
0        1        2        3        4        5        6        7        1
         8        8        8        8        8        8        8
|_____|_____|_____|_____|_____|_____|_____|_____|
```

2 Etta has 10 coins in her pocket. She takes out the first one she touches.

(a) Find the decimal probability that she takes out …

A a 1p coin   B a 2p coin

C a coin worth more than £1   D a silver coin

E a £2 coin   F a coin worth less than £1

G a coin worth less than £2.

(b) Draw a decimal probability scale.

(c) Write the letters A to G in their correct positions.

> **Finished Early?**
> ➡ Go to page 384

Further Practice

This roulette wheel has 36 numbers. Half are black, half red. The ball lands on one number. You bet by placing a coloured 'chip' on the board. Find the probability that these bets will win.

1 red

2 1 to 12

3 pink chip touching the numbers 5 and 8

4 blue chip

5 white chip

6 yellow chip (one row)

7 green chip (two rows)

8 a number divisible by 4

9 a multiple of 5

10 a prime number

11 19 to 36

12 black chip (one column)

> **Finished Early?**
> ➡ Go to page 384

P ③ Probability Experiments

Learn About It

1 This spinner is equally likely to land on A, B, C, D or E. This is because the spinner has equal sides. In mathematics you say the spinner is **fair**.

What is the probability of the spinner landing on the letter A?

2 There is a 1 in 5 chance the spinner will land on A. So, you would expect an A once every 5 spins. If it is spun 50 times, you would expect an A 10 times. How many As would you expect in 100 spins?

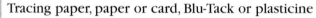

Tracing paper, paper or card, Blu-Tack or plasticine

3 You can make your own spinner. Copy the spinner using tracing paper. Don't forget to mark the centre. Write in the letters. Carefully cut out your spinner. Put a small round piece of Blu-Tack or plasticine in the centre; this helps it to spin. That's it!

4 Is your spinner fair? You can check by spinning it 50 times. First, copy this tally chart to record your results.

5 Use a pencil to point to where the spinner stops.

Letter	Tally	Total
A		
B		
C		
D		
E		

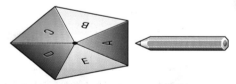

Make a tally mark for each spin.

6 Add up your tally marks for each letter. If your spinner is fair, you should have about 10 tally marks for each letter.

Word Check

fair a coin is fair if heads and tails are equally likely; a die or spinner is fair if each number is equally likely; a game is fair if the players have an equal chance of winning

Try It Out

H 1 Spin your spinner another 50 times. Record your results in a new table.

2 Do you get exactly the same results?

3 Do you get roughly the same results?

4 You have now spun the spinner 100 times. Make a new table combining all the results.

5 If your spinner is fair, how many of each letter would you expect?

6 Is your spinner fair? Explain your answer.

7 Stick your spinner in your exercise book. Keep the Blu-Tack for later.

Learn More About It

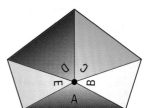

1 Morris has made a mess of his spinner.
His spinner is *not* fair. It is **biased**. So, the probability
of it landing on A is *not* $\frac{1}{5}$.
Do you think it is more likely or less likely?

2 Here are Morris's results.

His spinner landed on A 18 times out
of 50. So, Morris estimates that the
probability of getting an A is $\frac{18}{50}$. This is
called an **experimental probability**.
What is the experimental probability
of getting a B?

Letter	Tally	Total
A	⤷⤷ ⤷⤷ ⤷⤷ |||	18
B	⤷⤷ ||	7
C	⤷⤷ ⤷⤷		11
D	⤷⤷ |||	8
E	⤷⤷		6

3 Morris wants to compare his experimental probability $\frac{18}{50}$ with $\frac{1}{5}$.
He changes both to decimals using a calculator.

  Fair spinner: $\frac{1}{5}$ = 1 ÷ 5 = 0.20
  Morris's spinner: $\frac{18}{50}$ = 18 ÷ 50 = 0.36

Morris's spinner is more likely to land
on A than a fair spinner. This is
because the probability is higher.

Compare the experimental
probability of getting a B with $\frac{1}{5}$.
Is it more or less likely?

Word Check

biased not fair

experimental probability the
  probability you calculate using
  the results of an experiment

Try It Out

Tracing paper, paper or card, Blu-Tack or plasticine

1 Copy and cut out Morris's spinner.
Spin it 50 times just like before. Record
your results in a tally chart like this.

2 Calculate the experimental
probabilities for each letter.
Change them to decimals.

3 Is your spinner fair? Explain your answer.

4 Stick your spinner in your exercise book.

Letter	Tally	Total	Experimental probability
A			
B			
C			
D			
E			

Practice

One coin each

Play this game with another person. You will both need a coin.

1 Both of you are going to toss your coins at the same time. One person scores a point if they are both heads. The other person scores a point for a head and a tail. Decide on the scoring before you start playing.

2 Toss the coins 40 times. Keep count of the tosses.

3 Record the points in a tally chart like this.

4 Do you think the game is fair? Explain your answer.

5 Calculate the experimental probabilities.

Result	Tally	Total score	Experimental probability
Head Head and Head Tail			

6 Convert them to decimals.

7 If the game is fair, what should the probabilities be roughly?

Finished Early?
➡ Go to page 384

Further Practice

A coin

1 If you toss an ordinary coin, what is the probability of heads?

2 If you toss an ordinary coin 100 times, how many heads would you expect?

3 Copy this tally chart.

Side	Tally	Total
Heads		
Tails		

4 Toss a coin 100 times. Make a tally mark for each toss.

5 Add up your tally marks for heads and tails. Your totals should add up to 100.

6 Is the number of heads roughly as you expected?

7 Do you think your coin is fair or biased? Explain your answer.

Finished Early?
➡ Go to page 384

Unit 15 *Probability*

Summary of Chapter 30

- Probability tells you how likely something is. It is measured on a scale from 0 to 1.

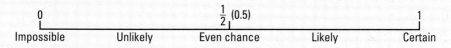

- You can calculate probabilities by dividing. For example, a die has 6 sides. Three of them have even numbers. So the probability of an even number is 3 out of 6. This can be written as the fraction $\frac{3}{6}$. You can change it to a decimal by dividing: $3 \div 6 = 0.5$.
- A game is fair if the players have the same chance of winning.
- A die or spinner is fair if every number has the same chance of coming up.
- Experimental probability is the probability you calculate using the results of an experiment. A coin was tossed 100 times. It turned up Heads 30 times, Tails 70 times. The experimental probability of heads = $\frac{30}{100} = 0.3$. The experimental probability of tails = $\frac{70}{100} = 0.7$.
  The coin is biased (not fair), otherwise the probabilities would both be about 0.5.

Finished Early?

Chapter 1 *Numbers and Number Names*

① Numbers and Words

1 For each of (a), (b) and (c), find the numbers that are shortest and longest when you write them in words.

   (a) single-digit numbers
   (b) two-digit numbers
   (c) three-digit numbers

2 Find a rule for larger numbers.

② Numbers for Ordering

1 Find out how this code works. There is a message hidden in the table. Start with the 8th letter, then follow the ordering numbers above the letters.

Example	The 8th letter is M (the first letter of the message), the 5th letter is A (the second letter of the message), and so on.

8th	6th	10th	11th	14th	13th	7th	5th	9th	4th	16th	12th	3rd	15th	2nd
P	S	C	O	A	I	B	M	T	O	L	Q	S	T	H

2 Find the message hidden here. The rule is the same.

3rd	12th	9th	6th	4th	10th	13th	16th	7th	2nd	11th	8th	5th	14th	15th
S	I	I	D	R	E	M	G	A	R	M	N	O	X	F

3 Find the question in this table, then answer it.

9th	11th	14th	12th	3rd	8th	4th	2nd	13th	16th	10th	15th	7th	6th	5th
E	E	T	T	P	M	I	B	I	?	R	S	S	E	E

4 Now make up some of your own and try them out on your neighbour.

Roman Numerals

Imagine you were a Roman mathematician. Your job is to make up a number system. Instead of using V for 5, you decide to use T for 2. Your counting would start I, T, TI, etc. Also, instead of L for 50, you use S for 20, and instead of D for 500, you use B for 200.

Investigate how the numbers look in this new system.

If you have time, try making up a different system of your own.

Chapter 2 *Place Value and Rounding*

Positions and Columns

1 Charlie's calculator has been damaged. She can only get the display to show a 5, a 2 and three 0s at any one time. How many different numbers can she type in? Here are some examples to start you off.

520, 25, 2050

2 Suppose your calculator is like Charlie's, but you can only get the display to show a 6, a 9 and three 0s. How many different numbers can you make? Is it the same as Charlie's?

3 What if you can only get two 1s and three 0s at any one time? How many different numbers can you make now? Is it the same as in question 2?

4 Try out some other ideas for broken calculators. Make a note of how many different numbers you can type in.

Digits

A **palindrome** is a word which spells the same forwards as it does backwards.

Examples MUM, DAD, HANNAH, POP, I

Numbers can be **palindromic** too.

Examples 505, 4114, 77, 12321, 8

1 Using the digits 1, 1, 2, 2, 3 and 3, how many different palindromic numbers can you make?

Examples 121, 3113

Work them out, then write them in order of size.

2 Choose three different digits (e.g. 2, 5 and 7). Using **up to two** of each (2, 2, 5, 5, 7 and 7), make as many palindromes as you can. Write them in order of size. How many did you make? Is it the same as in question 1?

3 Suppose you only have two digits but are allowed to use three of each (e.g. 1, 1, 1, 2, 2, 2). Work out the palindromes, then write them in order of size. Can you make more or less palindromes than in question 1?

4 Try some other combinations (e.g. 1, 1, 1, 2, 2, 3). Work them out, then write them in order of size. Do you get more or less palindromes than question 1 or 3?

❸ Rounding

1 (a) (i) Write down **all** the numbers that **?** could be.

(ii) Write down **all** the numbers that **?** could be.

(b) What are the smallest and largest numbers that **?** could be?

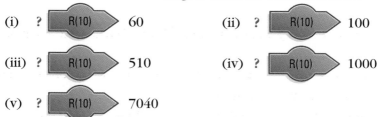

Is there a pattern in your answers? Describe it.

(c) What are the smallest and largest numbers that **?** could be?

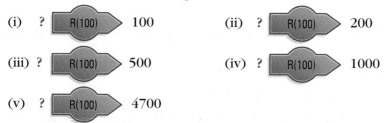

Is there a pattern in your answers? Describe it.

2 Look at these numbers and rounding machines.

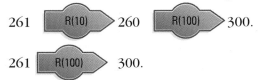

261 ⟩ R(10) ⟩ 260 ⟩ R(100) ⟩ 300.

261 ⟩ R(100) ⟩ 300.

The final answers are the same. Can you find any starting numbers that will give *different* answers?

Chapter 3 *Addition and Subtraction*

❶ Up to Four Digits

Some numbers have patterns in their digits. We will call these **interesting** numbers.

Examples 1234 and 8765 count up and down.
2468 goes up in twos.
3333 and 4848 repeat.

1 Make a list of interesting 4-digit numbers. Try to find at least ten, more if possible.

2 Try adding numbers from your list. Are the answers **interesting** or not?

3 This time subtract some interesting numbers.
Are there any rules for when you get an interesting answer, or not?

❷ Large Numbers

1 Using all the digits from 1 to 9 in order, how many different results can you make?

Examples 123 + 456 + 789 = 1368
1234 − 567 + 89 = 756

2 What are the smallest and largest answers? Are any of the answers the same?

3 Try the same with the digits in reverse order (9, 8, ... 1). Do any of the answers from question 1 match?

4 What happens if you can use 0? Would you put it at the start or the end?

Chapter 4 *Multiplication*

---

❶ Multiplication Tables

1 (a) For this activity you need to use
  digit clocks, like this one.

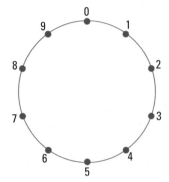

(b) Write out the numbers in the 2× table
  (2, 4, 6, etc.).

(c) Underline the **units** digit of each number
  (e.g. <u>8</u>, 1<u>0</u>).

(d) Now join the dots on the digit clock in
  order. Join 2 to 4, 4 to 6, etc.

(e) Look at the pattern you have drawn on
  the clock. Try to describe it. Label it '2×'.

2 Now work through the other tables in the same way. Start with 3, then 4, etc.

3 Are any of the patterns the same? Which ones? Is there a connection?

❷ Multiply by 10 or 100

1 What is the rule to multiply by 1000?

  What about 10 000, 100 000, 1 000 000?

2 Work out these.

  (a) 24×1000 **(b)** 4000×6 **(c)** 800×30

3 Find some more that have the same answer. How many can you find?

4 Write down some different multiplications with the answer 15 000 000.
  How many different ones can you find?

5 Pick a large number of your own and repeat question 4.

❸ Multiply by a Digit

1 Use any method you like to work out 29×2. Now multiply this answer by 4.

2 Work out 29×8.

3 Questions 1 and 2 both give the same answers. You can now multiply by
  any of these numbers, by working in two steps. In each part, work out what
  the two steps are, then test your idea. Try each one 'both ways' as in
  questions 1 and 2.

Choose your own number (like 29) and multiply it by these.

(**a**) ×15   (**b**) × 16   (**c**) ×18

(**d**) ×21   (**e**) ×25   (**f**) ×27

(**g**) ×28   (**h**) ×32   (**i**) ×36   (**j**) ×45

> (*Hint:* use ×5 and ×3 for (a))

5 Check your answers to question 4 using a calculator. How many did you get right?

Multiply by Two Digits

1 Use the box method to work out 123 × 123. You will have 9 boxes.

2 Now use long multiplication to work out 123 × 123. You will have three rows to add up, and the last one will end in 00. Check that your answer is the same as question 1.

3 Now try 1234 × 1234. Use both methods.

4 Now work out 12 345 × 12 345, 123 456 × 123 456, and carry on the sequence as far as you can.

5 Check your answers to these questions using a calculator. How many did you get right?

Chapter 5 *Division*

Divide by a Digit

1 (**a**) Work out the missing numbers in this chain. Copy it and complete it.

435 — | ÷ 3 | ▶ ? — | ÷ 5 | ▶ ?

(**b**) Copy and complete this.

435 — | ? | ▶ put the answer from (a) here

(**c**) Check your answer to (b) by multiplying.

2 (**a**) Work out how to divide by 25 in the same way.

(**b**) Test your idea by dividing 450 and 675 by 25.

(**c**) Check the answers by multiplying.

3 Answer these in the same way.

(**a**) 294 ÷ 14   (**b**) 651 ÷ 21   (**c**) 666 ÷ 18   (**d**) 2695 ÷ 35

4 Try to think of some of your own.

❷ Divide by 10 or 100

1 Look at the number 20 000. There are lots of different divisions you can do. For example,

$$20\,000 \div 10 = 2000$$
$$20\,000 \div 20 = 1000$$

How many others can you find?

2 Try the same thing with 24 000.

3 Use a 5-digit number of your own.

4 Now try this with a *really* big number!

❸ Divide by Two Digits

1
$98 \div 1 = 98$	(*that's easy!*)
$987 \div 12 = 82 \text{ r } 3$	(*quite easy!*)
$9876 \div 123 =$	(*your turn*)
$98765 \div 1234 =$	(*your turn*)

Now carry this pattern on as far as you can. What happens?

2 Invent a pattern of your own like this one. Investigate what happens.

Chapter 6 *Types of Shape*

---

❶ Flat or Solid?

1 This is a 2 by 2 square tray. How many different ways can you fill it up using these tiles?

2 What about a 3 by 3 tray?

3 What about other sizes of tray?

4 How many ways can you fill this 2 by 2 by 2 box using these pieces?

5 What about different sizes of box?

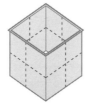

Two Dimensions

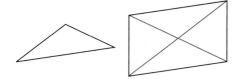

1 A diagonal is a line joining corners of a shape. The corners must not be next to each other. A triangle can't have diagonals. There isn't anywhere to put them.

A quadrilateral has 2 diagonals.

2 How many diagonals are there in a pentagon? Draw a convex pentagon and put in the diagonals.

3 How many diagonals are there in a hexagon? How many in a heptagon?

4 Look at the pattern of numbers you get. Can you work out the next few?

5 Work out how many diagonals a decagon would have. What about a 20-sided polygon?

Three Dimensions

1 (a) Copy and complete this table.

Name	Faces	Vertices	Edges
triangular prism cuboid pentagonal prism hexagonal prism			

(b) Look at the patterns of numbers.

(c) There is a connection between the number of faces, vertices and edges for each prism. Write down the rule connecting them.

2 Does this rule work for pyramids? Investigate.

3 Does the rule work for other shapes like the octahedron? Investigate.

Chapter 7 *Symmetry*

❶ Line Symmetry

1 Draw all the different quadrilaterals you can think of. See **Two Dimensions** on page 59 if you can't remember them all.

2 Mark any parallel lines with arrows.

3 Draw on all the lines of symmetry.

4 Find as many mathematical symbols as you can and write them down. (Look through this book to help you.)

Make a larger drawing of each one. Mark on any lines of symmetry.

❷ Rotational Symmetry

A die, squared paper

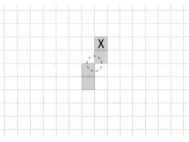

1 Copy this grid in the middle of a piece of squared paper.

You are 'at' the square marked with an X. The picture has order 2 rotational symmetry.

2 Roll the die. This grid tells you how to move. If you roll a 6, you can move one square in any direction.

Suppose you rolled a 4. You would now be 'at' the square marked X in this picture. You have to keep the symmetry, so add another square to the bottom.

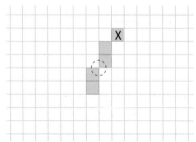 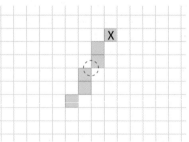

3 Carry on as far as you can. This is called a **random walk**.

4 Now start with a fresh grid. This time the rotational symmetry is order 4. Make a random walk diagram as before.

5 Can you make a random walk using just lines instead of filling in squares?

Making Things Symmetrical

Squared paper, triangle grid paper

Design these shapes. You can find some of them in Chapter 6.

1 a quadrilateral with 1 line of symmetry

2 a pentagon with 1 line of symmetry

3 a hexagon with 1 line of symmetry

4 a hexagon with 2 lines of symmetry

5 a hexagon with 3 lines of symmetry

6 a heptagon with 1 line of symmetry

7 an octagon with 1 line of symmetry

8 an octagon with 2 lines of symmetry

9 an octagon with 4 lines of symmetry

10 a dodecagon with 4 lines of symmetry

11 two octagons with order 2 rotational symmetry

12 two octagons with order 4 rotational symmetry

Chapter 8 *Negative Numbers*

Below Zero

Using these temperatures

24 °C   −20 °C   16 °C   −10 °C   14 °C   −8 °C   12 °C   8 °C   0 °C   −12 °C

write sentences including these words.

> **Example**   … less than …
> **Answer**   −20 °C is less than −8 °C.

1 … more than …

2 … less than …

3 … is colder than …

4 … is hotter than …

5 … is … degrees hotter than …

6 … is … degrees colder than …

② Number Lines

SuperSpy has worked out a code.

The letters of the alphabet are each given a number.

The code for a word starts with the number of the first letter.

The other letters are given as shifts left (L) or right (R) from the last letter.

0 means there is no shift and the letter is repeated.

The code for KING is –2,L2,R5,L7.

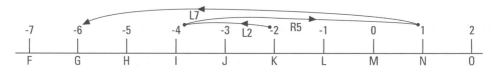

Work out these words.

1 4,R4,L16,0,R9   **2** 3,L15,R22,L9

3 5,L3,O,L4   **4** –2,R3,L5,L2,R1,R12

5 –11,R7,R10,L11,R7,R1

6 Make up some words of your own and write them in code.

7 Make up a sentence of your own and write it in code.

8 Exchange sentences with someone else and see if you can decode theirs.

③ Adding Negative Numbers

A bank keeps records of its customers' accounts. The **balance** is the amount of money in an account. When money is withdrawn a negative amount is added to the balance.

Example £100 is in an account at the start. £180 is withdrawn (taken out of the account). Then £50 is paid in. The balance sheet looks like this.

	Balance
	£100
–£180	–£80
£50	–£30

1 Make a balance sheet for this account.

Balance at the start	£210		Withdrawn	£60
Withdrawn	£150		Paid in	£100
Withdrawn	£100		Withdrawn	£20
Paid in	£30		Paid in	£50
Withdrawn	£80		Paid in	£100
Paid in	£40		Withdrawn	£75
Withdrawn	£20			

2 The bank takes £1 from the balance every time it is negative. Make a new balance sheet for the account. Start like this.

	Amount	Charge	Balance
			£210
Withdrawn	£150	£0	£60
Withdrawn	£100	£1	–£41

Subtracting Negative Numbers

The first amount is the money in a bank account on Monday. The second amount is the money in the account on Friday. Find the change over the week for these accounts.

Example	£120, £90
Working	The account now has £90. So take 120 from 90.
Answer	Change in the account is –£30.

1 £300, £450   **2** £150, £100   **3** £150, £90
4 £200, £125   **5** –£40, £30   **6** –£70, £30
7 –£40, –£20   **8** –£40, –£50   **9** –£200, –£150
10 –£175, –£100   **11** –£125, –£210   **12** –£250, –£210

Chapter 9 *Coordinates*

❶ Reading Coordinates

Here is a map of Balcombe.

Your task is to describe how to get from the cricket field to the farm.

Write down the coordinates each time you change direction.

Write down the coordinates and name of each place you come across. Here are the first few instructions:

'Start from the cricket field. Walk along the footpath and join Mill Lane at coordinates (11, 15), etc.

When you have finished, choose any two places. Write instructions on how to get from one place to the other. Read the instructions to a classmate. Ask your classmate to follow your route on their map. Can they understand your instructions?

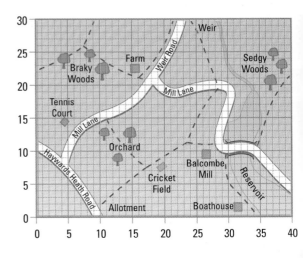

KEY

▨	Building
🌳	Wood/Orchard
▨	Water
– – –	Footpaths

N
W ——┼—— E
S

❷ Plotting Points

Squared paper

Copy the grid from question H1 on page 94 onto graph paper.

Draw a simple shape by joining up points. Write a program for the shape that Plotter could follow. Write down the coordinates of each point you plot. Don't forget to write down the coordinates of the point where you finish. Give your program to a classmate to run. Do they end up with the same shape?

Draw a more complicated picture. Write separate programs for each part of the picture. Try them out on a classmate.

Chapter 10 *Line Graphs*

● Reading Graphs

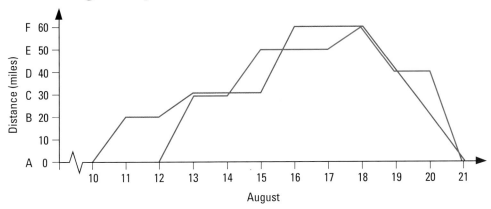

Look at the red line. Imagine this shows you on a cycling holiday. You live at A. You cycle to B and do something, e.g. fishing. Then you travel to C and do something else. And so on.

Describe your holiday, including these details.

(a) descriptions of the places A, B, C, D and F (you could look at a map)

(b) descriptions of what you did at B, C, D and F

(c) dates when you arrived and left

(d) how long you stayed at places

(e) how long each part of the journey took

The blue line shows someone else. Describe their holiday in detail. Perhaps you meet or have a race. Make up a realistic story.

● Drawing Graphs

60 cm of string, Blu-Tack, sticky tape, ruler, coin, watch, graph paper

1 Use sticky tape to fix your ruler to a desk. Attach a coin to one end of the string using Blu-Tack or sticky tape. Hang 20 cm of string over the edge of the ruler

2 Start your pendulum swinging. Use your watch to time 20 swings (one swing is back and forth). Record your results in a table like this.

Length of pendulum (cm)	20	25
Time (minutes)		

3 Increase the length of your pendulum by 5 cm. Time 20 more swings. Record the results in your table.

4 Increase the length of the pendulum four more times, up to 45 cm.

5 Draw a line graph on graph paper to show your results.

6 Use a dotted line to make your graph longer. Now estimate how long a 50 cm pendulum takes to swing back and forth.

7 Time the swing of a 50 cm pendulum. How accurate is your estimate?

❸ Conversion Graphs

Squared paper

There are three ways of measuring the temperature inside an oven: degrees Celsius (°C), degrees Fahrenheit (°F) and Gas Mark.
Here are the oven temperatures for two recipes from a cookery book.

> **Milk Pudding**   Gas Mark 1 or 140 °C or 275 °F
>
> **Pizza**   Gas Mark 8 or 230 °C or 450 °F

Use this information to make conversion graphs for these. Use these scales:

Gas mark 1cm : 1°C

Celsius 1cm : 10°C (break axis)

Fahrenheit 1cm : 10°F (break axis)

1 Gas Mark → °C

2 Gas Mark → °F

3 °F → °C

4 Copy the table. Use your conversion graphs to complete your table.

Gas Mark	1	2			5			8	9
Degrees Fahrenheit (°F)	275		325			400			
Degrees Celsius (°C)	140			179			217		

Chapter 11 *Reading Tables and Charts*

Tables

1 There are two branches of the Ocean Fish Bar, one in Poole and one in Bournemouth. The tables show their sales one evening.

OCEAN FISH BAR (Poole)	
Food	**Portions sold**
Cod	32
Haddock	25
Plaice	12
Chicken	14
Chips	125
Beans	8

OCEAN FISH BAR (Bournemouth)	
Food	**Portions sold**
Cod	25
Haddock	28
Plaice	18
Chicken	10
Chips	116
Peas	12

(a) Which shop sold the most cod?

(b) Which shop sold the most fish?

(c) Which shop sold the most portions of food?

(d) Fish and chicken are always sold with chips. How many customers bought just chips?

2 What are the other differences between the two fish shops?

3 Make a single table showing the combined sales of both shops.

Pictograms and Bar Charts

Nima, Craig and Amara take some exams.
Each test is marked out of 100.

Maths Marks

Nima	90
Craig	30
Amara	50

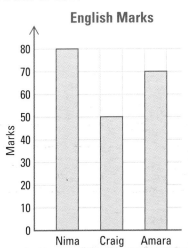

English Marks

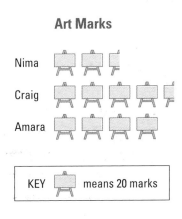

Art Marks

KEY [ ] means 20 marks

1 Answer these questions.
   (a) Who is best at Maths?   **(b)** Who is worst at English?
   (c) Who is better at Art than Amara?   **(d)** Who is good at Art and English?
   (e) Who got above 60 in two tests?   **(f)** Who did best in two tests?
   (g) How many results are above 50?

2 (a) Now write down five more questions about Nima, Craig and Amara.
   (b) Work out the answers.
   (c) Swap around answers with someone. Check their answers.

❸ Two-way Tables

Use the tables on pages 113–114. Find the best Disneyland holiday for two adults with two children that can be bought for £900. Make a table of their costs. Describe their holiday in detail and why you think it is the best they can afford. You can choose where they live and which airport they use.

Chapter 12 *Making Tables and Charts*

---

❶ Tallying Data

1 Turn to one of these pages in this book: 63, 110, 206. Write down the lengths of the first 40 words. Ignore any numbers.

2 Copy and complete the table.

3 What is the most common word length?

4 Are these words longer compared to the words in *Star Wars* (page 117)?

5 Now choose another page from part 1. Write down the lengths of the first 40 words.

Word length	Tally	Number of words
1		
2		
3		

Make a tally chart. Compare the lengths of words on the two pages you chose.

Drawing Bar Charts

1 Choose something that people have a favourite of, e.g. fruit, colour, number, drink.

2 Write down five popular examples, e.g. five fruits: apple, pear, orange, banana, melon.

3 Make a tally chart like this.

4 Ask each classmate to choose the one they like best. Make a tally mark.

5 Add the tally marks. Write the totals in your chart.

6 Draw a bar chart for your data.

Favourite	Tally	Total
Apple		
Pear		
Orange		
Banana		
Melon		

Drawing Pictograms

1 The bar chart shows the numbers of fish caught during a fishing trip.
  (a) Make a table of the data.
  (b) Draw a pictogram.

2 These fish were caught during the next fishing trip.

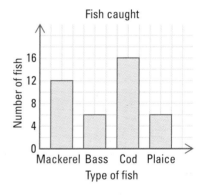

Fish caught

Fish	Number caught
Mackerel	13
Bass	4
Cod	14
Plaice	9

(a) Combine the catches of both fishing trips into a single table.
(b) Draw a new bar chart.
(c) Draw a new pictogram.

Chapter 13 *Calculating with Confidence*

❶ Shortcuts

1 **(a)** Write down a rule for adding 999 to any number. (Hint: look at adding 1000.)

(b) Choose three large numbers and add 999 to them.

2 Do the same for 9999 and 99 999.

3 **(a)** Write down a rule for multiplying any number by 999. (Hint: look at multiplying by 1000.)

(b) Choose three large numbers and multiply them by 999.

4 **(a)** Do the same for 9999.

(b) Choose three large numbers and multiply them by 9999.

❷ Mixed Operations

1 Make up ten questions with these answers.

3   7   13   25   43   36   57   135   341   445

Example $22 + 63 \div 21$ could be a question because
$$22 + 63 \div 21 = 22 + 3 = 25.$$

2 Write down your questions (without answers) in a different order.

Swap questions with your partner.

Match the questions with the answers.

3 Agree a list of other numbers with your partner. Make up and swap ten more questions.

❸ Brackets

Use the numbers 2, 3, 4, 12, 18, 20, the 4 operations $(+, -, \times, \div)$ and brackets to see how many different numbers you can make.

Example $(20 - 18) \times 3 = 2 \times 3 = 6$ So you can make 6.

Write down a list of the numbers you can make.

Checking Your Answer

1 Work out these accurately and check them by rounding.

    (a) 23×42 **(b)** 149×28 **(c)** $151 + 35 \times 15$ **(d)** $(24 + 94) \times 23$

2 Some checks are above and some are below the accurate answers.
   Write down a reason for this.

3 Using only the numbers 1 to 99 make up calculations which will give …

    (a) a check a lot larger than the accurate answer

    (b) a check a lot smaller than the accurate answer

    (c) a check equal to the accurate answer.

Chapter 14 *Powers and Roots*

Squaring

1 This table shows the difference between squared whole numbers.

   Draw the table with five more rows.
Fill in the rest of the table.

$2^2 - 1^2 = 4 - 1 =$	3
$3^2 - 2^2 = 9 - 4 =$	5
$4^2 - 3^2 =$	

2 Can you find the squares of these numbers without multiplying?

    (a) If $20^2 = 400$, what is 21^2?   **(b)** If $16^2 = 256$, what is 17^2?

    (c) If $25^2 = 625$, what is 26^2?   **(d)** If $30^2 = 900$, what is 29^2?

    (e) If $40^2 = 1600$, what is 39^2?   **(f)** If $60^2 = 3600$, what is 61^2?

4 Can you give a rule for getting from the square of a number to …

    (a) the square of the next number, e.g. 71^2 from 70^2

    (b) the square of the number before it, e.g. 69^2 from 70^2?

    (c) Use other numbers to test your rule.

Cubing

The answers to all these questions are numbers between 1 and 15.

Find the numbers in each case.

1 The cubes of two numbers add up to 35.

2 The cubes of two numbers add up to 91.

3 Twice the cube of a number equals 128.

4 Half the cube of a number is 108.

5 The cubes of two numbers add up to 189.

6 The difference between the cubes of two numbers is 189.

7 If you add the cubes of three numbers you get 1070.

8 If you add the cubes of three numbers you get 405.

❸ Square Roots

The ancient Chinese people had a method for finding square roots.

They would subtract from the number the odd numbers 1, 3, 5, 7, etc. in turn.

When they got to 0 they would count the number of subtractions.

Use this method to find the square roots of these numbers.

1 16 **2** 36 **3** 81 **4** 121 **5** 1024

Example	$25 - \underline{1} = 24, 24 - \underline{3} = 21, 21 - \underline{5} = 16, 16 - \underline{7} = 9, 9 - \underline{9} = 0.$
Answer	5 subtractions, so $\sqrt{25} = 5$.

Chapter 15 *Fractions*

❶ Fraction Diagrams

Squared paper (1 cm or 5 mm grid)

1 Here is a rectangle. It has been divided up in different ways. Make several copies. Find out how many different fractions you can make by colouring. Label your diagrams carefully.

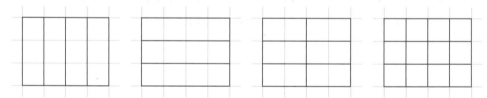

2 Try some different rectangles.

❷ Equivalence: Lowest Terms

A4 squared paper (landscape: a 5 mm grid is best)

1 Draw a coordinate grid. Use a scale of 1 cm to 1 unit. The axes should both start from 0 and go as far as possible.
Label the y-axis **numerator** and the x-axis **denominator**.

2 Plot a point for each fraction.

3 Join up the points you have plotted. What do you notice?

4 Carry on the pattern of equivalent fractions. Join these points up, too. Label the right-hand end of the line $\frac{1}{2}$.

Fraction	Point
$\frac{1}{2}$	(2, 1)
$\frac{2}{4}$	(4, 2)
$\frac{3}{6}$	(6, 3)

5 Start with a new fraction (for example, $\frac{1}{3}$). Plot its point (3, 1). Work out all its equivalent fractions. Plot them. Join all the points up. Label this line.

6 Work through as many different fractions as you can think of. Repeat step 5 each time.

Fractions of an Amount

1 **(a)** (i) Find $\frac{1}{2}$ of 24.   (ii) Find $\frac{1}{3}$ of this answer.

    (b) (i) Find $\frac{1}{3}$ of 24.   (ii) Find $\frac{1}{2}$ of this answer.

    (c) (i) What has happened?   (ii) What fraction of 24 is this?

2 Repeat question 1 with 60 instead of 24. Does the same thing happen?

3 **(a)** Repeat question 1 again, using $\frac{1}{3}$ and $\frac{1}{4}$ of 24.

    (b) Do the same again using $\frac{1}{3}$ and $\frac{1}{4}$ of 60.

4 **(a)** Repeat question 3(b) using $\frac{3}{4}$ and $\frac{1}{5}$ of 60.

    (b) Describe what has happened. Can you think of a rule for this?

5 Test your rule using other fractions and numbers.

Adding and Subtracting with Fractions

1 **(a)** Add $\frac{1}{2} + \frac{1}{4}$.   **(b)** Add $\frac{1}{8}$ to your answer.

    (c) Add $\frac{1}{16}$ to your answer.   **(d)** Add $\frac{1}{32}$ to your answer

    (e) Write down the next 4 answers *without* working them out.

2 **(a)** Add $\frac{1}{3} + \frac{1}{6}$.   **(b)** Add $\frac{1}{12}$ to your answer.

    (c) Add $\frac{1}{24}$ to your answer.   **(d)** Add $\frac{1}{48}$ to your answer

    (e) Write down the next 4 answers *without* working them out.

3 **(a)** Add $\frac{1}{4} + \frac{1}{8}$. Repeat what you have done for the other questions.

4 Work out the next few questions yourself. Is there a pattern?

5 What happens if you add $\frac{1}{2} + \frac{1}{3} + \frac{1}{4} + \frac{1}{5} + \frac{1}{6} + \dots$?

Chapter 16 *Decimals*

❶ One Decimal Place

1 Draw a horizontal line 10 cm long. Make a neat mark at the left-hand end.

2 Pick any decimal with one decimal place and a single units digit. Make a mark this number of centimetres from the starting point.

Example 2.6 cm

3 Now reverse the digits. Make a mark this distance from the starting point.

Example 6.2 cm

4 Measure the distance between your two marks.

Example 3.6 cm
Write down your results in a table like this.

Decimal	Reversed	Distance
2.6	6.2	3.6

5 Starting with a new line each time, try different decimals. Which choice makes the marks as far apart as possible?

6 Which choice of starting decimal makes the marks as close together as possible, without touching?

❷ Two Decimal Places

1 Pick three digits.

Example 4, 5 and 6

2 Make up as many different numbers as you can. You can make whole numbers, 1 d.p. or 2 d.p. numbers. You can only use each digit once.

Examples 5.6, 6.45, 45, etc.

3 Put them in order of size. How many are there?

4 Pick a different set of digits. Repeat steps 2 and 3. Did you find more numbers, less or the same?

5 What happens if two of the digits are the same?

6 What happens if all three digits are the same?

Adding and Subtracting Decimals

1 Pick …
   (a) a whole number, e.g. 1   **(b)** a number of tenths, e.g. 0.2
   (c) a number of hundredths, e.g. 0.03.

2 You can add or subtract as many of these as you like.

   Example $1 + 0.2 + 0.2 - 0.03 - 0.03 = 1.34$.

   Make as many different answers as you can. Are there any answers you *can't* make?

Multiplying and Dividing Decimals

1 **(a)** Start with 0.3. Multiply by 2. Multiply by 2 again. Repeat this until your answer becomes bigger than 100. How many times did you have to multiply?
   (b) Start with 0.3 again. Multiply by 3. Multiply by 3 again. Repeat this until your answer becomes bigger than 100. How many times did you have to multiply?
   (c) Repeat part (b), but multiply by 4. Try it again with 5, 6, etc. until you get to 9.

2 Start with 0.2 this time. Repeat question 1.

3 Start with 0.1 this time.

4 Start with 0.4, 0.5, etc. up to 0.9.

5 Make a table or graph of your results.

6 Try again using 0.01, 0.02, 0.03, etc. as starting points.

Decimals and Place Value

1 Find as many numbers as you can that multiply together to make 2.4.
   Examples 0.3×8 0.12×20 0.24×10

2 Repeat question 1, but dividing instead of multiplying.
   Examples $4.8 \div 2$ $24 \div 10$.

3 Choose a number of your own. Repeat questions 1 and 2.

Chapter 17 *Percentages*

❶ Percentages

1 Draw as many diagrams as you can with 24% shaded in. Your diagrams should have line symmetry or rotational symmetry, like these:

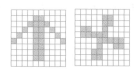

2 Pick a percentage of your own and draw diagrams to show it. It will be easiest to make them symmetrical if your percentage is in the 4× table.

❷ Percentages of an Amount

1 Write down as many percentage statements as you can that contain the number 50.

Examples 50% of … is … 50% is the same as … out of …
… % of 50 is … … % of … is 50

2 Pick your own number instead of 50. Repeat question 1 using your number.

❸ Fractions, Decimals and Percentages

1 How can you change the fraction $\frac{1}{8}$ into a percentage?

You can't change 8 straight into 100. Copy this and fill in the blanks.

What do you multiply by?

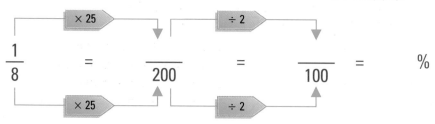

The answer is not a whole number. You may have written a fraction or a decimal.

2 Have your answer checked. When you are sure it is right, work out the percentages for $\frac{3}{8}, \frac{5}{8}$ and $\frac{7}{8}$.

3 Find the percentage for $\frac{1}{16}$. Try some other numbers of sixteenths.

4 Investigate $\frac{*}{40}$.

5 Investigate $\frac{*}{80}, \frac{*}{32}$ and $\frac{*}{125}$.

Chapter 18 *Formulae*

Giving Instructions

1 A small shop has figures for these costs.
 (a) the wages paid each hour
 (b) the cost of the electricity used in an hour
 (c) the cost of the gas used in an hour
 (d) the cost of the telephone each day
The shop is open for 10 hours a day 6 days a week.
It only pays these costs when it is open.
How could you work out the cost of each of these for one week?

Using Letters for Numbers

Read the last exercise and give each answer as a formula.
Decide on your own letters but write down exactly what they mean.

Substituting Numbers for Letters

Professor Brainstorm is putting numbers into his new formula.
What answers does he find for $s = 2a + 3b - c$ when ...

(a) $a = 3, b = 5$, and $c = 6$ **(b)** $a = 5, b = 3$, and $c = 6$
(c) $a = 4.5, b = 7$, and $c = 4$ **(d)** $a = 3.5, b = 7.5$, and $c = 9.5$
(e) $a = 2.8, b = 4.6$, and $c = 5$ **(f)** $a = 5.3, b = 4.6$, and $c = 9$
(g) $a = 17, b = 6.5$, and $c = 5.4$ **(h)** $a = 9.8, b = 6$, and $c = 4.8$?

Chapter 19 *Equations*

❶ Writing Equations

Example	Make 10 from 2 and a number.	
Answer	The number plus 2 equals 10.	$n + 2 = 10$
	The number minus 2 equals 10.	$n - 2 = 10$
	The number times 2 equals 10.	$2n = 10$
	The number divided by 2 equals 10.	$\dfrac{n}{2} = 10$

Write as many different equations as you can.

1 Make 12 from 3 and a number.

2 Make 18 from 6 and a number.

3 Make 14 from 2 and a number.

4 Make 24 from 8 and a number.

5 Make 36 from 9 and a number.

6 Make 40 from 5 and a number.

7 Make 32 from 4 and a number.

8 Make 17 from 9 and a number.

❷ Working Backwards

1 (a) Starting with 2, use number machines to get 14.
Can you do this in more than one way?

(b) Draw the number machines to go back from 14 to 2.

2 Repeat question 1 using 3 and 24.

3 Repeat question 1 using 4 and 20.

4 Choose a number to start with.
Use number machines to make 8 different numbers.
Write the reverse number machines for each one.

❸ Solving Equations

Make up four equations for each of these answers. Try to use all four operations ($+$, $-$, $\times$ and $\div$).

Example	$x = 7$
Answer	Some correct equations would be ... $x + 3 = 10$, $x - 4 = 3$, $5x = 35$, $14 \div x = 2$

1 $a = 5$ **2** $t = 4$ **3** $l = 6$ **4** $p = 12$

5 $m = 8$ **6** $n = 9$ **7** $c = 13$ **8** $d = 11$

Chapter 20 *Angles*

Types of Angle

In each question, you have to put together two turns.

Example   Imagine you are facing North. You turn clockwise through an acute angle. Then you turn clockwise through another acute angle. What **single** type of turn is the same as this?

Working   You could turn through two **small** acute angles, like this: You could turn through two **larger** acute angles, like this:

The result is also a clockwise acute turn.

This time, the result is a clockwise obtuse turn.

Answer   Always clockwise, could be acute or obtuse.

Investigate the possible results of these turns.

Question	First turn	Second turn
1	clockwise, acute	clockwise, obtuse
2	clockwise, acute	anticlockwise, acute
3	clockwise, acute	anticlockwise, obtuse
4	anticlockwise, obtuse	clockwise, obtuse
5	clockwise, obtuse	clockwise, obtuse
6	anticlockwise, acute	anticlockwise, reflex
7	clockwise, acute	clockwise, reflex
8	anticlockwise, obtuse	clockwise, reflex

② Measuring and Estimating Angles

1 Draw a pair of coordinate axes. Label them from 0 to 6. Use a scale of 2 cm to 1 unit.

2 Plot these points: A(1, 0), B(1, 5), C(5, 4), D(6, 2).

3 Join each point to every other point (6 lines altogether).

4 Measure every angle you can find and write it down.

5 Draw a new set of axes.

6 Plot four points on the grid.

7 Measure every angle you can find and write it down.

8 Write down the coordinates you used. Give them to a neighbour to try.

③ Drawing Angles

1 Draw these quadrilaterals full size.

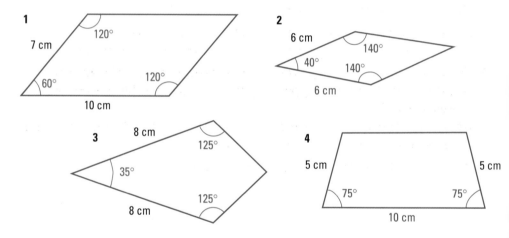

2 For each quadrilateral, measure …
  (i)   the missing side(s)
  (ii) the missing angle(s)
  (iii) the length of both diagonals.

Chapter 21 *Angle Relationships*

◗ Angles on a Straight Line

Protractor

This diagram is made up of two straight lines crossing each other.

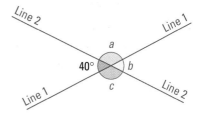

1 **(a)** Use angles on a straight line to find the angle marked *a* (40° and *a* are together on Line 1).

(b) Now use Line 2 to find angle *b*.

(c) Use Line 1 to find angle *c*.

(d) How else could you have found angle *c*?

(e) Make a copy of the diagram. Label all the angles in degrees.

2 **(a)** Draw another diagram. Choose your own angle instead of 40°.

(b) Work out all the other angles, as in question 1.

3 **(a)** There is a rule connecting the angles. Write it down.

(b) If you can't see it, draw another diagram and repeat question 2.

4 The angles *a* and *c* are called **vertically opposite angles**. The 40° and *b* are also a pair of vertically opposite angles. You can use this to work out missing angles.

Draw another diagram. This time measure the angles with your protractor and label them. Does your rule really work?

5 Investigate what happens in a picture like this.

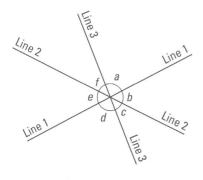

❷ Angles in a Triangle

Protractor

This diagram shows a triangle with one of its sides extended. The extra angle (marked y) that you get by doing this is called an **exterior angle** of the triangle, because it is 'outside' the triangle.

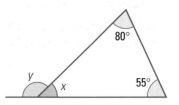

1 (a) Use angles in a triangle to find angle x .

  (b) Use angles on a straight line to find angle y .

  (c) Make a copy of the diagram. Label all the angles in degrees.

2 (a) Now do the same thing with each of these triangles.

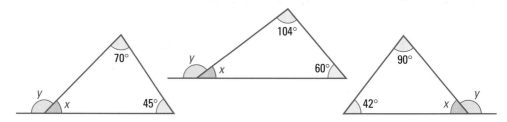

Put the answers into a table like this.

Marked angles			
1	2	Angle x	Angle Y
80°	55°		

Start the table off with the one you've already done.

(b) There is a connection between the marked angles and angle y . Write down the rule.

If you can't see it, draw some triangles of your own. Put the results in your table.

3 Draw another diagram. Measure the angles with your protractor and label them. Does your rule really work?

Angles Round a Point

Ruler, protractor, scrap paper, scissors

1 (a) Draw any quadrilateral on a piece of scrap paper. Make sure it is quite big.
  (b) Cut it out **carefully**.

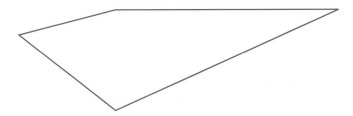

  (c) Now **carefully** tear or cut off the four corners.

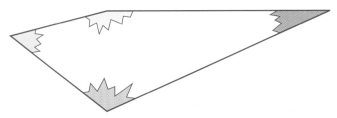

  (d) Turn these round and try to fit them all together. You should find that you can make them fit exactly.

  (e) What does this tell you about the angles in your quadrilateral? What do they add up to?
  (f) Stick the torn-off corners into your book so they fit together.

2 (a) Now try it again with a different quadrilateral. Work through the same steps as in question 1. Does the same thing happen?
  (b) Design another quadrilateral with a **reflex angle** (an angle of more than 180°) at one corner. Does the same thing happen?

3 Write down a rule that describes the results.

4 Test the rule. Draw any quadrilateral. Measure the angles with your protractor and add them up. Does your rule work?

Chapter 22 *Multiples and Factors*

❶ Multiples

1 **(a)** Write down the first 12 multiples of 2, in a column.
  (b) Write down the first 12 multiples of 3, in a column next to the first one.
  (c) Circle the numbers that are in **both** columns. These are called
    common multiples of 2 and 3.
  (d) They are all multiples of another number. Which one? Write down the
    first six multiples of this number. Were you right?

2 Repeat question 1 using multiples of 3 and 5. These are all multiples of
which other number?
The smallest number in both lists is called the **lowest common multiple**
of 3 and 5 (**LCM** for short).

3 Find the LCM of …
  (a) 3 and 7   **(b)** 8 and 12   **(c)** 6 and 9   **(d)** 15 and 20
  (e) 13 and 8   **(f)** 16 and 24   **(g)** 14 and 40   **(h)** 2, 3 and 5
  (i) 3, 5 and 6 **(j)** 4, 8 and 10.

4 How could you test to see if a number is a multiple of …
  (a) 20   **(b)** 25   **(c)** 50   **(d)** 100?

❷ Factors

1 **(a)** Write down all the factors of 18.
  (b) Write down all the factors of 30.
  (c) Circle the numbers that occur in **both** lists. These are called **common
    factor**s of 18 and 30.
  (d) The biggest number circled is the **highest common factor** (**HCF**
    for short) of 18 and 30.
    Copy and complete this sentence: *The HCF of 18 and 30 is … .*

2 Repeat question 1 with 25 and 40.

3 Find the HCF of …

  (a) 14 and 42   **(b)** 25 and 35   **(c)** 9 and 15
  (d) 26 and 65   **(e)** 27 and 36   **(f)** 72 and 90
  (g) 100 and 125   **(h)** 6, 18 and 20 **(i)** 52, 78 and 130
  (j) 14, 21 and 47.

4 **(a)** Find the HCF of 12 and 12.   **(b)** Find the HCF of 15 and 15.
  (c) What happens if you find the HCF of a number and itself?

Squares and Primes

This section uses square and prime numbers to make coded messages.

M	E	N	N	I
E	R	–	–	D
E	–	–	E	–
T	T	I	M	T
–	M	E	–	A

1 This message has been coded.

MENNIER--DE--E-TTIMT-ME-A

To decode it, count the letters and dashes.
There are 25. 25 is 5^2 or 5×5.

2 Write the letters in a square block.

3 Now read round the block this way.

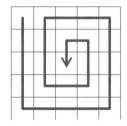

You have now decoded the message. The dashes at the end are to make up the 25.

4 Decode these. Remember, the block size depends on the number of letters.

   (a) NOWT-PE--MOOXWN-RRTEOWFD-EKS--SUPPLY

   (b) SKAM-SUEE-MHCSA-ETC-SYEAEIT-SMSS-IN-

5 This method of coding uses prime numbers $(2, 3, 5, 7, 11, 13, \ldots)$. The letters are in groups of 5 to make it easier to count. There are no spaces.

   MMEAE RTYHA MDEAL IATTT LEDLA MBIIT NSFLE ENCEW EARSW
   HTITE ASISN OWAMN ED

   (a) Read the 2nd, 3rd, 5th, 7th, 11th, 13th, … letters to decode the message.

   (b) What has been used to fill the gaps between the letters in the message?

6 Now write your own message.

   (a) Code it using a square number.   **(b)** Code it using prime numbers.

   (c) Give it to someone else to decode.

> # Chapter 23 *Patterns and Sequences*

Number Patterns

1 Use your calculator to find $200 \div 9$. Write down the answer, ignoring the decimal point. Describe the pattern.

2 Do the same with $200 \div 99$.

3 What about $200 \div 999$?

4 Divide 500 by 9, 99 and 999. Ignore the first 0 and the decimal point. Describe the patterns you get.

5 Try dividing other multiples of 100 by 9, 99 and 999. Do you always get a pattern?

6 Now try dividing numbers by 3, 33 and 333. Do you always get a pattern?

7 Try dividing by other repeated numbers, like 5, 55, 555.

❷ Rules for Patterns

1 This number pattern is called a **chain**.

$$18 \longrightarrow 9 \longrightarrow 10 \longrightarrow 5 \longrightarrow 6 \longrightarrow 3 \longrightarrow 4 \longrightarrow 2 \longrightarrow 1$$

The rule is in two parts:
- if the number is even, divide by 2
- if the number is odd, add 1.

$$\overset{\div 2}{18} \longrightarrow \overset{+1}{9} \longrightarrow \overset{\div 2}{10} \longrightarrow \overset{+1}{5} \longrightarrow \overset{\div 2}{6} \longrightarrow \overset{+1}{3} \longrightarrow \overset{\div 2}{4} \longrightarrow \overset{\div 2}{2} \longrightarrow 1$$

Make new chains starting with these numbers. Stop when you reach 1.

(a) 2　　**(b)** 3　　**(c)** 4　　**(d)** 5　　**(e)** 6　　**(f)** 7
(g) 8　　**(h)** 9　　**(i)** 10　　**(j)** 15　　**(k)** 16　　**(l)** 31
(m) 32

2 Look at your chains. What do you notice?

3 What kind of starting numbers make short chains?

❸ Writing Rules Using Formulae

Mr and Mrs Trout are giving their baby two first names. First they chose Alex and Phillip. The baby's name could be Alex Phillip Trout or Phillip Alex Trout.

They also like Jay. This gives them six possible names.

Alex Phillip Trout	Alex Jay Trout	Phillip Jay Trout
Phillip Alex Trout	Jay Alex Trout	Jay Phillip Trout

1 Choose a fourth name that you like. How many ways can you name the baby now?

2 What if you use five, six or seven names?

Copy and complete the table.

Names to choose from	2	3	4	5	6	7
Ways to name the baby						

3 How can you use the numbers on the top row to make the numbers on the bottom row? (Hint: look at two numbers at a time.)

4 Write down a formula, in words, that gives the number of ways the baby can be named.

5 What if the baby has *three* first names?

Chapter 24 *Length and Weight*

Length

Tape measure, metre rule, ruler

Measure different parts of your body. Use a tape measure if available.
Find as many different lengths as you can. Make a table of your results.

Weight

Make a supermarket shopping list for your family. Estimate the weight of each item and add it to your list. Use the tables of objects in your exercise book to help you.

Converting Units

Estimating can be fun. How long do you think a piece of spaghetti is? Let's guess 40 cm. How many pieces does Luigi eat in a meal? Guess 20. So, every meal Luigi eats $20 \times 40 = 800$ cm = 8 m of spaghetti. How many spaghetti meals does Luigi eat? Let's guess 3 times a week. So, he eats $3 \times 8 = 24$ m of spaghetti a week.

How much spaghetti does Luigi eat in his lifetime?

What weight of cereal will you eat in your lifetime? (One serving is about 30 g.)

How far will you write in a year at school? (Start with the length of a line of writing.)

Think of some more yourself and work them out.

Chapter 25 *Measuring*

❶ Reading Scales

A pair of compasses or dividers, A4 paper

1 Open your compasses to the width of your thumb.

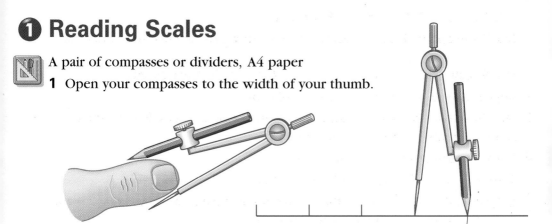

Use your compasses to make a thumb scale. Draw it along the long edge of an A4 sheet of paper. Number your scale. Cut it out to make a thumb ruler.

2 Use your thumb ruler to measure 10 objects in your classroom. Put your results in a table like this.

Measurement	Thumbs	Estimated length (mm)	Actual length (mm)
Length of pencil			

3 Now measure the width of your thumb in millimetres.

4 Convert the thumb measurements in your table to millimetres. These are estimates of the actual lengths. Put them in your table.

5 Measure the actual lengths of the objects with a ruler. Write your measurements in millimetres. Put them in your table.

6 How accurate is your thumb ruler? Write a sentence about it.

7 If you have time, try these:

   (a) Make a scale that can be used to convert thumbs into millimetres (like the one for miles and kilometres on page 276).

   (b) Draw a conversion graph for thumbs and millimetres (see page 102).

Measuring Length

1 These lengths have 1 decimal place:

7.1, 7.2, 7.3 … 7.9, 8.0, 8.1 … 8.8, 8.9 cm

  (a) Write down all the lengths that are 8 cm when rounded to the nearest cm.

  (b) Which is the smallest?   **(c)** Which is the biggest?

2 Repeat question 1 with 3 cm instead of 8 cm.

3 Marvin says he knows a bigger length than 3.4 cm that is still 3 cm when rounded to the nearest cm. Can you think of one?

4 These lengths have 2 decimal places:

7.40, 7.41, 7.42 … 7.49, 7.50, 7.51 … 7.99, 8.00, 8.01 … 8.49, 8.50, 8.51

  (a) Write down ten lengths that are 8 cm when rounded to the nearest cm. Your answers must have 2 decimal places.

  (b) Which is the smallest?   **(c)** Which is the biggest?

5 Write down five lengths that are 8 cm to the nearest cm. Your answers must have 3 decimal places.

6 Repeat question 5 with more decimal places. Is there a rule?

Weighing

Ruler, pencil, Blu Tack, as many of these coins as possible: four 1p, one 2p, three 5p, two 10p, two 20p, one 50p, one £1, one £2

1 Balance the ruler on the pencil. Use two pieces of Blu-Tack to stick the ruler to the pencil. Make sure it still balances.

2 A 1p coin weighs about 3.6 g. Use your balance to estimate the weight of the other coins. Make a record of how you estimated each weight, including any calculations.

Chapter 26 *Time, Timetables and Calendars*

❶ Calculating Time

Song	Group	Running Time
DREAMING	The Grifters	2.42
I LOVE YOU	Dave Grant	3.05
SPEND TIME WITH ME	Heaven	4.00
DON'T DO IT	Shame	2.45
GETTING DOWN	Fandango	3.17
SOUL FOR SALE	Chain Gang	3.29
NO TIME TO STOP	Mary Lee	2.15
LONDON TOWN	The Brothers	2.25
SIMPLY ME	Showdown	2.51
SCHOOL BLUES	Spellbound	1.46
BOYFRIEND	Groundhog	3.09
FIRST LOVE	Harmony	3.50
TAKE IT FROM ME	The Babes	2.41
HOME RUN	Mike Ross	3.28
HEARTBROKEN	Danielle	1.58

There are 15 songs recorded on this CD. For example, DREAMING by The Grifters lasts 2 minutes 42 seconds.

Fabia wants to record all the songs onto some music cassette tapes. Her tapes have 15 minutes on each side.

1 Work out how she can record all the songs on 3 sides of her tapes. There are lots of ways of doing this.

2 Find the length of music on each side of the tapes.

3 Find the total length of all 15 songs.

Timetables

You and a friend have to catch a plane from Gatwick Airport to Amsterdam. Planes leave at 3.30pm and 8.30pm. Passengers have to arrive at the airport 1 hour early. You live in Portsmouth. Your friend lives in London. Here is your plan.

> Bus from Portsmouth to Brighton → 15 minute walk to Brighton railway station → Train to Kings Cross → Meet friend and have lunch for 1 hour → Train to Gatwick Airport → Check in 1 hour early → Fly to Amsterdam.

Trains to Gatwick Airport leave Kings Cross every 15 minutes. The journey lasts 45 minutes.

1 Copy the plan.

2 **(a)** Use the timetables on pages 289 and 291 to find the times of each part of your journey. Write them on your plan.

  (b) Can you make the 3.30 pm flight to Amsterdam?

3 Now plan a journey to catch the 8.30pm plane to Amsterdam. Have tea with your friend at Kings Cross for half an hour. Avoid getting to places too early. You will have to add more times to the railway timetable.

Calendars

1 Copy this calendar.

2 Write in the name of this month.

3 Find the column for today, e.g. Wednesday.

4 Write today's date in one of the spaces.

5 Write in the other days of the month.

6 Now make a new calendar for the next two months.

7 Make a new calendar for the previous two months.

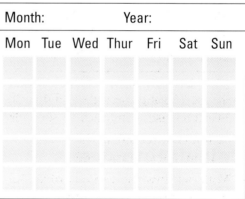

Month:				Year:		
Mon	Tue	Wed	Thur	Fri	Sat	Sun

Chapter 27 *Perimeters and Areas*

---

① The Perimeter of a Shape

 Squared paper

1 On squared paper draw as many rectangles as you can with a perimeter of 20 cm.

2 Repeat question 1 for **(a)** 24 cm **(b)** 30 cm.

3 You have nine square tiles. (You can use squared paper to draw them.)

Fit them together so that you have …

(a) the smallest perimeter **(b)** the largest perimeter.

4 You have 16 tiles. (You can use squared paper to draw them.)

Fit them together so that you have …

(a) the smallest perimeter **(b)** the largest perimeter.

5 Can you write down a rule for finding the smallest and largest perimeters?

② Counting Areas

 Squared paper

1 On squared paper see how many rectangles you can draw with area 24 cm^2.

2 Now see how many rectangles you can draw with area 36 cm^2.

3 Now see how many rectangles you can draw with area 45 cm^2.

4 Now try to find an area that gives more different rectangles than these.

③ Calculating Areas

1 (a) Find rectangles with a perimeter of 20 cm. Using width 1 cm, 2 cm, 3 cm, etc., find the lengths that go with each width.

(b) Work out the area for each of the rectangles.

Put your results in a table. Here the first line has been filled in.

Width	Length	Area
1	9	$1 \times 9 = 9$

What length and width give the largest area?

2 Repeat question 1 for rectangles with perimeter 16 cm.

3 Look at your answers for the first two questions.

Which rectangles give the largest area?

4 (a) Repeat question 1 for rectangles with perimeter 18 cm.

(b) Can you find a rectangle with sides which are not whole numbers that gives a larger area when the perimeter is 18 cm?

5 Choose some perimeters of your own and find the largest areas.

Chapter 28 *Volume and Capacity*

▶ Filling Space

1 If you have a cube with 4 cm sides, you can make it with 2 cm cubes.

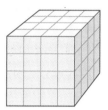 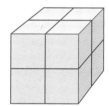

4 cm × 4 cm × 4 cm cube   eight 2 cm × 2 cm × 2 cm cubes

How many 2 cm cubes do you need to make these?
Some may not fit.

(a) A 6 cm cube   **(b)** A 8 cm cube   **(c)** A 5 cm cube   **(d)** A 9 cm cube

2 Repeat question 1, trying to fill the cubes with 3 cm cubes.

3 Repeat question 1, trying to fill the cubes with 4 cm cubes.

4 Write down a rule that tells you when the smaller cubes fit.

5 Try this with cuboids instead of cubes.

▶ Boxes

1 A cube with sides 1 cm by 1 cm by 1 cm has volume 1 cm³.
What does the volume become if you …

(a) double the length of one side
(b) double the lengths of two sides
(c) double the lengths of all three sides?

2 Work out the volume of a cube 2 cm by 2 cm by 2 cm. Repeat question 1 with this cube.

3 What happens to the volume when you double the lengths of the sides? Write down a rule for this.

4 Repeat questions 1, 2 and 3, multiplying the lengths by 3 instead of doubling.

5 Choose another number to multiply the lengths of the sides. Repeat questions 1, 2 and 3 with this number.

❸ Liquids

1 A petrol station stores its petrol in a big tank buried in the ground.

The tank has a base of 2.5 m by 2.5 m and it is 4 m deep.

(a) How many litres of petrol does the tank hold when it is full?

(b) How deep is the petrol in the tank when it is 0.5 m below the top?

(c) How many litres of petrol are there when the petrol is 0.5 m below the top?

(d) How many litres are in the tank when the petrol is 75 cm below the top?

(e) If the level falls by 4 cm how many litres of petrol have been sold?

2 A second garage has a storage tank which has a base of 3 m by 3 m and it is 2.5 m deep.

Work out the answers for question 1 using this tank.

3 Design your own storage tank. Remember it must be large.

Work out the answers for question 1 using your tank.

Chapter 29 *Averages*

❶ The Mean

1 Calculate the mean of the numbers: 1, 2, 3, 4, 5. What do you notice?

2 Now calculate the mean of 6, 7, 8, 9, 10. What do you notice?

3 Can you say what the mean of 20, 21, 22, 23, 24 is without doing any calculation? Write down a sentence explaining the rule you used.

4 Now investigate the means of …

(a) even numbers, e.g. 4, 6, 8, 10, 12

(b) odd numbers, e.g. 5, 7, 9, 11

(c) other number patterns, e.g. 1, 1, 2, 2, 3, 3

The Mode and Median

1 Find the mean, median and mode of this row of numbers.

    1 1 2 3 4

2 Find the new mean, median and mode when 100 is added to the row.

    1 1 2 3 4 100

3 Describe how adding 100 affects the mean, median and mode. What would be the effect of adding 1000 instead? Try it and see.

4 Find the mean, median and mode when *two* 100s are added to the row.

    1 1 2 3 4 100 100

What effect has this had on the mean, median and mode?

5 Try adding more 100s. Describe what happens.

Comparing Sets of Data

A page from a newspaper or magazine

1 Turn to page 117. Write down the lengths of the first 40 **words** on the page.

2 Calculate the mean, median, mode and range of the word lengths.

3 Write down the lengths of the words of the nursery rhyme from *Alice's Adventure in Wonderland* on page 116.

4 Calculate the mean, median, mode and range of the word lengths.

5 Write sentences comparing the two sets of word lengths.

6 Write down the lengths of the first 40 words from a page of a newspaper or magazine.

7 Calculate the mean, median, mode and range of the word lengths.

8 Write sentences comparing the word lengths from the newspaper or magazine with the word lengths in questions 1 and 3.

Chapter 30 *Chance*

❶ Probability

1 Choose something you are interested in. For example, football, watching television, eating.

2 Write down sentences describing things that could or could not happen. For example, England could win the World Cup, someone might break a leg in the next episode of *Neighbours*, someone eats a car.

   Write at least ten sentences. Give each sentence a letter, e.g. A, B, C.

3 Now decide how likely each thing is. You should use probability words (e.g. very likely, impossible) and probability numbers (e.g. 0.3, $\frac{1}{2}$).

4 Put the letters in the correct position on a probability scale.

❷ Calculating Probability

Look at Practice question F1 on page 334. The spinner has letters, numbers and colours. You found some probabilities when the spinner was spun.

1 Design your own spinner. Make a sketch of a spinner with 6 sides. Decide what you want to go in each space, e.g. numbers, letters, colours, names, animals, pictures. You can have more than one thing in a space, e.g. a letter and a number.

2 Imagine the spinner is spun. Write down the probabilities of five different things happening. Look at question F1 to give you some ideas.

3 Show your spinner to a classmate. Ask them to find your probabilities.

❸ Probability Experiments

1 Make this spinner. This is your roulette wheel.

2 Spin your roulette wheel 72 times. Record your results in a tally table.

3 Look at each of the bets in question G on page 335. Find the experimental probability of them winning. Use your table to help you. Leave your answers as fractions.

4 Do you think your roulette wheel is biased? Explain your answer.